THE FUTURE-PROOF CAREER

THE FUTURE-PROOF CAREER

STRATEGIES FOR THRIVING AT EVERY STAGE

ISABEL BERWICK

PAVILION

To my father, Gerry, who went to a secret place called 'the office'. I have never stopped trying to unravel its mysteries.

Pavilion
An imprint of HarperCollinsPublishers Ltd
1 London Bridge Street
London SE1 9GF

www.harpercollins.co.uk

HarperCollins*Publishers*
Macken House, 39/40 Mayor Street Upper
Dublin 1, D01 C9W8, Ireland

10 9 8 7 6 5 4 3 2 1

First published in Great Britain by
Pavilion, an imprint of HarperCollinsPublishers Ltd 2024

Copyright © Isabel Berwick 2024

Isabel Berwick asserts the moral right to be identified as the author of this work.
A catalogue record for this book is available from the British Library.

HB ISBN 978-0-00-860772-2
TPB ISBN 978-0-00-861931-2

MIX
Paper | Supporting
responsible forestry
FSC
www.fsc.org **FSC™ C007454**

This book contains FSC™ certified paper and other controlled
sources to ensure responsible forest management.

For more information visit: www.harpercollins.co.uk/green

Printed and bound in the UK using 100% renewable electricity at CPI Group (UK) Ltd

Publishing Director: Stephanie Milner
Editor: Ellen Simmons
Copyeditor: Shari Black
Senior Designer: Alice Kennedy-Owen
Design: Hannah Naughton
Cover: Luke Bird
Proofreader: Kate Reeves-Brown
Production Controller: Grace O'Byrne

THE FINANCIAL TIMES HAS NOT SEEN OR ENDORSED THE CONTENT OF THIS BOOK

Contents

Foreword

My desk in the Financial Times (FT)'s London HQ is piled high with new books, and they just keep coming. Books about management. Books about leadership. Books about feedback, productivity, how AI will transform work. Almost all of them are aimed at very specific audiences: the kinds of people who buy books about business and management. And then there are other piles: the How To Win At Everything books, and practical guides for the LinkedIn-braggers, the self-improvers, and would-be entrepreneurs who revere Elon Musk.

This is not a book like that.

I wrote *The Future-Proof Career* because I don't see many titles – whether that's on my piles at work or piled on the tables in bookshops – that deal with the reality of most people's working lives and how to make them better, forever.

I wanted to write something that's rooted in the practical, infuriating, and often disappointing reality of workplaces. Why, you may ask, am I qualified to do this? Well, I've been hanging about in offices, breathing in the aircon and the low-grade resentments, for three decades. More constructively, I have spent the last five years tasked with covering the workplace and the future of work, first as the FT work and careers editor, and now as the host of the FT *Working It* podcast and writer of a weekly newsletter of the same name. My day job is to offer practical advice, aimed at improving our working lives, while unpicking a bit of the pomposity and jargon around HR and management trends.

I wanted, above all, to write a book for those of us who rely on an employer to pay our bills and give us holiday and sick pay (we hope). We want to see work as a place where we can find career progression and fulfilment. Workplaces are the enduring backdrop to our lives – and we deserve to thrive in them. So, this is a book for people of any age who want to be a bit more self-aware about how work can best fit into their lives, long term.

Most of us will remain employees for our entire careers. Only about 13 per cent of people in work in the UK are self-employed. After reading

The Future-Proof Career, you may realise that the salaried life is not for you, long term – and that's a fantastic and clarifying realisation to have.

The really strange thing about our working life is that it often sits, semi-secretly, in parallel alongside our 'real' lives with our friends, families, dogs, and wider communities. Sometimes I call it a shadow life. There's often a disconnect between the people we are at work – even if we are, in the fashionable jargon phrase, "bringing our whole selves to work" – and the rather less polished person that our old friends see. For people who don't feel comfortable or accepted in work – and that situation disproportionately affects people of colour and people with a visible or invisible disability – then that disconnect can be deeply jarring and takes a mental toll.

Working life in an organisational setting can, and should, give something back to us. You will have grown, over the course of your career, in terms of confidence and skills. We too often underplay that, or don't even think about it. I hope this book will help you to think about your strengths – even the ones you haven't articulated yet.

Here's my story: I've spent my working life building a credible professional self as a journalist. My FT colleagues may splutter over this (sorry, all) but I *think* I am quick, articulate, good at being in a team. I believe I was a thoughtful and humane manager – and brave people sometimes told me when I was failing at that. I remain too much of a people pleaser. Above all, I'm paid to be good at words. I can now write almost as fast as I think, which is to say fluently, but sometimes a bit carelessly – as is the case for many journalists.

Why, then, does little of this confidence translate to the self away from work? I am a loving but anxious mother, a too-absent daughter and sister, thinly spread friend, and an obstinate, emotionally distant partner. An all-consuming focus on words and the life of the mind (I read a *lot*) means I have never devoted time to developing skills in anything practical. I lack, as one teacher friend witheringly informed me, common sense.

The transferable skills that we do bring home from work can actually end up being a bit . . . tricky. I get frustrated with people – on committees and trustee bodies where I've served, for example – who don't talk, organise, plan, and get stuff done at my cracking pace. Living on newspaper deadlines turns you into a speed merchant. I am finally ageing into an appreciation that slower, more considered outlooks are a valuable counterbalance to my own. Teams need all sorts of people – inside and outside of the workplace.

Being more aware of the 'mixed bag' of skills and possible overly developed biases that work has gifted us is something we don't think about enough. Examining that can be the starting point for a much wider audit of what we like and what we want to change; firstly about our work, but also in our wider lives. I hope this book will help you do some of that.

When I started writing this book, I thought hard about where the workplace sits now – both in our actual lives and in our collective imagination. On the latter, there aren't as many great novels about people at work as there should be, considering how much time we spend there. If you are interested in exploring the workplace in fiction, I loved Joshua Ferris's *Then We Came to the End* and *Small Pleasures* by Clare Chambers (this gets extra points from me for being about a woman reporter on a newspaper, back when there were very few of them).

Television is far better: the closed workplace environment is a gift to long-running ensemble casts and their in-jokes. Beyond *The Office*, I love *Parks and Recreation*, *Superstore*, and heck, even my old favourites *Star Trek: The Next Generation* and *Deep Space Nine* are really workplace dramas. I watched them when I was just starting out at work myself. The aliens and the battles were exciting, but really I loved the long-running camaraderie, love affairs, and petty tensions among the crew.

Post-pandemic, everything about work IRL (in real life) is being *re-imagined*, not least because we are now in the midst of a pivot to embedding artificial intelligence into millions of workplace processes, with as yet unknown knock-on effects for workers and their jobs. Meanwhile, CEOs and leaders are in a quandary over getting people back at their desks in expensive offices. The City of London, where I work, is pretty deserted on a Monday and, especially, on a Friday. (Not the really good salad place, though. That lunchtime queue never gets any shorter.)

This book is partly about navigating the new – and future – reality of work. But really, as we do every week in the *Working It* podcast, I wanted to highlight what we as human beings bring to our workplaces. That environment impacts us both positively and negatively, but we can learn effective tactics to help us get on with others, move ahead, get a pay rise, and think about whatever comes next. All the while, balancing that work life with everything else we've got going on, and not burning out. Tall order.

I've divided *The Future-Proof Career* into two parts: one for employees, or we might say team members, and the other for managers and leaders. Most of us are both of those things, sometimes at the same time. I'd encourage you to read both parts, wherever you are in your career – but the complexities of managing a team and learning to communicate upwards to make your voice heard by corporate leaders, for example, are specific to managers. We all behave and think somewhat differently depending on whether we have management responsibility, or not.

This is a book for all the stages of your career, the early bits, the good bits, the bits you'd rather forget, and for your fifties and early sixties, when you start to think about what comes next. I hope you find it useful. Let me know what you think, what I missed – and about your own experience. You can find me @IsabelBerwick on LinkedIn (of course).

After a lifetime of speaking and telling ... I'm all about listening. Spoiler alert: better listening is the secret sauce for future proofing anyone's career.

FOR THE EMP

LOYEES

Chapter 1: What Are You Working For?
Ambition, in its many disguises

This book is about the workplace, and how to succeed on your own terms. We will cover as many aspects of that as we can fit into one short book, but before you turn to any other chapter, go back a step and consider why you work in the first place.

Money, obviously – and we can consider that later.

But if you have picked up this book, you are looking for something beyond pure monetary reward. You have ambition.

What, though, does ambition mean to you? And have you considered that it's not just about careers anymore?

What, in short, are you working for?

In the olden days – which for the purposes of this book means pre-2020 – saying that someone was 'ambitious' was an important signal. It meant they were climbing a corporate career ladder. Or they were an entrepreneur with growth on their mind. There was a lot of ambition on LinkedIn, put it that way.

There were, however, always gendered aspects to this loaded term. I got used to being called 'an ambitious career woman' at the start of my working life during the back end of the last century. It was 100 per cent meant as a pejorative term.

When I first got together with my husband – who is also a journalist – I encouraged him to aim higher in his career. He soon got a great new job and handed in his notice. His angry boss said he was sure Michael had been bullied into leaving 'by that pushy new girlfriend'.

A bit of ambition was seen as attractive in a woman. Too much, however, was not.

I am not saying anyone thinks that way now, and in fact there has been another profound shift in how any of us, regardless of gender, defines or is defined by ambition. If you cast your mind back to how you used the term pre-pandemic, I would bet that you, like me, didn't think about what ambition meant beyond career or money.

Now, though, the pandemic has shifted our boundaries. The meaning of ambition is more nuanced.

Do any of these resonate?

- Your new ambition may be to be able to pick your kid up from school two days a week.

- It might be to leave a corporate career in two years' time and become a freelance consultant.

- It might be to prioritise your wellbeing and home life as being as important as your working life. Or even more important.

- It might be that you want to work less, not more.

I first learned that the definition of ambition had changed from a *Working It* podcast guest, the writer, comedian, speaker, and podcaster Viv Groskop. In short it seems that younger workers are resisting the sorts of unpaid, long hours, 'be seen' tasks that older generations took as part of the process of having ambition, of working our way up the corporate ladder.

According to Viv, 'A younger generation is not willing to take on extra workloads, to work those extra hours for nothing – they are questioning that. And an older generation is saying, "This is ridiculous, how do you expect to get on?" Those two points of view are really incompatible and at odds with each other at the moment, and it's going to take a while to work itself out.'

Ambition, in short, is having a bit of a crisis. It's all up for grabs. It's a good time to reassess what you want from your career.

For anyone who wants to think far more deeply about ambition – both inside and beyond the workplace, I recommend you read Emma Gannon's *The Success Myth: Letting Go of Having It All.*

Emma is one of the UK's foremost experts on balancing – if that's the right word – careers and life. I asked her for her prediction for the future of work, post-pandemic. She says, 'I would say [there will be] a huge collective reassessment of what success means; rejecting the hustle culture; really looking at burnout properly.'

Not long after we recorded together, Emma had own experience of burnout. Out of that came her book *The Success Myth*, which offers a practical template for re-making your goals and your life. She now describes herself as 'a recovering success addict'.

In my own case, I was incredibly and unthinkingly ambitious, and edited the business section of a national paper in my early thirties. Then I had two kids and scaled back my hours.

Back then, the overall corporate view – and not one limited to the media sector – was that working part time equals a lack of ambition. I didn't feel that; I had a great job and was very lucky to have understanding bosses who valued my ideas and my work.

Then a new manager arrived and said to me, 'I don't think part-time workers should have senior jobs.' That person soon moved me to another, less prestigious, position.

I had a breakdown and could barely function, but kept going. Nobody could know how ill I was – I truly believed I would be sacked if they found out.

So when people openly talk about their mental health issues at work, I am delighted. Things have changed so much for the better.

This rupture in my previously smooth career advancement had a profound effect. The valuable lesson it taught me was that ambition and hard work were sometimes not enough. There is a wild-card factor: We are all still dependent on others and their recognition of us as somehow 'worthy'.

In workplaces, it is managers and leaders, people senior to us, who offer us recognition and promotion. So there is almost no way to carve out a stable place for ourselves – let alone an upwards career path – that doesn't depend on other people's views of us.

We need to be clear-eyed and ruthless about the reality of this dependence on others in an organisational structure, and decide how to manage it and navigate it – or not.

Becoming self-employed is one way to sidestep the vagaries of office politics, but there are many ways to survive and indeed thrive inside workplaces. Part of the key to doing so is learning to generate your own sense of self-worth so you're not totally reliant on praise from others. It's a hard one to crack, but I persist with this and hope you do, too. If, like me, you are a 'people pleaser' who never saw a group or meeting they didn't want to be a part of . . . I see you.

The truth is that people are messy and have biases and prejudices. Often, we don't recruit, promote, or retain people fairly. That fact has a particularly hard impact on the careers of people of colour and anyone from a 'different' background to the dominant group at work. Despite some $8 billion spent annually in the US alone on diversity, equity, and inclusion initiatives at work, many of these just don't work.

Your ambition may not even be welcome in your workplace if you don't 'fit' the culture – and even that word 'fit' is an especially pernicious one, that we will come back to in Part I, Chapter 3.

Age and ambition

As I age, I care far less about conventional markers of success. I have been inspired by the work of Arthur C. Brooks, a Harvard professor and writer who advocates switching our focus as we get older. 'Devote the back half of your life to serving others with your wisdom. Get old sharing the things you believe are most important.'

This quote is from Brooks's book, *From Strength to Strength: Finding Success, Happiness and Deep Purpose in the Second Half of Life* and is one of my favourite work/life books.

We will return to the pleasures of achieving a mid-life success spurt – and how that relates to ambition – when I discuss late career blooming (see Chapter 9 in this section). Many of us in Gen X were forced to take a career step back when our children were young, but now, some of my friends are running arts centres, exhibiting in fancy Paris art galleries, and becoming visiting professors at top universities. And some others of them don't work, or have cut back on work. One is an environmental activist, while others are caring for elderly relatives and fitting work around that. All of it matters in the patterns of our longer lives and the waxing and waning of conventional ambitions.

After thirty years in media workplaces, I wish I could tell you I have aged into a position of calmly surveying my colleagues' swift progress up the ranks, while relying on my own sense of purpose and self-worth to make my own path.

I haven't. I am still petty and jealous.

But I am working on it. And you can, too.

<u>Takeaways</u>

- What does ambition mean to you? If it works for you, break it down into parts: professional and personal.

- If you are an employee, how far up the hierarchy do you want to get? Did your experience during the pandemic change your views on ambition?

- Analyse where your professional ambition comes from. Does your childhood experience mean you are overly dependent on external validation? Perhaps you grew up with economic insecurity, and so gaining financial stability has become the driving force in your working life. You may wish to take some professional therapy or coaching to understand your motivations more fully, and so embrace them. In the short term, try to talk to people who seem to have 'made it' in their workplace – you will often find they are still restless and unhappy.

- Accept the reality that corporate life involves being dependent on others for advancement. In big organisations, you will be a pawn in a larger game of chess. There's an element of randomness to it that you – and your ambition – can't control. Focus on what you can control. We will discuss that later – see Chapter 3, starting on page 26, for how to do an audit of your current workplace which can help to build your sense of control.

- Is finding a path to balancing career happiness and fulfilment in your personal life an ambition in itself?

- If you are in the later phase of your working life (post-45, let's say), has your view of 'ambition' changed? It might be time to reflect on changing priorities and making the best use of your experience and maturity. See Chapter 9, starting on page 107, which outlines how to do just that.

Chapter 2: Post-Pandemic Workplace 101
Why is everyone and everything all over the place?

If you are not a keen follower of every twist and turn in workplace trends (and why would you be?) then this chapter offers an overview and quick catch-up and look ahead, whether you are a team leader or a team member, or – as most people are – both of those things.

It covers where we are now in terms of work/life, how we got here (to which the answer usually is: the pandemic), and some of the resulting changes that are happening in workplaces. Not all of these will be on your radar yet but they will certainly impact you and your career, somewhere, sometime. It's always good to keep an eye on what's coming round the corner so you can remain ahead of the curve.

I've listed below the current top workplace themes and trends. I am sure I've missed some. But these are the ones that come up again and again when I talk to people on the *Working It* podcast, or chat to them in the breaks at conferences, or just when I survey what's posted on LinkedIn and what lands in my email inbox.

Uncertainty is in the fabric of our lives
We've come out of a global pandemic into war in Europe, renewed instability in the Middle East, and hard economic times. Politics everywhere is polarised. Everyone is exhausted from home schooling, there are knock-on mental-health effects of lockdown, and millions have Long Covid symptoms.

We don't suddenly become different people when we walk through the door into our workplaces. Uncertainty is in the air there, too.

For the moment, acknowledge it: It's uncomfortable for everyone. Sit with it.

Any business leader or manager who tells you everything is 'absolutely fine' is . . . behaving like a parent humouring a kid who is too old to believe in Father Christmas. Neither party can quite bear to face the truth.

Hybrid and flexible work are evolving all the time

To go back to basics, use of these terms is often interchangeable – but hybrid is better used to describe mixing up where a person works during a work week, often between in-person work alongside others in a workplace, and remote, sometimes called distributed, work.

Remote work can happen at home or at a 'third space', which could be a co-working space, a café, or a rental villa by the sea.

Before the pandemic, only about one in eight adults (12.5 per cent) in the UK workforce worked mainly from home, according the Office for National Statistics. The latest number is 31 per cent, according to a report using aggregated data from several sources from Summix, an urban planning and regeneration group. That's 5.3 million additional people working mostly from home in the UK alone, compared to pre-pandemic days.

Flexible work is also on the rise. This term is more often used to refer to flexibility around *when* we work – fitting our hours around childcare and elder care commitments, rather than a standard 9–5 work day, for example.

We've all read stories about employers asking staff to come in to the workplace on certain days – often two or three set days per week. One of my career high/low lights was going on BBC Radio 4 and telling the listeners that the practice of working in offices on Tuesdays, Wednesdays, and Thursdays has a terrible acronym – 'TWAT' working.

Astonishingly, I haven't been asked back on that show, but TWAT does reflect reality. My own office at the FT is one of many in the City of London where it's now busy midweek, and very quiet on Mondays and Fridays.

The evolving shape of the working week is another area of uncertainty. Are we all going to go back to our desks every day, or is hybrid here to stay?

Lots of academics and workplace experts are working on the 'problem' of hybrid and flexible work, trying to figure out what's going to happen, and advise companies and business leaders accordingly. Some of this is hot air, but let's hear the thoughts of someone I rate highly in this field, Dr Grace Lordan, an academic at the London School of Economics (LSE).

Grace has written several articles for the FT, and her research focuses on equality at work. She and her team at the LSE's Inclusion Initiative do research into what actually works in terms of helping people from diverse backgrounds thrive – and stay – in their workplace. She uses these findings to help companies develop better (read: unbiased) leadership practices that incorporate practical measures so all staff members can advance in their careers.

It turns out that developing the best hybrid and flexible working practices are absolutely vital if we are serious about creating fair and diverse workplaces. That fact often gets lost in the discussion. If the flexibility comes first, then lasting changes that create more diverse workforces will be easier to embed. People have complicated lives, and women, especially but not exclusively, want flexibility.

At the end of 2022, Grace's team published the results of interviews with 100 workers from diverse backgrounds in London's financial services sector. As the FT reported, some of them simply refused to go in to offices on mandated days. 'While at the C-suite level, executives in many large firms are asking for workers to come in to the office a specific number of days per week, in practice they are being ignored, with managers often favouring a remote-first approach that satisfies local operational needs.'

So another layer to the development of hybrid, flexible, and remote-first work is that lots of teams are currently ignoring commands from on high and simply working in a way that works for them to maximise staff happiness and productivity. If you are a manager doing this, you are not alone – and you are doing a good thing for your team.

There are no right or wrong answers about the future of our working week. My instinct is that most of us in knowledge work – and office jobs more generally – are never going back to pre-pandemic rigidity. At its most basic, that's because people really, really like working from home (WFH) for some, or most, of the time. We have children, pets, parents, and running regimes to attend to.

Crucially, we also have the workplace tech tools to be able to do our jobs effectively from anywhere (or nearly anywhere).

People really, really like being at home

Think back to the days before March 2020. Life was often a blur of time-pressed journeys to and from an office or workplace. Add in children or other caring responsibilities and it was almost impossible to navigate. I still have flashbacks about being trapped for long periods on stalled London underground trains, helpless and panicking, as six o'clock – when the nursery closed – loomed ever nearer.

Communities flourished during the pandemic years. Local shops and restaurants in residential areas have bloomed. This has led to a post-pandemic phenomenon called 'the doughnut effect' in cities, where the central commercial district is a 'hole' (low footfall, both in terms of the number of people visiting and buying stuff, and the number of people going in to offices) while the outer ring of the doughnut, where people live in the suburbs, is absolutely thriving.

There has been a profound shift in the way many people view their lives, and how they see work fitting within that. Part of this comes down to the chance that millions of former office workers have been given to place ourselves within our communities first.

This allows us to do more voluntary work locally (perhaps previously you only did that via an employer's volunteer programme), to join a yoga studio near your home, become a local politician or climate activist, or just to have a pet. One recent survey found that 78 per cent of US pet owners acquired their pets during the pandemic. There are ten million dogs in the UK – one in four of the adult population owns a dog. (This commitment has an impact on pet owners' needs when it comes to work, a topic I will look at later on – see page 44.)

The bigger picture issue here, and one that I think is good news, is that more focus on our home lives and environment takes us away from the kind of 'maternalistic' employer that was on the rise before the pandemic. By this I mean the company that offers staff everything from on-site nurseries to three meals a day, gyms, and dry cleaning – essentially, life admin and support. These perks kept people at work for many hours a day, and were especially prevalent in tech companies, banks, law firms, consultancies, and startups.

Of course staff perks are a good thing. Who doesn't want an employer that provides free food? But many knowledge workers have now got more balance in their lives. We have the chance to fully inhabit our roles as functioning adults in society and make our communities better because of it.

I hope this is one of the lasting 'good' consequences of all those long months and years we spent working from home during the pandemic.

And to give this renewed focus on WFH some long-term context, the importance of home in our working lives is not, in fact, anything new. It's a return to something that has been part of human civilisation for hundreds of years.

In her 2018 book, *Work: The Last 1,000 Years*, University of Vienna professor Andrea Komlosy crammed all that history into 270 pages. As she told me on a (pre-*Working It*) FT podcast, until the Industrial Revolution, men and women would often work together in a home-based business. 'Women had higher status – they cooperated with men in a family business and women's work was acknowledged. Each contribution was valuable.'

As paid work moved outside the home, into factories or other workplaces, the domestic sphere became devalued. It lost, as Andrea told me, 'its character of work' and became associated with women's nature for caring and home-based chores.

With a return to paid home-based work, might we even see a return to some higher value being placed on the domestic work that is often being squeezed in by women (and many men) around their employer's demands? We can't be sure, but it's fascinating to know that being at home more, and sharing duties, has in the past boosted the importance of the work – and it *is* work – carried out in the domestic sphere.

Friendship and connections at work are vital

Before the pandemic, not many people cared about having friends at work – it was sometimes considered a badge of honour to be so focused and cut-throat that you viewed the other people at work as objects to climb over on your way to the top.

What I always found especially weird were the people who'd say, 'I don't have work friends,' as if it was something central to their sense of being. Did they think that people at work were somehow unworthy of their attention?

A caveat here: If you are protecting something about your identity that you haven't revealed at work, that reticence is more than understandable. I once worked with a very quiet and diligent colleague who gave nothing away. Someone I met at a party said this person was her great friend, and had I also met their [same-sex] partner, X? Weren't they the best fun?

After checking that we were discussing the same person, I finally realised my colleague was comfortable in their queer identity in their personal life, but was not out at work. Whenever anyone is dismissive or a bit wary of the practice of 'bringing your whole self to work' – and that sometimes includes me – I think of this and check myself.

When my best work friend Sarah left the FT, I was so upset the next day that I went for a long walk in the pouring rain, ending up in a huge cemetery. My family suggested I might be going a bit overboard. So far, so melodramatic. But why can a work friend be so important? And why is friendship in the office such a hot topic now, after we've spent so long working away from our colleagues, in our bedrooms and kitchens?

My go-to expert here is Lynda Gratton, a professor of management practice at London Business School, and author of *Redesigning Work*, a book about how to make hybrid work patterns efficient and human-focused.

Lynda introduced me to something called 'affective forecasting', a term from psychology that's very useful in navigating the workplace. As she wrote in the FT, 'While from a business perspective we might understand what drives our work performance, when it comes to our broader lives we suffer from "affective forecasting". We are generally poor at predicting those activities that generate long-term positive benefits.'

One of those activities with benefits is investing in the relationships we have with colleagues at work. But because people are not neat and predictable, and the outcomes are not bullet-pointed, and because we are bad at affective forecasting, we think that (for example) having more meetings or a Zoom call is a better use of our time than coffee with a colleague. It has a guaranteed outcome, like a decision or an agenda for yet another meeting.

Since the pandemic, this urge to pack in meeting after meeting has become even more pressing. It doesn't seem to be going away, either.

We may have forgotten (or never fully realised) that making friends at work is incredibly important and has long-term benefits, for our own happiness and mental health but also, without being cynical here, for productivity and engagement. Happy teams are more engaged teams.

As Lynda wrote, 'When we make friends, we strengthen our resilience. We are also making the time we spend at work more pleasurable. Take, for example, Gallup polling which puts "I have a best friend at work" as one of the best predictors of whether you will stay in your current job. This resonates with me.'

When Lynda came onto the *Working It* podcast to talk about friendship, she talked about the post-pandemic importance of the workplace as a place of connection. There is no point going into offices just to sit on Zoom meetings all day. Lynda, in fact, would like us all to cut our meetings by 50 per cent and use that time more productively – by getting to know our colleagues.

As she says, 'If I go into the office, it's because I've got a friend at work. I want to speak to a friend . . . and I think if you [a manager] want people to come back into the office, it's got to be joy that brings them back. It isn't going to be by threats.'

This forward-looking interest in helping people connect is why many new offices and co-working spaces look like extremely cool cafés, complete with surly baristas, library walls, and trailing spider plants. If your workplace now looks like this, congratulations, someone high up has read up on friendship and connection and is taking notice.

My favourite part about work friends though, and this is not scientific, is when they become part of your 'outside' life too. That's something very special. They will understand you better than almost anyone else. We've all seen our other friends and even our partners glaze over when we recount the latest office dramas. Work friends don't do that. They really, really listen.

A good work friend, it turns out, is for life. I am now even closer to the friend I wept for.

The bonds that any of us forge at work are only going to become more important as time passes and the barriers between our home and work lives erode even further. Work experts call this 'boundaryless' work. It's a phrase we are all likely to hear a lot more about in future.

Worktech is making us smarter – but it's watching you

I'm writing this book three years after most office-based workers got sent home from work – for a few weeks, we thought – to sit out the risks from a growing pandemic. For many knowledge workers, whose work lives are powered by Wi-Fi and a laptop, this transition was pretty seamless, technically speaking. (We will deal with the social and emotional fallouts in Part II, Chapter 1. See page 125.)

Since then, 'worktech' has developed incredibly quickly. I talked to the futurist Amy Webb quite early in the pandemic, and she made a point that stuck with me: Sometimes a decade of progress can happen in a month. That's what happened at the start of the pandemic when a giant global experiment stress-tested all the software needed to make sure that people could keep doing their jobs from home.

You may well use Slack, Asana, Zoom, Teams, and other communication tools as the main way to stay in touch at work. We owe all of that to the high-speed internet. Now we are at the start of the next workplace tech revolution. That shift is summarised by Bain & Company, a management consultancy, in a recent report. 'Just as high speed data networks altered the nature of outsourcing and the way that companies organised work, the advent of automation and artificial intelligence will change the economics of how work gets done.'

This automation/AI shift will impact many jobs that remained (fairly) untouched by communications software and internet-based work. Many of these jobs are 'deskless', which means they don't have a specific office space. They may be in warehouse, construction, retail, or care work. There are an estimated 2.7 billion of these 'deskless' workers globally.

AI is already embedded in many deskless workplaces, which make up an estimated 80 per cent of jobs worldwide. Research from the Edelman Trust Barometer, a big global survey, shows that deskless staff are far less likely to trust their employer than other workers, which can lead to disengagement and lower productivity. So an example of AI in use in deskless workplaces is the use of better communication tools to keep staff in constant touch, so they know what's happening.

AI is also widely used for onboarding and training new workers. Gone is the familiar and onerous process of endless induction sessions and paperwork. Bots can help people give the right details and offer them the right information about the company, and the job expectations. Taking it further, machine learning can help people get up to speed on the new job. Those are just two examples. The speed of rollout is staggering.

There is a new jargon term for this: an 'augmented workforce'. Although it sounds robotic (remember when the robots were coming for our jobs?), in a more optimistic scenario, AI and automation could help everyone do their jobs more effectively. By taking the most boring admin tasks away from us, it could free people up to focus on human interaction and emotional skills. That's the ideal, anyway.

Here's (some of) what the generative AI system ChatGPT4 – which can already create written content that is practically impossible to tell apart from humans' efforts – had to say when I asked it about its role in the future of work:

'As an AI language model, my impact on the future of work will primarily be in the areas of automation, communication, and collaboration.

'In terms of automation, AI technology like myself can automate many repetitive and time-consuming tasks, freeing up human workers to focus on more strategic and creative work. This could lead to increased efficiency and productivity in the workplace.'

The downsides of AI, in terms of its negative impact on jobs, are starting to become clearer too. A recent report by Goldman Sachs suggested that the use of generative AI (AI that generates and creates new content) could raise global gross domestic product by 7 per cent over ten years, and automate some 300 million jobs worldwide. That's not good news for the people whose jobs it will not only automate but eliminate entirely. The robots *are*, in fact, coming for our jobs. And some of those jobs will be professional ones – lawyers and administrative staff are among those at risk.

Another worrying development is that worktech allows bosses to spy on their staff. Where managers don't trust their workers, surveillance tech – or spyware – is an easy way to keep paranoia at bay. Typically, this might be software that tracks what sites workers are visiting, or monitors keystrokes. There are even some that use the computer's built in camera to follow facial expressions to see how engaged a worker is.

The practice is widespread, and growing. In 2022, a survey by the British Trades Unions Council found that 60 per cent of workers reported some form of tech surveillance or monitoring at work.

So what can you do about it? Very little, although reported hacks to elude the spyware include wedging something onto a key so that it is permanently pressed down or using a device that jiggles a computer mouse so that it's in permanent motion.

Spyware is rapidly becoming a fact of life. Reddit forums offer workers' unvarnished views on this. If you are struggling with an intrusive employer, my best suggestion is to join a union and follow r/antiwork along with 2.6 million other people who are sticking two fingers up at it all. Some of the stories on there are shocking.

I wish I could be more optimistic about this subject but I fear the only solution for most people who are being spied on by paranoid bosses is to move jobs. And even then, the spies may stay with you.

Generative AI and spy tech are both areas where the future is coming at us very quickly, and may already be out of our control. Even as I write this book, things are changing. I recently interviewed Steven Bartlett, entrepreneur and host of the mega-hit podcast *The Diary of a CEO*, for a big live event. He suggested to the audience that the way to keep up with AI, and so keep your career on track, is to be curious and open minded. In other words, stay ahead of the curve.

It may also be true that in the very near future, monitoring will become the everyday and accepted price that workers have to pay in exchange for the freedom to work at home some or all of the time.

I hope I am wrong.

There's a gap between what CEOs want and what everyone else wants

While CEOs have always been a bit removed from the concerns of the average worker (median UK FTSE 100 CEO pay was £3.4 million in 2021), many of them – and their PR people – managed to get across a feel-good 'we're all in it together' communications strategy to staff during the pandemic. That has all but dried up.

Survey after survey shows a widening gulf between the (usually) secret wishes of CEOs, who want to get more staff back in the workplace more of the time, and the desire of workers to maintain autonomy and flexibility by working at home – or wherever they want – for some or all the time.

Nobody should be surprised. Why would workers give up hard-won freedoms? The fight is on, and this is likely to be the biggest and most enduring source of workplace tension in the coming years.

One of the best barometers of the global state of workplace thinking is a giant annual Microsoft global survey of 20,000 people in eleven countries, incorporating extra analysis and data points from Microsoft 365 and LinkedIn.

In its latest report, the software giant found that 85 per cent of leaders say the shift to hybrid work 'has made it challenging to have confidence that employees are being productive'. Meanwhile, an uncannily similar 87 per cent of employees report that they 'are productive at work'.

No room for ambiguity there. Workers and leaders have very different outlooks. Microsoft calls on leaders to 'end productivity paranoia' but I see no sign of this happening.

Still, this is an evolving area, and sometimes CEOs might have a point. When Silicon Valley Bank (SVB) collapsed in early 2023, there was some concern that its culture of working from home had contributed to poor internal communication about difficult issues. Nicholas Bloom, a Stanford professor and one of the world's leading experts on remote and hybrid work, told the *Financial Times*, 'It's hard to have a challenging call over Zoom.'

Even before SVB collapsed, some CEOs had been explicitly citing what we might call the 'creativity deficit' of remote work as a reason for asking staff, especially in creative industries and knowledge work, to return to offices. Disney's Bob Iger, when he returned for a second stint at running the company, announced at the start of 2023 that staff would be required in the office four days a week. In a memo to employees he wrote, 'In a creative business like ours, nothing can replace the ability to connect, observe, and create with peers that comes from being physically together, nor the opportunity to grow professionally by learning from leaders and mentors.'

Only a few CEOs, though, are prepared to go on the record to demand their workers return to offices full time. Elon Musk at Tesla was early to embrace this hard-line approach. In June 2022, the FT reported that he told staff that Tesla's office was not 'some remote pseudo office' and that if people fail to show up in person, 'we will assume you have resigned'.

Since then, Musk has taken over Twitter and implemented brutal job cuts and punishing work regimes. One senior executive, Esther Crawford, who posted a photo of herself actually sleeping on the floor of the office (can there be any higher commitment than that?) later lost her job. I thought her comment after being fired in February 2023 was a model of how to do it: 'The worst take you could have from watching me go all-in on Twitter 2.0 is that my optimism or hard work was a mistake.' Ultimately what can any of us in employment do except follow the orders of a leader?

The truth is that we are too early into our post-pandemic working lives to really see how hybrid or mostly remote working is impacting our workplaces. The early indications are that productivity is higher (of course it is – nobody is spending as much time commuting, for starters). But at its heart, this is a human issue. What Microsoft calls 'productivity paranoia' boils down to leaders' trust in their workforces.

Bold company leaders are starting to play hardball with moves to hit workers' pay packets if they refuse to return to the office. In April 2023, the *Wall Street Journal* reported the first (that I've seen) US prestige employer planning to tie bonus payments to in-person attendance. Law firm Davis Polk & Wardwell, which has many Wall Street clients, warned that bonuses could be reduced for those who don't spend the required three days a week in the office. JP Morgan Chase, meanwhile, has told senior bankers worldwide that they need to be in the office every day.

Why is this happening? Partly because humans are hardwired to only trust the people we can actually see in front of us and around us. That's why so many CEOs and senior leaders like to see people at their desks.

It's not that they are egomaniacs (although some might be). It's just human nature, and getting past that takes a lot of effort – something that is also down to leaders. As Harvard professor Heidi K. Gardner, author of a very useful book called *Smarter Collaboration*, told me, 'Highly engaged people don't need to be monitored. They need to be challenged, coached, and recognised.'

Which way is this going? Too soon to tell. Five-day in-office attendance may not become widespread. But I stand by my scepticism about the long-term viability of having a corporate career for anyone who moved far, far from the office during the pandemic, thinking they'd rarely have to commute again.

My own view is that offices have a big role to play in the human side of work – bringing us together, connecting us, forging friendships, and generally being good for our mental health. But the buzzword 'belonging' actually means something useful here. There's no point in CEOs talking about belonging and connection as part of a cynical strategy to lure people back to workplaces, unless they can back it up with actual action to make the workplace a welcoming one.

Long Covid leaves a big impact

People have always got sick. But a shift during and since the pandemic has been the sudden, simultaneous impact of Long Covid on millions of people worldwide. In May 2022, the UK's Office for National Statistics estimated that two million people in the country, about 3 per cent of the population, had Long Covid. That figure is around 100 million globally.

The Institute for Fiscal Studies, a think tank, estimates that one in ten people with Long Covid will stop work altogether, although most people with the condition will go on sick leave and return.

There are a number of levels to think about here, for the individuals whose jobs and lives are blighted by the debilitating condition, and their colleagues and team leaders who have to navigate their own workloads while supporting a colleague who might be working reduced hours or not at all.

At the end of 2022, I talked to a Long Covid activist, Jana Javornik, who is also an expert on work. She is associate professor of work and employment relations at the University of Leeds. Jana had first developed Long Covid in early 2021. I asked her how the condition has impacted her. Her symptoms, she said, have 'ranged from intestinal problems to rashes, hives, migraines, cough, sneezing, back pain, high fever, memory lapses, and a really debilitating brain fog. You can imagine for a worker in the industry of knowledge, where memory is your key tool and brain is your key tool, experiencing this debilitating brain fog really made me unable to work.

'And honestly, last year [2021] I actually slept most of the time. I think I spent more than 18 hours [a day] in bed. And this year, unfortunately, things have changed, so I hardly sleep at all. It really feels like [being] a mobile phone battery that never fully charges.'

That's grim, but it evokes the reality of this miserable condition for millions of people. I asked Jana for her professional view: How is Long Covid impacting people at work?

'It becomes really difficult [in workplaces] when a significant number of people have conditions that fluctuate day to day,' Jana says. 'And because it's unpredictable, it's usually not like there's one thing you can do to solve it.'

Later in the book we will cover strategies for managers to help team members who need adjustments, time off, or flexible working arrangements (see page 177). But I wanted to add Long Covid to the list of post-pandemic workplace changes to note. It's still out there and it's here to stay.

Don't forget your family, friends, and colleagues and the impact it may have had on them. If you've been affected, you won't need me to tell you this. I know plenty of people who have had Long Covid at some time over the past three years, and most of them have had to keep quiet about it at work, or minimise its effects when talking to anyone with influence over their career.

That should not happen.

Regrets, I have had a few

I've thrown this one into the mix of post-pandemic work trends as a wild card – a lot of people perhaps won't agree with me. But after spending several years as a journalist specialising in workplaces and careers, and after several decades living deep inside the politics and power plays of media organisations, I have come to believe that regret is a powerful emotion in our working lives.

It is also one that our years locked down working in bedrooms or kitchens, with plenty of time for rumination and reflection, may have brought to the fore.

Regret is nothing to be ashamed of or to dismiss. It is an emotion that can work wonders for you, and for your career (also your life; this book covers everything!).

As much as we might all want to put lockdowns and the pandemic behind us, much of what I am writing about in this book would not have happened without that extraordinary catalyst for change.

Examining the regrets we've had – I am talking about in relation to work here, but you can add in anything you want – allows us to think about the mistakes we've made, the jobs that didn't work out, and so on. But more importantly, in my opinion, it can lead us to consider the paths we might have taken, and perhaps still could. Looking back helps us to push forward.

The kinds of people who suggest they never look back and regret nothing are not likely to be self-aware enough to think about how the past can positively impact the future.

In his book, *The Power of Regret*, Daniel Pink surveys people of all ages. He highlights an interesting shift that happens as we age: In our youth, we regret things we do (mistakes happen), but the older people get, the more likely they are to regret *not* having tried something. So regret becomes more about inaction, the path not taken.

Daniel talked to my FT colleague Andrew Hill for both the *Working It* podcast and the FT newspaper. Andrew writes that 'for every person in his [survey] database who said they regretted setting out on their own in business, Pink says there were forty or fifty who kicked themselves for not having acted. "The lesson from career regrets," he says, "is that we should have a slight bias for action... We should just try stuff and be less worried about the risk."'

What strikes me about these thoughts is that in the podcast we are very careful to distinguish between regret and failure. And that's an important point – failures are often outside our control. There may be no lesson to be learned from failure; it just happens. Regrets, on the other hand, are something we can reflect on.

For some, there can also be a certain bittersweet pleasure in dwelling on past workplace regrets – or any other sort. I am one of these people. Here's mine: Why didn't I capitalise on my early career success? I was incredibly ambitious and had a good eye for a news story. At 31 I was briefly the business editor of a national newspaper, albeit the least successful one. It's now defunct. Soon afterwards I moved employers, had kids, and I didn't apply for senior jobs because I didn't think I had the bandwidth to do them anymore. I was scared of doing a bad job at home and at the office so I worked for other people (who were often terrible managers) and I didn't step up into a senior role again for many years.

I regret that now but the regret and sorrow has forged itself into a determination to fulfil my professional potential going forward. Life is complex and unpredictable, and in maturity I have come to accept that. Plus, I did get to collect my kids from school a couple of days a week and that time was very precious. Back before the pandemic, mothers with full-time jobs on national newspapers could never do that.

If you consider yourself attracted by the notion of something being 'bittersweet' then I recommend Susan Cain's book of that title. She is the author who became a global sensation with her 2012 book, *Quiet: The Power of Introverts in a World That Can't Stop Talking.* Her follow-up, *Bittersweet: How Sorrow and Longing Make us Whole*, is about learning to recognise and grow from that precise feeling of what I would call 'delicious melancholy'.

This bittersweetness, as Susan shows us, can be a creative force. It 'shows us how to respond to pain: by acknowledging it, and attempting to turn it into art, the way musicians do, or healing, or innovation, or anything else that nourishes the soul. If we don't transform our sorrows and longings, we can end up inflicting them on others via abuse, domination, neglect. But if we realise that all humans know – or will know – loss and suffering, we can turn toward each other.'

At the heart of what Susan is proposing is the idea that we can transform 'pain into creativity, transcendence, and love'. If you are having a hard time at work or in life, are in grief for a lost loved one, or just sad, this is a way to synthesise it and help construct some meaning and narrative. Because humans are hardwired for storytelling, and you can take more care of how you think about, and even tell, your own story, however sad or bittersweet it may be.

So, exploit regret. Embrace the bittersweet losses and near misses of your career and your life. If in doubt – and especially if you are older rather than younger – you may regret it less in future if you opt for action, rather than inaction, when given a choice.

Take that job offer. Set up as a consultant. Go for your startup idea. (But please don't blame me if it goes wrong.)

The long and winding path to more diverse and inclusive organisations

Cast your thoughts back to May 2020 and the murder of George Floyd in Minneapolis. Black Lives Matter marches went global, and there was sudden momentum in business and society to push for race equity. It seemed to herald a profound change in workplaces.

My FT colleague Taylor Nicole Rogers, US labour and equality correspondent, reported on these events and the corporate response to them. 'CEOs from every major company were putting out statements, for the first time acknowledging racism and the struggles that Black Americans like myself face in the workplace every day. And that was huge because we had never heard anyone acknowledge it. But these acknowledgements also came with pledges to make things better and that's the part that I am not sure has changed – we've had this seismic shift between pretending that racism does not exist in the workplace and now we are at the part where we know it exists but we are still trying to figure out if we are going to do something about it.'

Taylor was talking to me on the podcast in 2022 and things haven't changed much, other than that a lot more money has been spent in workplaces to place Diversity, Equity, and Inclusion (DEI) goals very much nearer to the centre of operations. Over the two years to early 2023, according to the consultants Deloitte, 'large multinational organisations made more than 1,000 public DEI commitments and pledged more than $210 billion to DEI initiatives.'

That's a lot of money, and the shift in terms of open corporate commitments to advancing more workers from minority groups since 2020 has been noticeable in many workplaces. The snag is that the money goes into inputs. Many companies measure progress on diversity by how many people they recruit from previously underrepresented groups, or by the fact that they run mentoring and sponsorship schemes. The mere existence of the initiative – let's say, management training for women – isn't enough.

Companies who are serious about DEI are now looking at outcomes, and structural and institutional change, not just developing and nurturing individual workers. Think about this: From talking to experts,

I've come to the understanding that the purpose of DEI is to make the organisation better for everyone.

DEI can never solve the problems of individual workers, and the focus has to be on structural progress and change.

Not enough organisations have caught on to this, in my view.

While the current trend is for DEI to be very visible within organisations – and leaders often offer vocal support for efforts to build and maintain diverse workforces – most of the time, not much happens. The dial moves a bit.

My advice for anyone reading this book who cares about building and maintaining a more diverse group of colleagues, and who wants to see leadership teams reflect the societies we live in, is to follow the outcomes. Don't be distracted by shiny HR-driven plans and training sessions. Many organisations now make a big fuss about how they recruit young workers from non-traditional backgrounds. The outcomes are what happens next. Do those people stay? Who gets promoted?

In a post-pandemic economic trough, amid mass layoffs at big companies, what progress has been made on DEI since 2020 may be under threat. It's early to tell, but in a crunch the instinct of many leaders is to protect the jobs that focus on money and operations. The HR and diversity departments are easy targets for budget cuts. Twitter and Meta are among the big tech companies who have let DEI staff go in layoffs.

We will take an in-depth look later in the book at the proven, practical ways to build, maintain, and develop more inclusive teams. Many of them involve tracking data, and greater transparency over pay and promotion, as a way to minimise the effects of personal biases (See Part II, Chapter 3, starting on page 170).

In too many workplaces, diversity efforts are still focused on ways to make senior leaders feel good – rather than uncomfortable and challenged.

<u>Takeaways</u>

- The pandemic disrupted what we had believed was 'normal' about work (9–5, five days a week) for more than a century. Things will never, ever go back completely to how they were. Whatever the 'all week in the office' crowd think.

- Homeworking used to be a norm for most people in the pre-industrial age. Think of WFH as a return to our roots, which are naturally close to the communities we live in.

- Expect more uncertainty. Live with it. It's uncomfortable but by its very nature is full of possibilities, both good and bad.

- Communities are thriving. Can you shift the energy that might previously have gone into workplace events and get more involved in local issues? (Many schools need governors, for example).

- Invest in workplace relationships. Try one fewer meeting and one more coffee with a colleague per week.

- Work friends are real friends. (Those people must really love you – they have probably seen you lose your shit over nothing at work.)

- Tech, AI, and automation will change everything. They will make large parts of this book obsolete. They might make your job easier, or they might put your job out of existence. At this stage (in 2023), it's important to learn about how they may impact your sector. Be open minded and curious. If you can see what's coming round the corner, you can be the first to react if your sector is going to be impacted.

- Accept, even embrace, your regrets and a sense of bittersweet sorrow – don't be a '*je ne regrette rien*' type. Those people lack basic self-awareness. When it comes to planning our future careers, what we regret about the past can teach us a lot.

- Bring compassion to work. Millions of people have Long Covid and the crisis will impact workloads and careers for years to come. It's a hidden workplace crisis.

Chapter 3: Does Your Current Workplace Suck or Shine?

How to spot a healthy workplace that's also fit for the future

Here's my work mantra, and I repeat it to anyone who will listen because it will always be true: All Workplaces Are Dysfunctional.

How could it be otherwise? People are different, people are messy, and the people who are in charge at our workplaces are no different to those of us who work for them. They are just better paid.

The difference between a decent, reasonably functional workplace and the wild excess of your local Nextdoor feed or street WhatsApp group (God, I love that stuff) is that a set of boundaries and rituals bind people at work and keep everything running – reasonably – smoothly.

You might live in the same street as Roger who keeps posting UFO conspiracy memes, but he's not living in the same dimension as you are. If Roger did that on a Slack channel at his work, he'd likely be taking a trip to see HR.

My point is that we should have high expectations that our workplaces will keep us physically safe and not subject to bullying, UFO conspiracies, or unreasonable workloads. That we should have the right tools and environment to do our best work. Employers have a duty of care to us. But we can't expect perfection. Before you audit your workplace, remember, this employer is probably not going to be your partner for life.

These are some of the things to look out for in order to perform an 'audit' on your workplace. Evidence of any or all of the below shows that an employer has given thought and commitment to its present staff – and the future thriving of the organisation, whether that's for profit or in the charitable or public sector.

If you don't recognise any of these things, you must know on some level that your place of work is a dud. It's probably time to go and polish your LinkedIn profile.

Handbooks and clear communication

Until the rise of the internet, many big organisations had physical handbooks for staff, outlining expectations, forbidden activities, and staff benefits. This was useful. It codified and solidified corporate culture and employer expectations.

We lost sight of this as everything went online, but it's interesting that there's been a corporate handbook revival – now online – since the pandemic.

As new staff arrive, they may be working partly or wholly from home, so a written guide is really helpful. It's sometimes hard to communicate any changes in policy or working practices to a big and dispersed workforce. And when experienced staff leave, institutional knowledge goes too. Handbooks may be the answer. If you have one in your workplace, that's a good sign that senior leaders are interested in creating a functional and dynamic place to work.

Absence of a handbook is not a warning sign; they are still relatively rare. But if you are new in a job, it's helpful to have all the company information easily accessible. (Your workplace may simply have all this information on an intranet site, without explicitly calling it a handbook.)

Corporate culture is invisible, which is one of the big and enduring problems in workplaces. It's hard to find an actual definition of it, too. The *Harvard Business Review* (my go-to publication for accessible but clear leadership thinking; I recommend a subscription to any manager who wants to be better informed) suggests this in a 2018 article called 'The Leader's Guide to Corporate Culture'. 'Culture is the tacit social order of an organization: It shapes attitudes and behaviors in wide-ranging and durable ways. Cultural norms define what is encouraged, discouraged, accepted, or rejected within a group.'

Crucially, corporate culture is unspoken. It gets talked about all the time, but without any explanation. You would not believe how many emails and pitches I get at the FT offering me the chance to talk to CEOs or heads of HR who have 'created a truly inclusive corporate culture', whatever that is. Often, we are just supposed to ingest 'it', whatever that Kool-Aid is, and start to behave at work in the appropriate way.

For an example of really good internal communication practice, have a look at GitLab's handbook, which was first created in 2013 and is publicly accessible. The company has an all-remote workforce – this pre-dates the pandemic – and its head of people, Wendy Nice Barnes, told the FT that a handbook which documents internal processes means that 'all which was implicit [has] to be made explicit.'

Wendy's point is important. Any sort of clarity is helpful, especially for newcomers. A sense that internal processes and expectations are 'unwritten' and 'known' is a form of obfuscation – and can mean that managers get the leeway to wriggle out of responsibility when things go wrong.

Another thing to remember is that simply writing things down doesn't make them happen. Organisations have to make a commitment to acting on their intentions. One of the most disappointing things in any workplace is hot air – big statements about flexible work or inclusive recruitment or sustainability. Does your workplace back up its big statements with real action?

The good thing about having expectations and commitments written down is that you can hold your employer to account, if necessary. Let's hope it doesn't come to that, but it is reassuring.

Learning and development

I once spent a week on a management training course run by one of my early employers, *Reader's Digest*, an old-fashioned US media company. My team stayed at the company-owned conference centre and did role playing exercises, which included how to confront an underling who was stealing stationery and/or toilet roll. (I'm still waiting for my chance to do this in real life.)

We also learned about the history of the company and its unique 'culture'. This included, I kid you not, a company song, of which I can now find no trace online. Perhaps I was hallucinating.

I am sure that sort of course has gone the way of fax machines and the petty cash box. Staff training has shifted towards giving individuals the skills to do their job – or to 'upskill' for the next job.

If your company is investing in its staff through offering any sorts of skills, management, or training (or Learning and Development, L&D, as it's probably called), then that's a good sign, too.

Some companies worry that staff will gain new skills and then move on, so they don't spend much on training. Employers get mad when people they've spent money on just take those new skills elsewhere.

Anyone can see that is petty beyond belief but it happens all the time. And it is a huge barrier to advancement.

Other managers want their best staff to stay with them. They may be great champions of their teams, and be kind and caring leaders, but that's worthless if they don't also encourage staff to take up offers of training. Some managers are so scared of the prospect of newly trained staff leaving the team that they will actively block them from going on courses (I have had this happen to me).

Both of these scenarios are flashing warning signs that your organisation is not investing properly in its staff.

As New York University professor Raul Sanchez told me, 'Upskilling is a way to say, "You have a career path at this organisation."' It should be a retention tool. And, he says, training opportunities can also be a good way to show commitment to building a diverse workforce. 'We are giving access to opportunities [for upskilling] to every member of the workforce. This is another way to build long-term career paths.'

On an individual level, we should all maximise the chances offered to us. Even if a course doesn't look promising, it might be an opportunity to network.

What skills should you be focusing on? We will deal with that in a later chapter (see Part II, Chapter 5, starting on page 193) but bear in mind there are two broad groups of skills: tech and professional skills, related to your work, and what used to be called 'soft skills' – a term that is now firmly out of favour, but which relates to the human skills of communicating, negotiating, teamwork, and being in touch with others' emotional responses.

Transparency at work

Transparency is one of those buzzwords that might mean something important or it might just be an organisation trying to sugar-coat its internal practices with a fancy expression. If your workplace makes a lot of its 'transparency', that's potentially a good sign for your audit, but dig about to see what that means in practice.

What transparency should mean in a workplace context is that there is a demand on managers and leaders to be clear and open about one or more aspects of the organisational structure and culture. That might be around promotion – making a pledge to advertise all jobs and give fair interviews with the same questions asked to all applicants, for example. This sort of transparency helps to reduce the mysterious ways in which favoured or 'in group' staff get promoted, sometimes without a post being advertised.

The problems around promotions highlight why any sort of transparency at work is especially helpful for people who are not part of the 'in group' or the majority group. As my FT colleague Brooke Masters, the US investment editor, points out, 'If you are in the "in group" you don't need transparency because people will help you out. It is the people who are on the margins who need the transparency.'

The best-known form of transparency is around salaries. This is such an interesting subject (come on, who doesn't want to know what their boss earns?) that we've already covered it twice on the *Working It* podcast. There are some obvious upsides. For those who are from minority or marginalised groups, being able to see the banding levels, or the process behind determining pay – or even what others earn – could well highlight the discrepancies in pay levels and help them to get a pay rise.

Total salary transparency – in which everyone's pay is disclosed – or the less drastic act of making public a range of salary bands for different job categories, is one of the best, proven ways to close the gender pay gap.

Tomasz Obloj, associate professor at the Kelley School of Business, University of Indiana, has done a lot of research on pay worldwide. He told me on the podcast that 'one of the big results is that pay transparency does lead to a decrease in discriminatory pay gap, in particular the gender pay gap. So there, I think that there is unequivocal evidence that pay transparency works.'

Employers now have to put pay ranges on job advertisements in several US states, so this is going mainstream very quickly. The intention is to give jobseekers more information. There are some companies who try to obfuscate by giving ludicrously wide salary ranges. These often stop workers from finding out what the actual pay for the job is. However, over time, this undermining of the system is likely to be called out and disappear.

One of the things my podcast interviews have highlighted is that salary transparency encourages a very open culture overall. Joel Gascoigne, CEO of Buffer (salary: $298,958), a company that helps businesses build a social media presence, said, 'We are trying to work in an open way – we are not doing things in secret that are then big surprises to everyone else on the team.' Buffer publishes all its salaries online, and potential recruits can see how much they might earn in any particular role.

Is there a downside to transparency? Probably not for anyone doing an 'audit' of their company; attention to transparency is only going to become more important in future.

One potential downside of salary transparency is – wait for it – more pay for CEOs. Their pay is usually disclosed, so there's plenty of data. Brooke Masters, the FT's US financial editor, offers a great explanation of why that happens. 'The more disclosure there is about CEO pay, the more other CEOs go to their boards and say "Look, I'm making less than Charlie at Company B. And I want to make above average for my sector – and everyone's average keeps moving up."'

A trend to keep an eye on, and which might be even more relevant than pay transparency for some people, is 'pay equity'. This is a new-ish term that's quickly gaining currency. Achieving pay equity means that every employee in an organisation is rewarded according to their performance, measured against their goals, company strategy, and how much they contribute to the success of the business.

It goes a lot further than money. Pay equity is about achieving an overall package that is fair, and is equivalent to peers in the organisation who are at the same level. Rewards, for example, might also include training opportunities and advancement at work.

Josh Bersin is a US human capital consultant who first alerted me to the idea of pay equity. He runs surveys among hundreds of companies, and found early in 2023 that a pay equity policy was far more important to staff than having high levels of pay and benefits across the company. Why is this? Partly, it seems, because of our innate human desire for fairness. And, 'if pay is unfair, then usually growth, development, and other benefits are unfair,' Josh says.

Fairness also becomes closely linked to wider trust measures at work. If you think you are paid fairly, you are more likely to trust managers and leaders, and it has knock-on benefits in terms of diversity and inclusion, for example. It's a virtuous circle.

More employers are starting to take pay equity seriously, not least because staff who think they are paid unfairly are likely to be disengaged from their work, and then often leave.

As a first step, a growing number of companies are using tech to help them assess their salaries. These programmes, with names like Syndio and Salary.com, will crunch the numbers of all the salaries within the organisation and look for factors that might explain pay discrepancies.

Josh explains that the analysis might find, for example, that 'men are paid 8 per cent more than women, and that then becomes a pay equity problem that can be addressed.'

Overall, there are often massive discrepancies between pay levels among peers, and that's hard to correct quickly because people might come from outside on a higher salary than existing staff, or they have switched sectors or internal departments with no pay cut, or, at the other end of the spectrum, some workers might be paid less than colleagues because of past managers' biases.

So, to be realistic, if your manager, head of HR, or CEO even mentions that they are thinking about pay equity, that's a very good sign for the future.

Sustainable offices – and the streets beyond

What does your workplace look like? This has become a big question, post pandemic, and a lot of the 'future of work' thinking being done by academics, consultancies, and the companies themselves focuses on the actual spaces where we do our work together.

For anyone looking at their current workplace, there are some easy ways to see if the leaders are thinking about the future by investing in staff wellbeing and optimised workspaces. The big consultancies and law and tech firms often lead the way on this – but a big spend isn't always going to end in a great result.

The easy way to think of the different ways we work is to think about how we divide our time. There is self-directed, deep focus work which is where we get on with tasks and projects (also known as 'actual work'). And there is anything that involves other people. Meetings, chats, coffees, team stand-ups, Zoom calls, and the like (let's call that 'collaborative work').

Since the pandemic, forward-thinking office managers and designers have stripped out endless banks of desks and added in collaborative tables, sofa areas, and so on, plus those tiny retro-looking phone booths where you can make a call or take a virtual meeting. In other words, the workplace layout is more of a mix than it used to be.

The next level of future-proofing is a workplace that takes into account the needs of physically disabled and neurodiverse colleagues. This requires a lot of thought. Something as simple as a loud or distinctive pattern on the walls might affect someone with ADHD or autism. There is a long way to go on these aspects of the workplace but organisations such as Neurodiversity in Business are leading the way in collating resources and expertise.

One of the buzzwords in office design, and in many other arenas, is 'sustainability'. This might include efficient energy use and using sustainable materials for building and refurbishment projects. That's all good, and patching up your office with good air filtration and windows that open is nice. But the sign that an organisation is *really* thinking about environmental, social, and governance (ESG) issues is when they consider the supply chain, their own business practices, and how to get staff to change their behaviour. It's also about being a part of local communities and benefiting them. This latter point is a trend that's likely to accelerate.

To find out more about the most innovative space and sustainability ideas, I turned to Yasmin Jones-Henry, a London-based expert on both place and space. She's a cultural placemaker, which a new-ish job but one that is becoming very influential. She makes sure there is a good mix of cultural offerings, commercial space, and various other elements within new and existing urban developments.

And she is passionate about making everything sustainable – from a building's construction to the work that goes on inside it.

Yasmin told me there is a very easy benchmark that helps experts like her spot 'greenwashing' by companies, though it's useful for anyone to know. 'The UN's Sustainable Development Goal 11: Sustainable Cities and Communities, offers a universal benchmark and filter that enables me to cut through, and identify very quickly, which organisations are serious about sustainability and their eco-credentials. I can spot the greenwashing fairly quickly because whatever promises workspace providers make around sustainability and eco-credentials are weighed in the balance against the 'S' [social] in ESG.

'There is no credibility if the organisation is preoccupied with the material composition of the concrete, for example, while the wellbeing of the people who manufacture that and other products used in construction, or the people who work in the space, are poorly treated. The construction [sector] is the second biggest driver of modern slavery.

'Too often London – and cities in general – have fallen victim to the jargon, with little chance for big workplaces and other developments to create wealth generation for the local community. Increasingly, the "best in class" organisations are the ones who understand that their social responsibility is a fundamental part of building sustainable cities.'

Leadership in this area, as in so many other areas, comes from the beliefs and example of those in charge. The clue to whether your workplace is actually forward-looking, and making workspaces that are built for humans, on sustainable foundations in all senses, is in whether your leaders practise what they preach.

The thinking that Yasmin and other sustainability experts bring to their work is at the cutting edge of design, building, and corporate culture. It's a great sign for the future if your employer is acting on these principles already.

'Psychological safety' is a key concept

How do you know if your workplace is the place to invest your talent for the long term? The shortcut to answering this is not pay, perks, or whether you feel nauseous because you are 'hot-desking' among other people's coffee cups and skin flakes. No. The first hack is to work out whether or not it is a place of psychological safety.

Unfortunately, 'psychological safety' is one of the most written about, yet least understood, terms in the workplace world. Here's an FT definition (so we know we can trust it) by my colleague Andrew Hill. He defines it as 'ending, or at least reducing, interpersonal fear in teams and increasing candour'.

On one level, it's a fancy way of saying 'be honest and nice to each other' but there's a lot more sophistication than that. The term was coined by Amy Edmondson, now a professor at Harvard Business School, and it centres around the discovery that high-performing teams actually report more errors because they can talk openly about mistakes (and fix them, work out how to avoid them in the future, and so on).

If you have ever worked in an environment where everyone keeps quiet about potential errors or indeed anything negative for fear of being shouted at or worse, or where the boss talks at you all but doesn't ever listen, then you will know what psychological safety isn't. It is very easy to recognise its absence.

Health and safety measures and error prevention are two big bonuses of teams who can talk freely to each other. And so is improved feedback. Andrew Hill reports that 'psychological safety is a core part of a new training programme Warner Music is rolling out to its 1,500 people managers. Members of its all-important A&R (artist and repertoire) teams, for example, are encouraged to offer frank feedback about each other's hits and flops, a process known as "retrospectives" or "retro-ing".'

'Psychological safety' is sometimes used nearly interchangeably with 'safe space' which usually means a supportive and non-threatening environment. But too often a workplace that aspires to be a safe space may, in practice, be one where difficult and polarising facts and opinions are not aired and some people feel 'silenced'. One person's safe space might be another's threatening one.

Psychological safety is different. In a candid workplace you will be able to tell colleagues and leaders when things are wrong, when you see something that worries you, or when the business is threatened (by inefficiency, a process that is going wrong, actual wrongdoing by colleagues, and so on). You need to trust your colleagues; you don't need to agree with them. A good word to think about is 'challenge'. Would you feel comfortable challenging your manager or the boss?

The flipside of this candour is that within a psychologically safe organisation, feedback will be taken seriously, and it can often be very hard to hear. You need to be aware of that. It's probably the price you have to pay for a psychologically safe workplace, in the best sense.

In the How to Manage Anyone, Especially People You Don't Like chapter (see page 165) we will deal with the upsides of feedback, as well as with the dire consequences it can create when done clumsily, or with bias, dislike, or just in a half-hearted way.

Is it a healthy workplace?

This 'healthy workplace' concept is invisible, but absolutely key in any audit of whether your workplace is somewhere you want to invest your time, talent, and brilliant personality. And it doesn't mean what you think it does. I am not talking about healthy snacks or free yoga classes. Or even about leaders' efforts to make sure staff have good mental health support.

A 'healthy workplace' is much more than somewhere that focuses on the physical and mental health of its staff, and on preventing illness. Sure, it encompasses those things, and it also takes in just about everything else: workload, inclusion, leaders who model healthy ways of working, respect, and professionalism. The whole thing.

I came to this understanding pretty recently. I think, like most of us, I had parcelled up all the different parts of a workplace and corporate culture into different boxes. Now I can just say 'healthy workplace' and mean all of them.

This first occurred to me after reading a book called *Make Work Healthy* by a specialist workplace consultant in this field, John Ryan. I asked John to outline exactly what staff should look for in an employer – what makes a workplace healthy?

He told me that 'the key is to understand that it is made of two components: healthy people and a healthy organisation. There is a symbiotic relationship. People impact the organisation and the organisation impacts the people. A healthy employee is an individual with the vitality to flourish at work and beyond and a healthy organisation is one that sustainably delivers on its objectives.

'Employees should look for a culture of wellbeing, one where it is easier to be healthier than not. A brand or independent certification is useful but not just a tick box of policies and practices – real life views of employees' lived experiences. Ask to meet employees randomly, walk the floor; you can get a sense very quickly whether the mood is right. Attrition data [how many people leave] is useful too.

'Leaders and organisations have numbers for everything that they care about. Do they have workforce health data? Do they review? Do they take actions to address the findings? Look for organisations that take a data-driven, evidence-based approach to workforce health.'

The unhealthy workplace can have a serious effect on your mental and physical health. You don't have to be a workplace expert to audit this one – look at the bosses. Do they actually do the healthy things they say they want for the staff?

John says that leaders are often an obstacle to workplace health. His research found them to be 'modelling the worst behaviours'. His interviews showed that 'in many cases leaders had knowingly sacrificed their own health in the pursuit of power and profit.' Many were exhausted and close to burnout (these interviews were done during the pandemic).

I'm fascinated. Why are CEOs so bad at managing their own health?

John explained, 'Because being a CEO is hard. There is a lot of stress and load to carry. The buck stops with you. There are always things to be done, priorities to deliver, people to keep happy. Often the thing that is easiest to sacrifice is your own health. As one of the CEOs said in my book, "That's why they pay me the big bucks." CEOs fall for the trap of matching their lifestyle to their remuneration and then they can't leave – even if the job is killing them. Boards also seldom really care about the health of the CEO unless it may be a risk to performance.'

That (almost) makes me feel sorry for CEOs, but it does highlight something very important: It's easy to look up to leaders and think they have all the answers. Otherwise, why would they be paid so much or be in charge of a billion-dollar operation? But as John's work shows, when CEOs are able to speak confidentially and honestly, they are as flawed as the rest of us.

We can't help CEOs do better to take care of their own health, but we can learn to see when they've allowed a sick workplace to flourish. Think here of the term 'see/do management' as a shorthand for what to look for in terms of how leaders behave at work, and the examples they set. The Chartered Management Institute's Ann Francke uses this term in her work with companies, and it's a good one to keep in mind when you look at overall culture and working practices. Does what the leaders 'say' match up to what they 'do'?

If leaders say they are inclusive, and that bad behaviour, harassment, and worse will not be tolerated, how is that monitored? Because 'walking the talk' in terms of organisational culture is, as Ann told me on the *Working It* podcast, 'not HR's job and it's not the DEI person's job. It's your job. How are you behaving? How are you including your team? How are you role-modelling good behaviour, and how are you dealing swiftly and robustly with bad behaviour?'

The idea of a 'toxic' workplace is pretty widespread and people use it all over the place. Ann's point about the 'see/do' gap is key to remember here. A grim example of this gap is the story of what happened in the UK's largest employers' organisation, the CBI (Confederation of British Industry), a high-profile supporter of diversity and inclusion in the workplace. The CBI got into huge trouble in early 2023, when the *Guardian* ran the first of many explosive news stories about a toxic workplace culture, based on testimony from women who had worked there. These allegations led to the firing of the director general, while far more serious claims emerged against other staff, including two claims of rape.

What happened over the next few weeks was the public unravelling of an organisation. As Ann told me once the scandal broke, 'If you are preaching inclusivity and diversity and fronting all of these campaigns, but you don't hold your own senior leadership to account or you allow, routinely, transgressions to happen, then all of that is for naught because culture isn't a slogan on the wall, it's not the campaigns you front. It's how you behave every day to your colleagues.'

No organisation is perfect but if you see a big gap between the rhetoric and the reality in your workplace, then it's not a healthy organisation. As a staff member, it's not down to you to fix it, but if you don't feel you would be listened to if you made public any worries or complaints, then that's a massive red flag.

Perks and benefits

Talking about perks used to mean health and financial benefits – private health insurance (vital in the US), generous workplace pension schemes, season ticket loans for commuting, discounted gym membership, and so on.

Over the past few years, starting early in the pandemic the conversation has swung from purely 'bolt-on' benefits to those far more integrated with employees' lives and priorities. Broadly, these include childcare and flexible working support, health care – in the broadest sense, including mental health support – and investment in training and development. Being sponsored to go on a course or professional seminar is a personalised benefit, and that's the key to all of this.

Look closely at whether your employer tailors the benefits offered to each individual worker. This is part of the personalised 'employee experience' and it is a growing trend. It's good to be wise to it, as extra perks and benefits can really boost the value of the salary package you get, and you may be able to negotiate more of them.

The brilliant benefit that is a workplace pension deserves a lot more space than I can give it here, but the important part to note is that paying into your pension is always a very, very good idea. As my FT colleague and host of the *Money Clinic* podcast, Claer Barrett, makes very clear in her book, *What They Don't Teach You About Money*, a company pension is 'free money'. Perks don't get better than that.

You should immediately buy Claer's book to read more about it, but the very basic information I'm going to include here is that when you pay into a UK company pension scheme, your employer has to make a contribution, too. The minimum amount the employer pays is around 3 per cent of your monthly salary. The more you pay in, though, the more free money your employer is likely to give you. Claer says in her book, 'Often, if you choose to pay a bit more into the pension scheme, your employer will also pay in a bit more – up to a point. This extra 'free money' is often described as a much duller-sounding "matched contribution".'

Saving into pensions is also free of tax. 'Think of your pension as a tax haven,' says Claer. And on top of that, the money inside your pension grows tax free (until you get to £1 million). I can't recommend her book highly enough for all of your financial needs.

If you work for a reasonable-sized company, you may also have access to some sort of 'wellbeing platform' that offers you access to meditation and yoga, for example, as well as counselling, legal advice, and possibly GP services. Clients can buy into as many services as they want for their staff. All of this is usually done online, or via an app.

I think the idea of bringing existing benefits together in one place is good (the FT, for example, allows us to access gym memberships and private health insurance via a wellbeing app). I am not, though, excited by things like rewarding better health – by giving discounts on leisure brands, for example – if you log your walks or exercise. To me, that's a bit sinister. You may disagree; it's probably a generational issue.

Keep an eye on how your employer behaves more generally. Are they investing in the staff by providing decent working conditions and not overloading you with work?

Because no amount of wellbeing by app is going to help if you have too much work and consequently burn out. In that case, it just looks like a very cheap fix for deep-set issues. Every HR conference I attend is full of people pushing 'wellness solutions' for corporate buyers. That says it all, really.

Free wellbeing support and therapy

If you have watched the TV series *Billions*, you'll know what having an in-house therapist can do for staff. To be precise, Wendy Rhoades on this show is a psychiatrist turned in-house performance coach, because hedge funds can afford to have her skills available 24/7. She helps the bosses and traders at Axe Capital to make the right decisions, both professionally and in their personal lives.

More down-to-earth businesses are also starting to buy into the idea of having counsellors and psychotherapists available for their staff. It's the new version of the old-school practice of having an on-site nurse in big companies (maybe some of them still do it but I haven't heard about it for a long time).

If your company offers counselling and therapy, it is also likely to be as part of an EAP (employee assistance programme). A lot of organisations buy packages of EAP support for their staff. It typically includes a confidential telephone line that will direct you to the right support for issues such as mental health, family problems, or bereavement counselling. There are usually financial and legal helplines. Buying this sort of service allows employers to show they are aware of their 'duty of care' to staff, to ensure their wellbeing.

A typical EAP offer might include a fixed number of sessions with a counsellor to address short-term problems. So if you have a particular issue at work, such as getting to burnout levels of stress or a boss you can't bear, then EAP is a great first step in getting help. Though EAP counselling is confidential, some people are wary of using it for fear that their personal information could be shared with the employer.

Another issue with EAP is that it is often 'baked in' to the staff benefits package and because it's not a shiny new service in many cases, it may not be obvious that it's available. Check your company benefits policy, handbook, or intranet, or talk to HR to find out more, as what's available will vary considerably (a cheapskate employer will, of course, buy a minimum-standard EAP).

A step up from outsourcing wellbeing support to an EAP is to bring some of it in-house. The on-site or virtual-but-free therapist is a growing trend. It's already well-established in the US, where about three in ten organisations have, or plan to have, in-house therapy.

When the FT last wrote about the topic in 2023, in-house therapy was firmly on the rise in UK legal, finance, and professional services firms. The sorts of issues covered included helping managers with staff problems they can't solve themselves, and mental health problems arising from remote or hybrid working. It's not right for everyone; some people won't want to confide in a therapist being paid by their employer. But just having an external, impartial person to talk to about workplace or life dilemmas is a perk I could get behind. Because your best work friend is no expert at psychology and is always, always going to take your side in workplace disputes. Also it's sometimes best to save the secrets of your dysfunctional marriage or your ambivalent feelings for your baby for someone who is paid to listen to you.

What sort of flexible work is offered?

There's a great tension at many organisations between (often) leaders' desire for staff to return to the office and (often) their employees' desire to work from home, and for flexibility in how and when they do their jobs.

Many places have settled into a hybrid arrangement, with some days in the office and some at home, but if employers are taking into account individuals' family commitments, health considerations, and other reasons why it makes sense to be at home, then that's a good sign for the future.

If your manager allows you to balance all the things you need to do in order to make sure you can work effectively, and in the most productive way, then you should treasure that employer. A fixed line on where, when, and how you must work – not so much.

Are your team leaders and top executives good communicators, including being good listeners?

This is a hard one to assess and requires looking behind the PR puff and heavily edited pronouncements that your CEO or top managers make. People can be good communicators on the surface, but overuse of jargon is an easy way to mask what they are really saying behind a wall of platitudes.

Do you feel that staff are listened to? Often the best ideas in organisations come from people well below the top layer of management, but those ideas will never be heard unless senior people are open to listening.

That's just one example. There's a lot of talk about 'authentic' leadership and being 'vulnerable' as a CEO or senior executive. I am never quite sure what it means. None of us are completely 'authentic' at work (that's actually a bad idea) but it's important for leaders to behave well and professionally, and to bring out the best in others.

So when I suggest that being a good communicator is a great sign in a manager or leader, what I mean is that they talk directly, they talk in plain language, and they give every indication of being open to hearing from others.

Good communicators also don't need to rant, shout, bully, or generally behave like the workplace is their personal fiefdom. Often, a leader becomes closely identified with their business but, unless they are the founder or owner (though shouting remains non-acceptable in 99 per cent of cases), then they are not in control.

If you decide to leave a company, it's usually not personal against the leadership. You may just have a better offer! Yet I've heard of many cases where people are accused of 'disloyalty' after handing in their notice to go to another job. Those bosses are suggesting their workers have some sort of personal obligation to the employer. They don't. Your workplace is not your family, or even your friend, even though some employers do explicitly reference these close relationships.

In his book, *The Good Enough Job*, Simone Stolzoff explores this phenomenon. 'Salesforce defines its corporate culture using the Hawaiian word "ohana", which means "chosen family".' Still, as Simone says, 'Family relationships . . . are unconditional. At-will employment, by definition, is not.' You can't (usually) be fired from your own family.

Plus, the concept of 'boomerang' employees is on the rise: people leaving, then one day returning. Smart leaders want people to leave with a positive view of the company, because word of mouth is powerful.

When a leader surrounds themself with 'yes people' who manage their corporate image and messaging, and who don't allow any criticism near the corner office . . . that's not a great place for you to be.

Very many corporate scandals and collapses, once the dust has settled, turn out to have at their heart a leader or leaders who refused to listen to dissenting voices and who believed their own hype. Enron, the giant US energy company that collapsed spectacularly in December 2001, is an example of this. A vice president at the company, Sherron Watkins, warned its CEO, Kenneth Lay, in August 2001, that Enron's accounting methods were improper. Watkins later discovered that instead of following up on her warning, senior managers tried to have her sacked. Within months, Enron – at one time the seventh-largest company in the US – declared bankruptcy.

Is there any feeling of people being excluded or of there being an 'in group' and an 'out group'?

If you are new at your employer, you may still feel you don't know people well. It's okay to be a little wary or feel like an outsider for the first few weeks in any new workplace. But once you have got past the trial period, how your colleagues treat you, and your sense of belonging in the organisation are big issues.

This one requires you to look around at the types of interactions going on around you. Let's hope there are no longer any 'initiation ceremonies' going on, or competitive drinking to see if you can hold your alcohol, or anything else that belongs in the 1970s. Beyond that, keep focused on the idea of how much you feel you 'belong' in this organisation. It's become something of a buzzword, but it does actually convey a useful meaning. If you are excluded from meetings or general social events, or see that others are left out while you are included, then that is a red flag.

Lots of companies with predominantly young staff – startups and tech companies, for example – often have a lively workplace social life with events put on for staff. This is a great way to encourage people to come to the office, and also to encourage connection and friendships. But is everyone welcome? Or are there events going on that are only open to a select group?

All 'organised fun' on a department or corporate level is different from making evening and weekend social plans with work colleagues who are on the way to becoming your friends, or who have already crossed over. You can go out after hours with whomever you want, but be aware that the hurt of being left out – something that everyone probably suffered at school – doesn't go away just because we are adults. Our psychological response to this sort of rejection is still very much the same as when we were ten.

So if you have arranged to go out with some people in your team or group at work, and not others, remember not to shout about it on social media. Even better, consider before you go whether you have left someone out. If there's a pattern (is there a particular person or group of people who are excluded?) then think about what lies beneath that. Can you act with more consideration and kindness? (Answer: Yes, we all can.)

If you are on the other end of this and find yourself persistently left out, that's not a great long-term outlook for your mental wellbeing. You may not even like or want to see your colleagues for one minute beyond contracted hours (remote work can really help in this respect) but all measures show that feeling connected to our colleagues helps us in every aspect of our work and boosts our wellbeing. If you hate them, think about moving on.

And if you think there is another motive behind feeling excluded – perhaps you are from a different ethnic, social, or linguistic background from the 'in group', or you are a person with a visible or invisible disability – then that is a serious issue and very much worth addressing formally, if you can face it. This kind of bias is all too common. There is a very basic reason for it – humans have 'homophily', a liking for people who are the same as us, or resemble us. Getting past that to understand and value difference is the work of grown-ups in good organisations, i.e. any of us who are thoughtful enough to think about these things.

Diverse teams work well. Often, they actually do better than ones where everyone 'fits' within the existing majority group. But these mixed teams take a lot of work and investment on the part of managers. Too often, the 'in group' is allowed to rule unquestioned.

It's depressing, but there is a lot that is depressing about human nature, and the good news is that we can overcome these biases and help everyone to belong at work. If you don't find yourself welcome, or don't like the attitudes of your colleagues, seek a transfer or you may have to leave.

And finally . . . can you take your dog to work?

Dogs in offices have become far more common since the pandemic. Not surprising, when you consider how many people got a pet dog during the lockdowns. There's no actual link between dogs in the office and somewhere being a great place to work, but the freedom and trust that allowing staff to bring pets to work implies is something very special. Even if you don't have a dog.

When I interviewed Ben & Jerry's ice cream 'K9 culture committee' member Lyndsay Bumps on *Working It*, she gave me the lowdown on the company's long-term commitment to allowing staff members to bring pets to work. Ben & Jerry's have been doing this for far longer than the pandemic, but understanding their reasoning helps anyone, even a cat person like me, to get why a company that allows dogs in the office is probably a relaxed and friendly and caring place.

As Lyndsay says, 'It's a bigger perk than free ice cream.' Dogs have been going with their owners to work since 1978 at Ben & Jerry's, making it a pioneer in this field. But there are clear rules: pets have to stay within their owner's desk or office area, and they have dog gates to keep them there. There are also plenty of toys (not to mention a nameplate for each dog).

There are health, cultural, and psychological reasons why some people don't want dogs in offices. I don't love dogs so this is not something I feel passionate about, but I am equally convinced that well-implemented dog policies are a real indicator of the type of company you have joined – or are thinking of joining.

Dogs bring people together and encourage connection, as long as they are well-behaved. Even Ben & Jerry's won't tolerate repeated bad behaviour from canine co-workers.

Takeaways

- All workplaces are dysfunctional. Work is not your family but, like families, all workplaces have their quirks. Just don't make the mistake of expecting either of these to be perfect. That ends badly.

- Corporate culture means the unspoken set of behaviours and norms in a workplace. Their unspoken nature is highly unsatisfactory; are we are just supposed to learn how to behave, as if by magic? Companies which publish explicit guidelines and commitments for staff are doing the right thing.

- A good employer invests in its staff. Work is changing fast and we need to keep up. Any manager who doesn't encourage you to learn new skills or who actively blocks you from training is being defensive and short-sighted. The team is never 'too busy' for you to take a day out for professional development. Put your own needs first.

- Transparency around promotions and pay is a good sign. Few organisations publish everyone's salary but making 'pay bands', or salary ranges on job ads, public is good, and now law in some US states. The concept of 'pay equity' is about overall fairness around your pay and benefits package compared to peers. Do you feel fairly paid?

- How is the physical space in your workplace (if you have one)? Post-pandemic shifts mean forward-looking employers mix banks of desks with informal meeting spaces and quiet zones for focused work.

- Sustainability in building design and supply chains is finally starting to get on the agenda. Greenwashing is everywhere, though, so beware.

- Are the access and workspace needs of people with visible and invisible disabilities being included? Spending money on refits is a sign of commitment to inclusion for everyone.

- Psychological safety is a highly desirable trait in the workplace. It means that everyone in a team is able to speak up or disagree without fear of consequence. This is a very misunderstood concept, but an important one.

- A healthy organisation is one that takes care of its staff and doesn't overload them with work, which causes burnout. How do the people in charge behave? Sending emails at all hours and making unreasonable demands indicates a not-so-healthy workplace.

- Perks, benefits, and therapists are all good. Pay into your company pension, because there's free money on offer. Watch out for over-reliance on 'wellness by app' from your employer. Mindfulness isn't going to fix a burnout culture.

- Hiding behind jargon is a common leadership tactic, rendering communication near-meaningless. Do your leaders speak plainly – and want to listen in return? Never expect total honesty, though. Humans need reassurance, and we want leaders who inspire us.

- Is there an 'in group' and an 'out group'? Realising you are being left out is demoralising. The reasons behind it can be complex, so take time to unpick them, and then decide what to do next. And if you realise you are the 'in' person excluding others? Self-awareness is the starting point for change.

- Dogs in offices are divisive, but the practice is on the increase, post pandemic. A dog-friendly office is likely to be an indicator of a healthy workplace that puts human values at its heart. And it also helps cut down on exorbitant doggy-daycare bills.

Chapter 4: Toxic Managers
Why don't more people realise that people quit to get away from a bad manager, not the job?

I can remember all the good managers I've had in my career because there haven't been many of them. There are eight. Out of a total of twenty-four. (I include both my line managers and involved department heads in reaching that total.) So that's a third. Not exactly a stellar percentage.

Good management matters. I remember the best bosses very fondly, and some of them have propelled my career onwards, or propped me up when I was falling short in my work or personal life (or both). Managers rarely get thanked, so if you do have a good manager and they've gone above and beyond for you, send them a note. I once got an email from a team member thanking me for helping them advance in their career, and it meant the world to me.

Stories about other people's terrible or repellent managers are often bleakly funny. I once wrote an FT article about the worst office habits, and more than one person who contacted me told me they'd had a boss who clipped his toenails at his desk. They can do that because they have power and entitlement. It doesn't make it less disgusting. (Nobody had a woman boss who did that. Nor were there any women nominated for the 'wears their cycling lycra all day' category of unwashed bosses and colleagues.)

Bad habits can be amusing, but bad managers are no joke when it's your own work and mental health that's being affected.

We all have deep-set triggers that affect our reactions to different management styles. These come from how we grew up, how we were treated by our parents and other authority figures. Many people don't recognise the link, though. I first made this connection through the work of the psychotherapist and workplace consultant Naomi Shragai, author of *Work Therapy: Or the Man who Mistook his Job for his Life*. It's a must-read for anyone who wants to delve deeper into the unseen and often unconscious ways in which our pasts hijack us at work.

As Naomi wrote in the FT, 'While we might grudgingly accept that our unreasonable behaviour in our personal lives is a reaction to early family experiences, we rarely consider how work tensions might originate from the same source. At work we are generally convinced that problems and threats we experience come from others – manipulative colleagues, bullying bosses, or demanding clients.'

We need to accept that we are not neutral observers in all this. And before deciding how to deal with a toxic boss – or deciding instead to walk away – it's worth first finding out which traits in a boss help you thrive at work, and which make you mad, sad, or perhaps (whisper it) difficult to work with.

The question to ask yourself is: Is it *all* their fault? Or is part of the problem the psychological baggage that you are bringing to the situation?

It's hard to be objective about our own input into tricky relationships, but I have learned a useful tactic from Gabriella Braun, a psychoanalyst and consultant who specialises in untangling and getting to the roots of the problems in dysfunctional workplaces. She details a lot of these case studies in her book, *All That We Are*, which is a good starting point for anyone wanting to understand why we all struggle with interpersonal dynamics at work. The tactic involves a kind of 'out of body' experience, which sounds weird so I asked Gabriella to explain it to me as clearly as possible.

She says, 'Taking the "third position" is a psychoanalytic concept that means stepping back in our minds, so that rather than just being part of an interaction, we can observe ourselves. This reduces the heat of the exchange. It also allows us to appreciate the other person, or people's, point of view and see our behaviour as others see it.'

So that's the first part of the 'third position', which is odd when you start to do it but is actually a very effective way to begin your examination of why your boss is behaving badly or strangely to you. It has to be followed up, as Gabriella points out, with some more self-examination.

'The potential for change is increased by considering whether our behaviour and feelings remind us of relationships from our past. If, for example, thinking about our boss – an authority figure – brings to mind interactions from childhood with a parent, it's likely that unconsciously we have transferred aspects of our relationship with Mum or Dad to the relationship with our boss. This is common because our parents are our first authority figures, so feelings about their authority gets triggered by the current authority figure.

'These insights into our part in a difficult situation means we can modify our behaviour and unlock a stuck dynamic.'

So, next time you find yourself angry beyond justification with your manager, consider whether you are turning them into your parents. I wish I had heard of this long ago when I spent years trying to please an extremely critical boss in a, frankly, childlike way. Still, like many things in life, it's better to come to these realisations later, rather than never. Some people spend a whole working life living out the lasting effects of their childhood.

What kind of bad boss gets under your skin?

I have had lazy bosses, some who only managed upwards, and others who weren't able to cope and blocked out their team's needs. I liked almost all of them and we had few problems. It took me a long time to realise that only micromanagers derail me. I am questioning, obstinate, and self-driven and don't like being told what to do. This reaction goes back a long way; my strict and old-fashioned school demanded that we obey a huge number of pointless rules, including wearing a hat at all times when outside the school grounds. I resisted mightily, often ending up in the Head's office.

I was able to trace a link between my childhood hatred of pointless authority and petty rules and my hopeless track record with workplace micromanagers only after I moved into my current area of work, focusing on management and the workplace. It was then that I started to meet people who helped me unlock the mysteries of why we get on with some managers but not others.

Micromanagers are very insecure about their status as authority figures and need to reinforce it with – often pointless – control over staff. One boss, for example, questioned me about my movements nearly every time I left my desk. They didn't like me to be out of their sight. The tension escalated alarmingly. The more I pulled away, the more they tightened the leash.

I read research recently that suggested our managers have as much impact on our mental health as our partners do. When that's a negative impact, the toll is huge.

In short, decades after leaving school, I know now that I still react badly to inflexible authority figures. I need to think I have some control, even if that control is an illusion. Knowing about this has been helpful and liberating in both my work and personal life.

Your story will be different, but once you step back and recognise its causes and patterns, you can help yourself and decide what, if anything, to do about your bad work situation.

Is it just you?

Having identified what really enrages or blocks you, talk to other team members if you feel comfortable to do so, and see how they react to the bad boss. Is everyone affected equally? This sort of conversation needs careful handling, so only go ahead with it if you feel you'll be heard and respected. It may be that the boss has allies on the team and they'll report straight back to them about your concerns.

Organisations, though, should be worried about bad managers. It's the biggest reason why people leave their jobs. About half of all workers, it seems, have left a job because of a poor manager. So any leaders who care about retaining talented staff should be worried when managers are causing issues – and they should listen to you.

If you are a member of a union, that can be a very good starting point for raising concerns and finding out if similar issues have been raised before. Your union representatives may also be able to work within the company to help you, but of course once you have raised the issue, you will probably have to keep working alongside the problem boss for at least some time to come. This is a massive disincentive to reporting for many people. (This happened to me. When I was being bullied by a boss, I didn't make an official complaint via our union for fear of what they'd be like to work with when they found out. Now I wish I'd just gone ahead and done it!)

Isolation is a common situation for people dealing with bad bosses, and it's another burden you may have to carry. Even if you can't talk to someone on the team, do you have a mentor, a former colleague or manager, or someone independent of the organisation who can listen? A therapist or counsellor will help you here, but don't count on partners, family, or very good friends because they will always tell us what we want to hear, and support us. That's a necessary role, but a different one.

Work situations often call for more impartial counsel. Even if that wise person tells you things you find hard to hear about your own behaviour and reactions.

The missing piece of the puzzle here is the HR department. I have left this until last because of the dual role HR plays in organisations. It's there to support you (the clue is in the 'human' in human resources) but there is also the mandate to carry out leaders' wishes for the good of the organisation, as they perceive it. It's a company department, after all.

While having a great deal of respect for many HR managers and the work they do, it's also necessary to warn anyone who is thinking of reporting an issue with a bad boss that you may not get the response you'd like.

The bigger the company, the more formal the reporting procedures are likely to be, and this is reassuring. There may also be support or coaching available for you so it's always worth seeing what is on offer. A sideways move or a secondment to another department, for example, is not ideal, but it is a good holding tactic to stop any further damage to your confidence or mental and physical health, while you figure out what to do next.

In smaller or family-run businesses, there may not be an HR department to talk to. Or the HR manager may be doubling up doing another job. This, I am afraid, is a red flag.

Your boss really is toxic – what do you do?

If you have worked through all the stages of trying to make change at work and nothing has improved, then the next choice boils down to a simple one: Do I stay or do I go?

That requires a long and involved decision-making process, and it's not one I can simplify for you.

Beyond toxic – when your boss is an actual narcissist

There is one category of boss that needs a special mention, because their effects are so corrosive on everyone around them: narcissists. We are likely to call any malevolent boss 'a narcissist' but it's helpful to separate the merely damaged from the actively harmful. We've already discussed how to go about dealing with a bad boss – or one with whom you don't get on. Sometimes that can mean doing nothing, or simply changing how you react to their behaviour. Narcissists, though, require a different level of understanding, and you will likely need to take action.

When Dr Ramani Durvasula, a clinical psychologist known to everyone as Dr Ramani, came on the *Working It* podcast to talk about narcissist bosses, she blew me away. Her YouTube channel is a great place to look if you think you have a narcissist in your life.

Her own painful experiences of working for a very powerful narcissist led to a new career as an expert in helping people to understand, deal with, and heal from these destructive human beings, both at work and in their personal lives.

What, exactly, defines a narcissist? Dr Ramani says that you will notice they have a rigid personality style and lack empathy. Those are the basics. Then, 'They're deeply entitled. They tend to be grandiose. They are validation- and admiration-seeking, very egocentric, controlling, unaware of the needs and wants of other people.

'They are very sensitive to criticism or feedback and will often lash out when anybody gives them that kind of feedback. They can often be very jealous, they're very thin-skinned . . . These are people who are very, very impacted by shame.'

Once you have recognised that you have a narcissist boss, Dr Ramani has one big piece of advice: document everything. Make notes, forward their emails to your personal address, save voicemails and anything else you need to keep. These may be necessary if you escalate your problem to HR or a lawyer. Even if you just decide to walk away, keeping this evidence also helps you to understand the patterns of abusive behaviour, and not minimise its effects on you.

It's also vital to note how you react physically and mentally. Dr Ramani says, 'There's some really interesting research showing that it's this workplace emotional abuse that results in more significant sleep problems than many other forms of emotional abuse. You sort of take your job home. Is it pulling you away from children, from family, from other things in life that give you joy? Pay attention to that because that's not normal.'

The 'not normal' part of this is key. We've all been in denial or normalised things in our lives – a romantic relationship that is not working, for example – and work is no different. A narcissist boss will try to gaslight you. They will try to make you think that what you feel or perceive isn't real. Take that as your starting point, so as well as the documentation, Dr Ramani recommends trying not to be alone with them and always involving third parties. Don't try to tackle them, suggest they need to change, or criticise them. It's generally counterproductive and nobody is going to stand up for you. (In workplaces where the staff are cowed by a monstrous boss there is often a collective refusal to engage.)

Psychotherapist Naomi Shragai suggests that confiding in people outside the organisation who can validate your experience is important, otherwise the narcissist will undermine the basis of your reality. 'The difficulty is you start to believe that the badness, the wrongness, the inadequacy lies with you. And there is a sense somehow that you really cannot leave, because if you left, who would have you?

'What's really important is to find somebody who can shift that mindset and help you to acknowledge that the problem really is located in the bullying, extreme narcissistic boss and not in you.'

Naomi reiterates what Dr Ramani told me, that confronting your narcissist boss, or even giving them what might be considered constructive feedback, is usually a bad idea.

'You don't want to put yourself in a position that the narcissist themselves experience you as a threat. This is really crucial. Sometimes by simply disagreeing, challenging, confronting – all of those ways will oftentimes leave the narcissist feeling threatened by you. Essentially, they'll feel bad. If they feel bad inside, immediately they'll think you've intended to make them feel bad and they feel justified in attacking you.'

Naomi sums up by saying, 'Very simply, find out what their agenda is and just go along [with it].' Less is more when it comes to dealing with a truly toxic boss.

In many cases, the only solution for those who work for narcissists is to leave the job. If the narcissist is in a position of power, they may be very valuable to the organisation. You are unlikely to get a hearing from colleagues or senior executives. As Dr Ramani puts it, 'Nobody wants to "behead the king" so nobody's going to be willing to speak about it.'

Finally, it may also be helpful to know that narcissism is not all bad. It is on a spectrum. We all have a bit of it in us and we can use it to our advantage.

Naomi notes that 'narcissism is terribly misunderstood. In fact, it's a personality trait and it runs along a long continuum. We, all of us, have an element of narcissism. In fact, we wouldn't be able to function in our jobs without some narcissism. It helps us promote our ideas. It helps us to believe in ourselves, to express our opinions. Without narcissism, we couldn't function.'

Think about it like this, Naomi says, 'Somebody could just simply be charismatic, intelligent, very good-looking – even maybe arrogant – and will be accused of being a narcissist. Now, that person may have some narcissism, but that doesn't imply that they're necessarily a pathological, malignant narcissist.'

How common is extreme narcissism? Some experts suggest 5 per cent of the US population are narcissists, and the rates among CEOs may be three times that.

So while we don't know exactly what percentage of people have had experience with a narcissist boss, the numbers in leadership positions are quite high. Good luck out there.

Takeaways

- Stop spiralling with reactive anxiety or anger about your bad manager. Instead, try to understand their motivations and emotional baggage – and your own.

- Can you (or should you) do something about the boss? If their behaviour is not a personal attack on you, can you learn to react differently?

- Is something 'not normal'? Even if you can't pin down exactly what's wrong with your relationship with your boss, you know when your emotional and physical self is 'off'. Note down changes in sleep patterns, whether you dread work on Mondays, or anything out of the ordinary. That's the first step. Noticing comes before action.

- Seek impartial outside advice about ways to deal with your situation from a mentor, therapist, coach, or former colleague. But not from someone on your team or anyone with allegiance to the boss.

- Unions and HR departments can be great sources of help and support. Investigate what is on offer before you commit to any official report. The bigger the company, the more official and (you'd hope) helpful the HR department and its processes are likely to be. If you are nervous or worried, take a colleague with you into any meetings.

- If you work for a narcissist, accept there may be no easy way to make things better. Don't confront or challenge them. Don't let them see you as a threat. In most cases, people have to leave because these bosses are too damaged – they can't change.

- Before you go, make sure you document everything, try to avoid one-on-ones with the boss, and keep talking to people outside the organisation who see your value and can reinforce that this behaviour is Not Okay. Narcissists undermine, so you must protect yourself.

- And finally . . . Have you read this chapter and thought, 'I've actually got a good boss?' (Caveat: There will be things about them that annoy you. No one is perfect.) Why not send them a thank you note? Mention something thoughtful or career-boosting they've done for you. The power of kindness at work is underrated.

Chapter 5:
Good Communication:
The Secret Key to Everything
And it will help you win at work in the long term

The very, very short summary of this chapter: Overcommunicate at work.

There are so many problems between people in workplaces, and yet when you boil them down to basics, they usually come down to two things:

• Not enough talking, or not enough communicating generally

• Not enough listening

A third, and little-discussed, issue is disliking the person you have a problem with. This is harder to solve (see Part II, Chapter 2, starting on page 153 for more on how to get along better with people you find hard to deal with). In many cases, however, it could at least be alleviated by more talking and listening.

And by setting out to communicate a little bit better every day, you are doing one big thing that could change the course of your career. I said 'could' because nothing is guaranteed, but think about how many people describe themselves on their CV as 'a great communicator' and use that as a key indicator of what a great hire they would be.

You can do that, too. Anyone can.

Don't bring any imposter syndrome to this one. We are all human beings, hardwired to communicate, and you can do it as well as the next person.

You may, however, need a few smart tips to polish up your technique. (Then you, too, can go on LinkedIn and call yourself a first-class communicator.)

This is not a one-size-fits-all chapter. If you are, or think you might be, someone with a neurodiverse condition or other lived experience that means you differ in how you like to communicate – don't worry, we deal with this in a later chapter (see page 170). But do read on anyway, for some tips that may be useful.

Improved communication will help every team or department to do better, be more efficient, and waste less of anyone's time. If you take one thing away from this chapter, let it be this: Overcommunication is better than undercommunication. And second (all right, two things): Face-to-face and digital communication are two separate, but linked, skill sets. Got it? Let's get talking.

The joy of listening

It doesn't matter whether you are a senior team member or an intern, this is the number one skill you need in the workplace, whether that's IRL (in real life), on video, or (old school) on the phone. The reason you haven't heard much about it until now is that it has been consistently undervalued and ignored.

The pandemic appears to have helped accelerate change, and for anyone wanting to future-proof their career, being an active listener is now a 'must have' not a 'nice to have'.

Listening includes things like not interrupting, maintaining eye contact (but not in a weird or alarming way; you'll have to be the judge of what's 'normal' with the person you are talking to), and repeating back what the other person has said to them, though it's better if you use your own words for this.

Pay attention to verbal and non-verbal cues. Not everything important is said out loud. There is deep meaning in what is left unsaid, and in the gaps between words. And you don't have to be a massive empath to realise that someone facing you with crossed arms and legs isn't giving off 'OPEN' signals.

I spoke to *Talk Fast, Think Smart* podcast host and Stanford lecturer Matt Abrahams, about simple ways in which each of us can improve our communication at work. Number one is (surprise!) actually listening. He told me that, 'most of us don't listen well. We listen just enough to think we understand what the person wants.'

He goes on. 'The other thing I would say is that we have to be empathetic, we have to take our audience's perspective. Often in our communication we are so focused on what we want to get across instead of thinking about what our audience needs to hear – and this impacts everything.'

When considering what your audience 'needs to hear', you need to think about both *what* you are communicating – the content – and *how* you are doing it.

'The focus we have in our messages, the language we use – do we use jargon, do we use acronyms? And [think about] the length of our messages, putting yourself in the service of the audience, being empathetic,' says Matt.

Making this shift from thinking only about what you want to say and the message you are dying to get across to thinking instead about what the audience, even if it's just one person, needs to hear, is a simple concept. But it represents a profound change in focus for most of us. We are being asked – in terms of both listening, and talking – to prioritise the other people with whom we are communicating. To put ourselves second. (Sometimes, when I talk about the workplace, I realise how much of this is also applicable in our personal lives. Imagine how much better most couples would get along if they each listened to the other and put their needs first . . .)

So, back in the workplace, set aside your burning desire to get your point across before someone else says the same thing, or to make a passive-aggressive comment about a colleague's poor timekeeping. It's going to be hard, and I am still a work in progress myself in this regard. But keep on it and you'll reap rewards, now and in the future workplace.

Why does my boss write such rude emails?

This was the title of an episode of the *Working It* podcast with Erica Dhawan, a top US digital communication expert. I wasn't keen on it at the time (the title, not Erica – she's amazing). But the episode did really well with very high listening figures. I realised that we had caught onto something important about the nuance required to make sure we all understand each other when talking via messaging platforms, email, and video calls. Research suggests that tone can be misinterpreted up to 50 per cent of the time in written digital communication. That's a lot of potential misunderstanding.

Before we get to the details of how to communicate better online, a word about the platforms you and your team or company are using to do that. There are almost certainly too many ways for you to send messages to each other, and that's a big time suck. It can cause many problems, such as missed messages, groupthink, and duplication of effort. I could go on.

If you are in the sort of organisation where you could work with others to re-organise the communication methods, then go ahead and do it. Everyone will thank you (eventually). What is more likely is that you will only be able to work within your direct team. If half of you are using Slack, while some others prefer instant messaging, and a few are email holdouts, that's hopeless.

Make decisions about which processes belong where. Some people are going to have to change their habits. If you can position yourself as the communication champion and keep everyone on the same platform(s), it's going to pay off and save everyone time, as well as stopping (most) misunderstanding.

If you want to deep dive into this topic, or want to re-organise digital communication for the team wholesale – and I imagine this is a dream job for people who love anything to do with productivity hacks – then I recommend Erica's book, *Digital Body Language*, which goes through examples, process, and questions to ask. (There's a lot more in there, too.)

Let's move on to the evolving and complex world of Doing Digital Right.

Emojis and disputed punctuation

Sometimes the simplest things are the easiest to get wrong. Emojis have become mired in difficulty, mainly because there are generational differences in how we view them. I will give a thumbs up emoji to my kids' messages telling me about their plans or achievements. I'm conveying a pure sense of 'that's great' or 'all good', and it comes from the heart.

For their part, Gen Z sees a thumbs up as an ironic or sarcastic statement. Viewed from my kids' perspective I am probably being snide about both their social plans and their personal achievements.

Thumbs up is also, according to some, the number one emoji for making the user look old. (Number two, in research done among Gen Z respondents in 2022, is the red heart, and number three the 'OK' fingers.)

Emoji use has become far more widespread in workplaces in recent years, across all generations, so if you are on the younger side, be aware that your boss's poor use of symbols is probably sincere, and go with the 'original' meaning, if you can.

The reality, though, is that workplace change is usually driven from below. Younger colleagues come in and talk, act, and communicate differently. Think carefully about emoji use. It's not strictly needed but it can lighten a mood or convey informality. Many people are in workplace WhatsApp groups, and not all of them are groups of friends engaging in 'information sharing' (gossip) about the boss. Be aware of tone on workplace WhatsApps and use emojis sparingly and – if you are older – sincerely. It's fine to ask younger colleagues about how these are likely to be interpreted.

But don't expect things to go back to how they once were. Younger cohorts are starting to change the way we all communicate, and older workers would be wise to understand that sticking firmly to the Old Rules and Norms – and expecting new recruits to change to accommodate this – is a losing battle. Language evolves, just as people do.

Erica Dhawan, shares her expertise in communication with this interesting macro-observation about 'digital natives', those who have grown up with the internet in their lives. 'Now Gen Z specifically – and digital natives, who are sometimes in their thirties and forties, grew up, often, with the AOL instant messaging tool, not only from when they were in high school but from when they were in middle school. They built a fluency, they built a language – which included a period [or full stop], meaning frustration or resentment.'

Erica is referring here to the vexed issue of putting a full stop [or period] as a punctuation mark on the end of texts, messages, and emails. Many older people know that younger staff find the use of a full stop to be an act of hostility. (To circle back to the title of the previous section, use of full stops is frequently the source of staff worries in the form of 'Why does my boss write such rude emails?')

I try not to put a punctuation mark on the end of anything now (except formal book sentences, like these). But old habits are hard to break, so we just have to hope we are forgiven. And it's always helpful to look at things in a much broader way. There isn't one 'right' way to use emojis or to punctuate our messages. Although – caveat – over use of '!!!!' is always going to make you look old or slightly panicky. I consider myself guilty in both respects.

Erica talks about evolving digital communication as a set of accents and dialects, and I like that way of looking at it. There isn't a clear-cut right way to 'be' online. We are all products of our age, upbringing, career, and personal history. Do what feels right for you, and be respectful.

There are now routinely four generations in workplaces, ranging from people who grew up playing with their parents' iPhones to those – like me – who were well into adulthood before the internet became A Thing. It's helpful to keep this in mind when we interact 'cross generationally' at work.

There is, though, a right way to communicate via email, and a very wrong one, too. Rules apply.

With emails, make them polite, concise, and purposeful.

I'd preface everything I'm saying here with the disclaimer that every workplace has its own – to be very fancy about it – 'idiolect'. Those are the speech habits and words particular to your corporate culture. So if it's the accepted practice in your workplace not to sign off emails with a pleasantry or your name, and there are places where those things are considered a massive waste of time, then you'll need to comply. Read the digital room.

Everyone else, pay attention. The humble written email still forms the backbone of millions of knowledge workers' working lives. Productivity expert (and computer scientist) Cal Newport cites the average knowledge worker as sending 126 emails a day in 2019. That's a lot of scope for misunderstanding and misery if you do it wrong.

Tone is everything. Politeness costs nothing

Erica Dhawan underlines the importance of treating emails with respect. They are a proxy for our relations with colleagues, bosses, and outside contacts and clients. 'We need a new playbook to understand that, in today's world, reading messages carefully is the new listening. Writing clearly is the new empathy.'

This advice suggests we should all be taking more time than we probably do at the moment to read, digest, and reply to emails. If you are serious about improving your digital communication skills, you'll need to factor that extra time into your day, and perhaps that might mean you adjust colleagues' expectations of your response time. And that's no bad thing. Many of us are stuck in the hamster-wheel of instant email responses, which gives the appearance of constant productivity. But usually, this makes us less productive, and often miserable.

I don't have space here to go down the fascinating rabbit hole of discussing why email is flawed – both as a communication system for workers and for human wellbeing – but keep that in mind and, if you are inclined, read Cal Newport's thought-provoking book, *A World Without*

Email: Reimagining Work in the Age of Overload. (It's great, but it will make you rage at the pointlessness of our work lives in thrall to the despotic gods of the inbox.)

According to Erica, the key to successful email etiquette in the workplace is to be polite and be succinct. In terms of politeness, always address formally: 'Dear/Hello X' or 'Hi X' if you know the person well is always better than just 'X' – which immediately gets me slightly worried or riled, depending on who has sent it. And remember to sign off in a non-cringe way. You can't go wrong with something bland, such as 'thanks' if you have asked for something or 'regards/best wishes/best'.

There are reports that Gen Z workers are embracing funny and sarcastic email sign offs, such as 'Let me know if you have any questions! Or don't' or 'Hasta la Pasta'. I haven't seen evidence of this, yet. But it may be coming. Emails have been with us for thirty-odd years and are ready for disruption from below, like the rest of the workplace.

What I have seen is a blurring of boundaries from younger workers. They may be more likely to put 'xx' on the end of an email to someone they don't know well, something I'd only do to a colleague who is also a friend. It's not something I'd advise routinely, mainly because it can be misinterpreted. Over the years, I've had to send a few swift emails to people I barely know apologising for an 'xx' on the end of a work email. But that slip goes back to Erica's point about careful writing. Don't write anything on autopilot.

On the subject of email tone, there can be few people who haven't vented by composing a fury-fuelled email to the colleague who has done something egregious. We all do it. Just make sure you leave it in draft. Nine out of ten times, it can stay there.

If you have been so badly wronged that the stiffly worded email is going to have to be sent, then read it again in the morning. Tone it down. Then get a sensible and non-involved colleague to check it over. I've done this often, and it saves a lot of unnecessary angst. Furthermore, when we are feeling extreme emotion, we meander and don't get to the point quickly. That's fine when talking to a kind friend – but not in a work email. An impartial person will spot that and save you from yourself.

Getting to the point is the single thing that is most often forgotten in emails. Busy people don't have time to scan down in search of 'the ask'. If you've put it in the third or fourth paragraph, you've lost your audience.

Someone once advised me that director-level people give emails two sentences before they move on. That's anecdotal, but to be sure of catching attention, you certainly need to be dexterous.

Just as with the tips earlier on face-to-face workplace communication, think of your audience first, not the message you want to give. Your boss needs to know what you are asking, and why. And they need to see that at the top of the email. You can even put it in the subject line.

And finally, always address the email last. Some 40 per cent of workers have admitted to emailing the wrong person (and 20 per cent said they'd lost their job as a result, which seems harsh). This survey was cited by the FT's Pilita Clark in a column about the agony of the mis-addressed email. It can also, as Pilita points out, be agony to receive a misdirected email that is all about your own shortcomings.

Pilita mentioned a staggering real-life example of this that had just happened to a friend. This woman had been mistakenly copied into a series of emails about her. 'They revealed one person in the chain believed her to be an inexperienced lightweight in her twenties. In fact, she is a mid-thirties professional who has worked very successfully in her field at home and abroad for close to fifteen years.

'I am not sure everyone in her place would have responded as graciously as she did. Instead of exposing the hapless error in a way that put the sender's job in jeopardy, she wrote back to correct the record and make it clear no serious harm had been done. This must have been a relief for the sender, who had fallen into a trap I have only narrowly avoided myself. She typed out the name of my friend in the 'send' field to check its spelling, then failed to delete it.'

I shudder just reading this. And remember, the 'cancel send' button is your friend. Set this up on your emails and it will give you precious seconds to undo your errors.

Don't be slack on Slack

We mainly refer to email in this section, but internal communication platform messages also carry pitfalls (such as through Slack and its ilk). A lot of what goes wrong on those is about private messaging that turns out . . . not to be. Reporting on internal discord at companies now often relies on leaked Slack messaging in internal forums. 'Slack leaks are the new email leaks', as one headline put it, as far back as 2018. This type of story sourcing is only likely to get more common, as use of internal communication platforms becomes near-universal.

If you have become used to making very quick responses to messages in your online personal life (and who hasn't?), the informality of Slack may seem to blend in with the rest of your life. There are pitfalls to this.

It is not, for example, a good place to badmouth the bosses. One prominent incident took place at Netflix, where it was reported in 2021 that company leaders had sacked three senior marketing executives over private messaging on Slack that criticised the management of their department.

Interestingly, the main reported reason for the firing was that the executives had been saying in private what should have been made public. It wasn't the fact of the messaging itself, it was that it violated the culture of transparency that Netflix values. Which is interesting in itself – and perhaps a reminder to us all not to comment online in a way that you wouldn't dare to say to someone's face.

Communication pitfalls are not confined to making personal slights. In the US, financial institutions have given staff training on when to move work messaging from personal phones to work email. Regulators have cracked down on bankers conducting official business away from official channels – on WhatsApp or by text, for example. Strict rules on their record-keeping demand that all communication is transparent and stored properly. Some bankers have received personal fines of up to $1 million, and total fines across financial services total $1 billion. The FT called it 'Wall Street's $1bn messaging "nightmare".' Quite.

When messaging, keep in mind the similar values you'd use while emailing: be transparent, concise, and polite.

Timing: Think twice before you hit the 9 p.m. email reply

Before we talk about the actual timings of when we send emails, let's first consider what is driving our relationships with bulging work inboxes. (Mine has 333,000 emails.)

There are two parts to this: the external pressure on you – meaning your employer's or boss's expectations – and what you are personally bringing to the endless toil of checking, replying, realising you have randomly been cc-ed by a bunch of people trying to cover their own backs, and so on.

Post-pandemic, there's more awareness of the need for a digital switch-off from work. Part of that has been driven by publicity about the 'right to switch off' laws that are in force in some countries. France, Spain, and

Ireland, for example, have some form of limit on out-of-hours workplace communications.

These aren't universal; small businesses are exempt in France, for example. And regardless of national laws, some companies choose to implement their own internal rules to protect workers' wellbeing and free time. Volkswagen, the German carmaker, has a lock on employee access to work emails between 6:15 p.m. and 7 a.m.

Structural change like this would save many of us from ourselves by putting actual boundaries around the instinct to send and check emails at all hours. But where those rules or norms are absent, staff will feel obliged to keep checking and replying to emails during all waking hours (and sometimes beyond).

It's telling that consultancy work, accounting, and the law are sometimes called 'greedy jobs' because they take up so much of an individual's life.

I'm including this context about the culture of checking our inboxes, because sending emails is about so much more than pressing a button. There's a whole backstory for each of us about the sort of workplace culture we are in, how and when people feel obliged to respond, and so on. You may never have consciously thought about it, but if you are picking up your phone to check your email as soon as the alarm goes off, you probably do need to think about taking more of a break. (Wait fifteen minutes after waking up before you check your email. Baby steps.)

The 'always on' culture around emails may be explicit or, more likely, unspoken. When I had small kids and worked part-time, I never confronted that one boss who would email or call many times on my day off. They just expected a swift response. There was a sort of stream-of-consciousness between us, and I never failed to deliver. I very much regret not saying something and setting firmer boundaries, since none of this was stuff that couldn't wait a day.

If you are in a workplace where immediate responses are expected, even though the matters are not urgent, then you may want to reflect on why that is. There's an element of control that work has over us, and the intrusion of constantly checked email is part of it. You are probably generating a lot of that pressure yourself because you are (for example) anxious to be seen as diligent by senior people.

Or it may be something more petty. I recently went on holiday with a friend. She'd switched off totally from work and could relax. I went back to my room after lunch every day and replied to emails for a couple of hours. This did not count as 'work', I told her, it was just 'inbox maintenance' so that things would be manageable when I got back.

'Really?' She looked sceptical. Rightly. Who was I kidding? Much performative holiday email checking – and mine was self-driven, not employer-driven – is about reassuring ourselves about how important and indispensable we are. (Newsflash: We aren't.)

There's more about how to manage an inbox effectively in the chapter on productivity (see page 70). Spoiler: You have to live with imperfection; there aren't enough hours in the day.

So when is the best time to send those emails? The schedule function is your friend, and when a bunch of emails come into my inbox at 8 a.m. on a Monday morning, I know those senders have spent a bit of their Sunday doing pre-work (if we can call it that).

It's always considerate to schedule send, but the other option, and this is especially good for multi-time zone organisations, is to set up a sign-off saying something like, 'I've sent this email at a time to suit me. Please reply when it suits you.' That sort of thing.

If you have something important to impart and want to make sure it gets seen and opened by the maximum number of people, then recent data from Axios (a newsletter-driven media organisation) found that the best time to send internal emails was either on Sunday afternoon or in the middle of the night.

The 'I'll look first thing when I wake up' bias is real, it seems.

Anything sent in the middle of the day (10 a.m.–2 p.m., roughly) is likely to arrive when colleagues are in meetings.

Meetings, meetings

We can all agree there are too many meetings in the world. The number of meetings we attend, and time spent in them, has been creeping up over the past half century. A 2017 University of North Carolina study of 180 senior executives found that they spent twenty-three hours a week in meetings, up from fewer than ten hours in the 1960s. And those are the people who usually have gatekeepers, such as executive assistants who can guard their diaries and prevent them from attending bad, wrong, or useless meetings. The rest of us are not so lucky.

Given we spend so much time in meetings, virtual or otherwise, there is often very little clarity on how to run meetings, or how to communicate in them. For this chapter, we are going to focus on those of us who have to attend meetings. Essentially, the etiquette of being in a room, real or imagined, with other people. (I won't go into the torturous world of metaverse meetings. Having been in just one, I would describe the experience as 'as yet unevolved'. If the future of work involves putting on headsets and hopping around as an avatar-torso, that will require a lot more advice than I can give here.)

We are all old hands at communicating in virtual meetings now. When researching this chapter, I went back and read some of the FT articles published in 2020 as everyone pivoted to Zoom. Much of it seems basic, but these two communication tips from stand-up comedian, coach, and *Happy High Status* author, Viv Groskop, stand out. 'Behave like you are in a job interview. You are being scrutinised all the time when you are on screen. Look alert, look positive, put a smile in your eyes.

'Look at the camera, not the screen itself. If you struggle with this and you have a presentation to give, cover the screen with a newspaper or a piece of cardboard to force yourself to look at the camera and not at the faces of your fellow contributors.'

Viv is also a proponent of treating virtual meetings like appearances on TV shows. 'The brains of others will process your image as if you are on TV. So you would do well to imagine that you are.' This is one of the best tips I've ever had on effective communication. (If you are running the meeting, that makes you the show host, and you should behave that way.) Virtual communication is far easier when you can see the people you are dealing with, so keep your camera on if you can. Obviously we have no control over others' in the meeting, and some do like their cameras off.

Viv recently answered the problem of a *Working It* newsletter reader who, as part of a remote team, felt upset because the boss refused to have his camera on in meetings. I would also have been mightily annoyed by this but Viv pointed out that virtual meetings are still evolving, and in the future we will have to adapt with them. 'Asking yourself, "What if he's actually right and we're wrong? What if his behaviour is okay? Can we work around him?" might help unlock a solution. Long term for all of us, we are going to have to be as open-minded about what constitutes a healthy digital working relationship as we are about what constitutes a healthy face-to-face professional relationship. I suspect it will be a very broad range of behaviours and not a 'one-size-fits-all'.'

The big takeaways about digital communication – take your time, be polite, be succinct – also work for all sorts of meetings, including in-person ones. As Erica Dhawan wisely says, 'Taking a moment of pause can make all the difference.'

Of course this can be a long way from the reality of being a participant in a meeting where loud voices dominate and people get talked over or ignored. For more on how to bring more 'presence' to the room and communicate your ideas effectively, see page 184.

Takeaways

- Communication at work can be the bedrock of all success, or it can lead directly to failure. It's that important.

- True listening means giving your full attention to the other person so you are taking in their words, not thinking of what you're about to say next. This is the most underrated skill in workplaces. (And in life.)

- Prioritise the message that the other person (or people) you communicate with need to hear – not what you want to tell them. These are often very different things.

- Generational differences in communication habits will always be with us, and we've yet to see the full impact of Gen Z in the workforce. Just be aware, be respectful, and keep a steady hand on the emoji finder.

- If you are an older person, learn to drop the final full stop off your emails and messages. It's easier all round and you won't cause misunderstanding among your colleagues or family. (Unless you are trying to spook people . . .)

- On emails, be polite, be succinct, and always type in the recipient's address last, when you are happy with what you've written. Autofill is a cruel beast and misdirected emails can cause misery (and possible job loss for the sender).

- Think about your dysfunctional relationship with email (it's always dysfunctional) and try to reclaim a bit of your life from work tyranny. Maybe start by not checking email relentlessly on holiday. You just aren't that important.

- If you must do some emails late at night and on weekends, set them to 'schedule send' for 8 a.m. on a workday. Exceptions apply, of course. If you want an especially important email to get noticed, then go for it. The best times to send are the middle of the night or Sunday afternoon.

- Private workplace messaging is often not private.

- Think like a TV star in your virtual meetings, and be an active listener in any sort of meeting.

Chapter 6: Productivity and Other Dirty Words
Productivity is not about more, more, more

I have spent almost my whole career hung up on how many hours I am spending at my desk. Worrying in case I am not there, not 'busy looking' enough, just . . . not enough.

Something happened a couple of years ago to shift that perspective. Yes, I am contracted to my employer to spend forty hours a week working. Like most knowledge workers, my actual hours are probably closer to fifty a week.

But I have managed to expand my view of what 'work' is to move beyond sitting on a chair at a computer. We should include creative thinking time, walking at lunchtime, sitting outside for a few minutes with the sun on our faces, and also doing nothing. Standing up and getting a drink or taking a short walk around the block, if your job allows, is far more beneficial than slogging on with no breaks, for comparatively lesser returns as the day goes on.

Productivity is actually about managing the time you have available in the best way for you. So you get done what is needed, and even have a little bit of thinking time. That's the ideal, anyway. It is mindset-driven and task-driven, not time-driven. Just because I sit at my desk for nine hours doesn't mean I am being productive.

The cult of productivity, however, has got out of hand. While it's good to maximise our paid time and it can be extremely fulfilling to feel you have achieved something at the end of the day, the likelihood is that you are only scratching the surface of your to-do list.

The term 'productivity hack' or 'life hack' is egregious in itself, suggesting – as Oliver Burkeman points out near the start of *Four Thousand Weeks*, his brilliant book on 'time management for mortals' –

that 'your life is best thought of as some kind of faulty contraption, in need of modification so as to stop it from performing suboptimally.'

Do not think about productivity as a way to erase your inefficiency and faults. It's better thought of as a way of maximising what you do, to best effect, in the time you have available. And an important part of that equation is staying well – physically and mentally – while you work. You will never get to the end of your to-do list, and the quicker you understand that, the quicker you will accept that productivity is not a conundrum to be solved but a calculation on where you place your limited available time.

I recently read a reader's problem answered by the very wise Annalisa Barbieri in the *Guardian*. (If you like Esther Perel and podcasts about psychology and relationships, you should also listen to Annalisa's podcast, *Conversations*.) The letter came from someone who was worried about a friend who was working until 4 a.m. every night. They wondered if they should tell the employer. Absolutely not, said Annalisa. 'It's unlikely the company demands your friend works such hours anyway. It's probably something she's decided to do for whatever reason, if indeed you are sure she is at work all this time.'

The reasons we work too hard are often to do with avoiding other things in our lives, as Annalisa explains to this writer. Whether the overworker is oneself or a friend, the manic drive to spend more time working as a way to boost productivity is seemingly hardwired. A very long time ago I worked for a boss who insisted on staying long after everyone else had gone home. At the time I felt guilty for not working long hours like my boss but I know now that they would have been running from something in their own life.

Overwork under the guise of 'productivity' is essentially a shield against involving ourselves in our own lives. When it becomes an addiction (meaning, in this case, compulsive behaviour that you can't stop) then that's clearly an attempt 'to fill a void', as with any addiction. If you compulsively overwork, it's time to separate out all the complex factors that are preventing you from seeing work and productivity as time-limited things that should not impinge on the rest of your time-limited life. This latter point is what Oliver Burkeman is making in *Four Thousand Weeks* (the title refers to the human lifespan if you live to age 80). Our time is short; don't waste it.

The best tip I ever got on productivity? I can't remember who gave me this (you can @me if it was you). 'Nobody should be so busy that they have to eat their lunch at their desk.' If you do this routinely, it should be a wake-up call to your working arrangements. Never mind work/life balance, you haven't even got work-lunch balance.

Desk eating in the workplace is especially unnecessary – and it can cause rifts in offices. Early in my career I worked for a small magazine where a colleague brought in home-cooked leftovers (good; thrifty), which they insisted on eating at their desk while working (Very Bad). The food aromas wafted across the badly ventilated room. Everyone was irritated. When tackled, they cited busyness as their reason. It's the worst possible outcome of performative productivity.

Even if you don't take an hour for lunch (it shouldn't be a luxury but somehow often is) then you can get up and go out for a walk, or eat in the workplace café or canteen. I like to get fresh air and, if it's not actually raining, and sometimes even if it is, I'll sit on a bench among greenery. When I'm at the office I'll get a sandwich with a colleague and we will talk fast, and chew over work and life. This is human connection, the building block that underpins us if we are to thrive, and also be productive.

What even is personal productivity?

Let's go back to basics. When economists talk about national productivity levels, they are discussing all of our personal productivity statistics, added up. That's the 'output'. So the UK's Office for National Statistics measures output per hour per worker. In a very basic sense, that is our productivity rate. Then it looks at how that compares with workers in other countries. British workers are less productive than those in France, Germany, and the US. National productivity in the UK has been on a much more shallow upwards path since the financial crisis in 2008 than it was previously.

Something went wrong in the UK after 2008. That's a mystery we'll have to leave hanging, although plenty of people have thoughts about why it might be. One FT report in May 2023 suggested that recent factors may include the fact that 'Brexit, Covid, and the energy shock [fast rising prices for energy] have all deterred businesses from making the investments in IT, machinery and other equipment needed to lift workers' performance.'

Personal productivity, where we are all striving to be as smart, effective, and time-efficient as possible, seems a world away from these dismal statistics. But I asked the FT's *Undercover Economist* columnist,

Tim Harford, when he talked to me about productivity on the *Working It* podcast, whether there is a link between personal and national productivity? He answered yes, but it's complex. 'Most economists would say that national productivity has to do with things like education levels and infrastructure and appropriate regulation, and all of that sort of good stuff.'

The connection Tim would make between personal and national productivity, though, is in the shift we've seen in our working lives over the last thirty years or so. This predates smartphones. Managers used to have secretaries do their typing, there were staff to prepare and submit our expenses, and there were skilled graphics and technical staff who would put together presentations. Now we do all of that ourselves, and most of us aren't very good at it. Plus, it's time consuming and keeps us from doing the actual business of our jobs.

Tim says, 'There's this tendency towards generalisation. And Adam Smith, the great economist [he lived from 1723–1790], told us that specialisation is the foundation of productivity. And I think that this tendency for even very senior and very highly skilled people to do a little bit of everything, including a lot of stuff they are not very good at, that's been enabled by technology. I suspect that is one reason why all these digital technologies haven't improved productivity as much as we want.'

So there you go, one reason why humans remain stubbornly unable to do much more with our time is that we may be terrible at a lot of the tasks we are meant to be completing. New tech means we often take on these tasks, but that doesn't mean we become any more productive. This may be something that disappears as digital native generations Z and Alpha (born after 2010) enter the workforce.

We will also discuss the coming impact of AI on our work and productivity at the end of this chapter. My guess (and this is very much a guess) is that AI will hit like a meteorite and blow a lot of the established 'facts' about productivity out of the water. So hang on in there until it lands.

Productivity hacks and methods – getting intentional

Apart from 'trying to be more efficient', I've tried a few formal productivity systems over the years, and asked colleagues to write about their own efforts with them. The market is developing all the time and many people use app-based task management for work or home needs. Something as simple as the Apple Notes function suits some; I know people who share Google Sheets of chores with their partners, and the truly organised have Asana and Trello or similar platforms, where the tasks and sub-tasks are clearly marked – for their work and, sometimes, home lives.

The following are the best-known traditional, non-tech systems you may be familiar with, and which have worked for many people. All of them are easy to implement and hard to build into a routine.

Pomodoro Technique: You work for twenty-five minutes, set a timer, take a five-minute break, then do it again. Some people swear by this. I find it interrupts me when I am in a 'flow' state, which is not often, but the timer is a potential distraction. And the name? It's after the tomato-shaped timer used by the system's inventor, Francesco Cirillo.

Bullet Journal®: The prettiest of all the hacks, completely tech-free, and the one most likely to appeal to stationery fans. Bullet journals are notebooks set up to display your task lists. If you are 'BuJo' curious, there are many Facebook groups and Instagram feeds, not to mention YouTube tutorials, on how to set up the various pages you'll need, such as lists of immediate, mid-range, or long-term tasks. Many people make their journals look like works of art. Time-consuming, but devotees swear by it.

I do a 'beta' version of BuJo using a new double-page spread in my work notebook every week. One page is for a list of work tasks. I carry over the unfinished tasks from the previous week and add more as I go along. The opposite page is folded to produce two columns: one a list of people I need to get back to and the other a list of admin and personal, family stuff that needs doing. Basic, but it works well.

Morning Pages: A morning practice beloved of writers specifically and creatives generally, this involves starting to write in a notebook as soon as you wake up. I did allow myself a cup of tea when I did it, but that's probably cheating. I am not sure I found it especially helpful in boosting productivity, but it's certainly surprising to see what comes out of your semi-conscious mind.

The originator of the technique, artist Julia Cameron, explains how to do it, 'Morning pages are three pages of longhand, stream-of-consciousness morning writing, for your eyes only, done as quickly upon waking as possible. These pages do not have to be "good writing." There is no wrong way to do Morning Pages.'

For more information about Julia, the practice, and why people love it, I'd suggest reading her book, *The Artist's Way*. It's a deep-dive manual for boosting creativity (Content warning: it's not suitable for the spritually averse).

Getting up at 5 a.m.: Too many tech bros swear by this and it does actually seem to work for some people. I do get up (almost) this early to go and swim outside all year round and it does set me up brilliantly for the day. (It's just hard to get out of bed when it's dark and nearly zero degrees outside.)

The key to the 5 a.m. productivity burst is that it gives you uninterrupted focus time for thinking, writing, exercise, or whatever you want to do first in the day. The best results come from focusing on one thing; later in the day, you tend to get overwhelmed by people, work, information, the dog, etc.

Professor Grace Lordan wrote in the FT about her experiment with getting up early like CEOs do. She found meditation was the best way to start: 'I simply bring to my mind the top three things I need to achieve each day and visualise what "good" looks like. I come away from my 20-minute meditation clear in my mind what my mission is for the day ahead.'

My main issue with 5 a.m. starts (or 4 a.m. in some cases) is that I'd probably fall asleep by 3 p.m. But then naps have also been found to be a beneficial productivity tool.

Where productivity meets self-improvement

Atomic Habits by James Clear is a 2018 book that has become the ultimate productivity/life primer for many people. I've read a summary of its main ideas via a summary app I use to get through more books than I have time to read in full.

Yes, that's my secret productivity tip: Summary apps such as Blinkist and Shortform are a great shortcut for people who like to take in a lot of productivity/self-help/management ideas, and often the twenty-minute version contains all the tips you need.

In the case of *Atomic Habits,* James tells his readers (of whom there are millions) to make small changes, which can turn into bigger changes over time. One of the book's best tips is to 'stack' a habit you want to build onto something pleasurable. One example would be to watch a Netflix series you are bingeing only when you are at the gym (or on your home exercise bike). It should help increase the 'stickiness' of your intentions.

James's book is the most famous title of its genre, but there are many others like it. Although I have read a lot of these books, and skimmed off a few ideas, I've never got my act together enough for that sort of commitment, and never will.

Some of the best advice I've read on habit-changing and its relationship to motivation comes from the academic Ayelet Fishbach, who spoke to my colleague Emma Jacobs in a fascinating 2022 FT interview. This one resonated with me (impressive, because I have commissioned and edited hundreds, if not thousands, of articles and interviews over my career) because of the very sensible and realistic approach that Ayelet – a professor of behavioural science at Chicago Booth business school – gives on the topic.

Ayelet is the author of *Get It Done: Surprising Lessons from the Study of Motivation*, and her work stresses the importance of understanding your own personality, and how that affects change. Whenever you think about productivity, habit change, or working differently, something that is 'one size fits all' probably won't work.

As Emma writes, Ayelet's 'overriding message is that multiple factors affect motivation. Different personalities need different approaches. She recommends understanding whether you go all-out for something (an "approacher") or if fear of criticism and mistakes is a driving force (an "avoider"). Everyone could benefit from greater preparation for overcoming the obstacles to goals, as well as understanding how your new goals might clash with other existing priorities — and sometimes pull you in opposite directions.'

I am an 'avoider' – of conflict, of anger, of criticism – and have always withdrawn from crisis into a self-sufficient cocoon. Consciously trying to overcome those blocks to uncover our true motivations is really hard, but worthwhile.

If you are going to go all-out on habit change for productivity gain, think about which methods suit you. Process-driven productivity tactics don't appeal to me because I am overly-verbal and not interested in methodical outcomes, plus I am infuriatingly bookish and impractical. (All my 'life advice' used to come from books, which probably explains why you are reading this one. My hard-won conclusion? Mix the words up with some Real Lived Wisdom.)

The only creativity/productivity habit I've ever enjoyed is Morning Pages, writing down whatever comes into my head as soon as I wake up. I did it for months during the lockdowns, and it helped clarify my thinking for the 'muddy' day ahead during that strange time.

As soon as things became more normal, I decided to go back to staying in bed or going for an early-morning outdoor swim as my 'clarifying' practice for the day. Some habits don't stick – or are for particular moments in your life – and that's also fine.

The 'change your habits' and motivational genre is incredibly popular and there is a fun side to it, but it sits in a grey area where productivity meets the self-help movement. My concern is that attempts at motivating ourselves to change by introducing new and more efficient systems make us feel (whether this is the intention or not) that we aren't trying hard enough to be our 'best selves' if we don't follow them, or fail to keep them going.

Don't go hard-charging at a new regime to turbocharge your life and work patterns unless you have already done some groundwork. And understand that when you decide to do something as a priority, or change your habits to take on something new, it means that something else won't get done. There is always a trade-off.

You won't get everything done by speeding up or adding new things. That to-do list is never, ever going to end.

Tiny email changes can transform your life (I promise)

And all those emails clogging up your inbox? This is the biggest productivity issue we face, because there is never any end to them. You can, though, be more efficient about how you deal with them. Tim Harford, the FT's *Undercover Economist* columnist, who is the most productive person I know, likes to move them to different inboxes as soon as they arrive. It's pretty simple but I am now following this (it is based on Gmail – if you have a different provider you'll likely have something similar).

'I have an action folder . . . basically you just put stuff that needs action that's going to take time somewhere else. And then all the stuff that's coming into your inbox, you either immediately reply or you put it in the action folder – or you delete and then there's nothing there.'

The best 'lightbulb moment' I've ever had about email – and this is key – is that you owe nothing to the people who email you uninvited, with requests, demands, and so on. Think of them as digital intruders. Focus on the people who are invited: colleagues, friends, the people to whom you need to be accountable in your life and work. If (and only if) you have time to answer unsolicited emails, then be ruthless about it.

When I have a spare hour or two I will, however, prioritise emails from people who are seeking my advice about something, or want me to speak at their event. Those are uninvited emails where a response is polite – and

I do expect to engage. I also actively invite emails from readers of the newsletter I write and those who listen to the podcast I host. Those are the members of the *Working It* community, and I always try to reply to them in a timely manner. I don't always manage it, but I try.

You will have your own workplace communities (clients, customers, and so on) so be clear in the way you distinguish between competing inbox demands. Using different inboxes is a quick and effective way to separate it all out so it is manageable (or can be forgotten about).

Also, please check spam sometimes. The occasional important email gets stuck there. I've missed some important communications over the years among the generous offers of money-making schemes and anatomical enlargements.

Other potential distractions

In recent years, part of the career advice dished out to young people coming in to the workforce, and to people thinking of changing careers, has been to contact others in the field that interests them and ask for a coffee, a call, or for answers to questions via email. An increasing number of people engaged in academic research, from undergraduates upwards, will also email strangers who are perceived as experts, asking for their responses to questionnaires, or for a meeting to go over their queries.

You have to decide how to respond to these requests. Anyone who has got to a relatively senior level in their profession has an obligation (I think) to give back a bit and try to help others just starting out, especially those from minority and lower socio-economic backgrounds, who may well lack the social connections that professional parents often 'invisibly gift' to their children via networks of friends and colleagues.

It's not too long (shockingly) since interns were often not paid and people were hired into jobs for their connections – who they knew, not what they knew or the potential they showed.

Once requests start to come in, you'll need to decide how much time to devote to career guidance. You may decide to block time for one or two coffee appointments a month, real or virtual, with people who would like to hear from you. If there are too many to deal with in person, you could put together an FAQ about your company, role, or sector, and send that out to anyone who asks. Some people post career advice on LinkedIn, or outline the slots they have available for a call or meeting with someone seeking advice – perhaps it's pro bono coaching for those who would otherwise not be able to afford it. This approach offers great 'optics', as they say, but just make sure you follow through.

For those who are self-employed, the 'ask' is often from agencies or other commercial operators, and there will be friendly requests to 'pick your brain' over coffee. I've heard too many horror stories about people being called into meetings on the vague promise of some work, only to find that the person on the other side is just trying to extract information or contacts.

I admire people who charge for their time for these events. It's an impossible situation for many freelancers, who need the work, or the promise of work, but exploiting people by demanding their time, unpaid, is not a sustainable way to operate.

The same goes for events. I will moderate panels and events for friends, and for charities, educational institutions, and non-profits – for free. However, if the organisation is running a conference they are making money from, and charging delegates to attend, then they should also pay moderators and speakers, especially when those people are self-employed. Although I am not self-employed, if there is prep involved for me – and panel moderation should take several hours of preparation – I expect to be paid.

The FT pays its journalists to moderate panels for our commercial events arm, FT Live. It's a fair model. Far too many organisers don't do this. And remember, 'exposure' is not the same as payment.

Finally, conferences, panels, and events generally are great in many ways (and the networking opportunities can be very worthwhile) but they are a massive time suck if you do them properly. Taking this time out of your job can impede productivity. I often end up preparing for events in the evenings and at weekends. That's okay when you are getting payment for it, but it can make you tired and possibly less productive at the day job.

Think carefully about the ask, about the event, and about the potential benefits for you. Consider whether they are enough before you say yes.

Will AI make me more productive?
Let's hope so. Those LLMs we keep hearing about (large language models, such as ChatGPT) are going to do some of the work you

don't like doing, which will hopefully free you up to do more exciting work.

The FT's AI editor, Madhumita Murgia, gives a very clear explanation of what we can expect in the short term. '[What] will affect many millions of people right now is AI, or generative AI, being integrated into the software that we use daily in the workplace. So things like Microsoft Office, Google Docs, Gmail, Outlook – these kinds of products that we all use. Both Microsoft and Google, who are obviously the giants in the productivity software space, have announced plans to integrate AI into these products.

'And what that will mean is AI predicting what your email should look like, for example in Gmail, or suggesting what a document could look like, or generating a document for you when you just give it a little prompt.' That's a huge time saver.

And we are now seeing AI coming into remote meetings – the bot can transcribe the meeting for you, or you can even send the bot instead of you to the meeting to save your time. In August 2023, Google announced that it would be introducing this feature. The bot sends you meeting notes and action points afterwards. (It can't talk or actually take your place – yet.)

The research results of working with generative AI are starting to come in, and they are positive. Leaving aside the massive ethical and legal questions around AI for the moment, let's focusing on productivity gains here. A paper from MIT, published in the journal *Science*, described a study that assigned writing tasks to more than 400 college-educated professionals. It randomly exposed half of them to being written by ChatGPT.

The researchers, Shakked Noy and Whitney Zhang, found that 'ChatGPT substantially raised productivity: The average time taken decreased by 40 per cent and output quality rose by 18 per cent. Inequality between workers decreased, and concern and excitement about AI temporarily rose.' Workers who'd been given the ChatGPT help were more likely to use it in their regular work after this experiment.

Interestingly, the participants with the weakest skills benefited the most from ChatGPT's help with their work. Obviously that won't apply to anyone reading this book, but it has huge implications for productivity overall because everyone's output will be lifted.

Takeaways

- Your to-do list will never end. The first step to boosting personal productivity is an acceptance that you can't do it all – and learning to prioritise what is most important.

- Sitting at your desk is not the same as being productive. Get up, walk around, go for a coffee with a colleague to connect and share ideas. If you don't take lunch away from your desk, it's time to ask: What are you doing with your life?

- Generative AI can already write workplace emails and documents for us, digest enormous datasets, and tell us what we need to know – and even attend meetings on our behalf. It's big news. Hang in there to see what happens.

- Habit changing to boost productivity is big business, but before you attempt it, think about how you work and how you react to things. Doing less, and taking time to breathe and think, might sometimes be a better tactic than 'stacking' habits on top of each other to do more.

- Tech apps for family organisation and work productivity are enormous time-savers – if you set them up right. Again, some people do better with a paper calendar on the wall and a to-do list in their notebook. Don't be pressured to change for the sake of it.

- Ask your younger family members and colleagues how they organise their personal productivity – it might surprise you. Gen Z likes its boundaries and isn't all about tech.

- Email is a time suck on a gigantic scale, and dominates our lives even though it shouldn't. Read Cal Newport's work for the basics. My advice is to treat anyone who comes uninvited into your inbox as an intruder; you owe them nothing. (Also, politeness costs nothing so try for some combination of the two.)

- Anyone who asks for a piece of your time is sapping productivity. Make a clear decision on whether the coffee/meeting/event is worth it. Ask to be paid for your time on a panel or chairing things. 'Exposure' is not enough.

- Never let overwork become a way to escape from the rest of your life. It happens way too often, and it's easy to slip into an 'evenings, weekends' form of seamless work/life. Take a breath, read Oliver Burkeman's *Four Thousand Weeks*, and go for a walk. (And do get some therapy if your partner/family/general situation is something you are trying to avoid.)

Chapter 7: How to Get a Pay Rise, Move Up, or Move On
Getting beyond 'I need' and 'I deserve'

You've been in the job for a while. You are feeling undervalued, overlooked, or perhaps you just want to assess where you stand internally before you make a decision about your future.

Asking for a pay rise is a good way to move things along. You may not actually be 'in it to win it' – asking for more money is often a proxy for wanting more recognition or training. In this chapter I will offer some guidance on the process and how to do it well, and consider how to plan your next move, whether you get the pay rise or not.

How to get a pay rise

How we all wish that getting a pay rise were as easy as saying, 'I'd like a pay rise, please.' Some of the best-read articles I've ever commissioned for the FT have been on this subject, not to mention the incredibly popular podcasts I've hosted or guested on around this theme. And in a time of relentless cost-of-living rises, the need to get a raise has never been more pressing.

Getting a pay rise is a bit of a lottery, especially in organisations where there are few funds available. Do not take that as a reason not to ask. You can always make a good case for yourself, get noticed, and potentially get more cash, or be offered other perks that are just as valuable to you. More on this later (see Part II, Chapter 5, page 193).

Caveats apply, of course. In public service and other workplaces with 'banded' pay grades, you are limited in terms of pay rises. The pay is attached to the job, not to you, so once you have hit the pay ceiling for your band you'll have to stick with it, apply for a new job on a higher grade or band, take on some extra duties as a long-term promotion play, or ask for some other measure of compensation (such as skills training or a course funded by your employer). Or you can seek out a higher-paid job, whether internally or externally.

The above-listed options are, in fact, also the choices facing anyone who feels 'blocked' by the pay in their current role, whether or not it's in a public sector organisation.

Let's separate the pay rise conversation into two types. The first is where you work in an organisation where an individual rise is not the norm (perhaps you have a union-negotiated annual rise), or where your workplace is 'purpose driven' – where there is little to no cash for pay rises (places like non-profits, arts organisations, charities, and so on).

The other sort of conversation will be for those in far more commercial, sales-and-target driven roles, financial services, professional work – anywhere where pay is negotiated individually, and its level may also reflect whether you've been in the job for a while or have been headhunted. In the latter case, you may find you are earning a lot more than colleagues doing similar roles. In short this conversation relates to the sorts of jobs where getting a substantial pay rise is a reasonable expectation.

Pay and recognition is a minefield for us all. I have always found asking for pay rises incredibly hard. I have barely ever done it. Why? Having dug into my soul, and read a lot about the psychology of negotiation, it seems I was trapped in thinking about it as a parent-child dynamic. We may have had childhoods where we worried about what our parents thought of us if we displeased them, and about the rejection if they said no. So we project that into the workplace, and do ourselves no favours at all.

The workplace should be a place where we operate adult-to-adult interpersonal dynamics (we all know that workplaces are in fact full of petulant toddlers and sulky teens, but bear with me). You have the right to ask for a pay rise and if your boss finds that annoying, or even a personal slight – tough. They don't have the right to view you as a 'child'. You are in a transactional relationship and you are being paid for your work.

Repeat this as often as necessary: Work is not your family.

Whether you are in a workplace with reserves of cash to attract and keep talented staff, or one where pay rises are hard to come by, it's helpful to plan and execute your pay rise plan using simple steps. I've drawn up this list with the help of everything I've learned; it's a distillation of my own experience, plus ideas I've found useful from experts such as Grace Lordan, a professor of behavioural science at the LSE, who first introduced me to the fantastic acronym 'Fobsag', meaning 'fear of being seen as greedy'. This concept sums up what holds a lot of us (especially women) back from asking for more pay.

My other pay 'mentors' include Jonathan Black, author of the *Dear Jonathan* career advice column in the FT (and who also answers readers' dilemmas with me on the *Working It* podcast), and also my wonderful FT colleague, *Money Clinic* host, Claer Barrett. Pay rises are such a huge topic that Jonathan and I have appeared twice on *Money Clinic* to discuss it. Do listen to those episodes. They are free on all podcast platforms if you want to get a good overview of the subject before you dive in with your own demands.

Simple steps to your pay rise

Before going through the process of asking for a pay rise, anyone in a relatively high-paid job, or who has ambitions to be in one, might also want to think about getting some one-to-one coaching around making the 'ask'. It will help you with confidence and presentation, too, and a good coach will help you to clarify your goals.

Pay is only a part of how we feel valued at work, and it may be that your near-term ambition is a promotion or training. Or it may be better to get out of the organisation altogether. A coach can help with thinking about that, too.

You may also have either official or informal mentors in your life who can help you prepare for your pay rise negotiation. What have they learned from their own experiences? Listening to others and hearing about their wins and mistakes is never time wasted.

If you are a LinkedIn user, then the platform has lots of video training resources available at LinkedIn Learning. (There's even one called 'How to Get People to Like You'.) LinkedIn also does in-depth courses that businesses pay for on behalf of employees (if you don't ask, you don't get).

If you want to think more 'holistically' about your attitudes and ambitions, and where pay sits within that – but don't have the money for coaching sessions – then I'd recommend a book called *You Coach You: How To Overcome Challenges and Take Control of Your Career*, by Sarah Ellis and Helen Tupper (they run Amazing If career coaching and host the *Squiggly Careers* podcast). Their book is very good on career progression and overcoming the self-imposed blocks to advancement, and you can do it all yourself.

I have broken the process of asking for a pay rise down into steps, which makes the whole thing a bit more manageable:

1. Know your worth

Before you go a step further with your pay rise request, judge where you sit in the internal market of your workplace, as well as in relation to those working in similar jobs elsewhere. Glassdoor and recruitment websites will have some salary data, and some US states and cities have passed laws that mean employers have to put salary ranges on job adverts. It's not perfect – nobody is learning anything useful if the salary range is $40,000–$100,000, but it's a step in the right direction.

Internally, a common issue is finding that someone who has recently joined the company with a similar job and skills profile to your own is being paid a lot more than you are. If your sector is facing a tight labour market, where there are fewer good candidates than there are good jobs, then your employer may well have had to pay a premium to get people to join.

Jonathan Black, the FT's *Dear Jonathan* career advice columnist, touched on this when he counselled a twenty-something marketing executive who had been joined on the team by a colleague with no formal qualifications and less experience, but who had secured a management role and would be paid more than the letter writer. This sort of issue is common, and Jonathan gave excellent general advice when he reminded the correspondent that we can never know everything. 'Remember that the information you are using for the comparison is asymmetric and incomplete. You know all the measures about yourself, have some measures about your new colleague, and are unclear on the measures used by your boss in the recent appointment.'

Even so, if you are in a position where a new recruit is (as far as you know – or you can directly ask them) being paid more than you for doing the same thing, then you need to look at what's going on inside the company. In particular, look out for 'internitis' – Claer introduced me to this concept. It refers to situations where you've been with a company since you were an intern or very junior staffer, and because of that it can be very hard for people to think of you in a different light. You will always be 22 in the eyes of your boss.

Overcoming this is hard, but using the steps below will help. In some cases, though, you may need to leave the organisation and start afresh somewhere new, where your skills and talents are valued, and nobody thinks you are the trainee.

One final thing. The easiest way to find out whether you are paid much less than colleagues is to share salaries. Ask people what they are paid, although make sure you choose to talk to colleagues you like and trust, rather than approaching people at random.

Talking about our salaries has historically been totally taboo. Recent research suggests a quarter of us discuss salaries openly at work. I think that seems a pretty high number. The psychology behind this secrecy just doesn't hold up. The problem we have as individuals is that we will feel we are worth less (or even feel worthless) if we discover we are paid far less than our close colleagues. So we never talk about it.

Try to get past that. Your pay is not a reflection of the integrity and value of you, your character, or your work. And who is benefiting if you keep your salary secret? Bosses, who may not want staff to share what they earn (it's explicitly banned in some workplaces, which is unjust). Silence is their weapon. Sharing can be yours.

There are many reasons why we may be paid less (or more) than others, and historic discrepancies between men's and women's pay rates – which persist in the gender pay gap – may be part of it. 'Internitis' may be another.

And don't discount the deep biases that persist in pay decisions. In 2018, the BBC's China editor Carrie Gracie resigned in a dispute over unequal pay. She had found out that senior male international editors were paid far more than female counterparts, such as herself. Her resignation and a subsequent investigation brought the issues of entrenched pay bias to the wider public, and Carrie wrote a book, *Equal*, about her own experience taking on bias at the BBC. The book also offers lots of practical advice on how to tackle pay inequity in your own organisation.

If you are in the UK, the law requires employers to pay men and women equally for equal work, and if you are a woman who suspects a man is being paid more for doing the same work, you have the right to ask what he earns. The Fawcett Society campaigns on equal pay, and its website is a good resource for anyone who thinks they are underpaid compared to men. (Carrie donated her payout from the BBC to the Fawcett Society to fund some of this work.)

And what if you are the person being paid more than a colleague for doing the same job? Don't feel guilty about saying what you earn. You can help others by doing so. You are, literally, paying it forward.

2. Do I actually want a pay rise – or is it just about recognition?

Pay and pay rises are emotional issues because they hook us into the slightly uncomfortable truth that we work for money – and money is an emotional topic. I won't go into the link between money and self-worth, but anyone who has been shopping-while-miserable will be aware of it.

Work itself – and the recognition and validation we get when it goes well – is a powerful craving that can become all consuming. Consider your relationship to work, whether the level of validation you expect and seek is healthy or not, and how your desire for a pay rise plays into that. It may be that a new job title is what you are really after, and that may be absolutely fine.

Someone who spent years in a role that gave them near godlike control over people's pay and promotions gave me an inside trick of the trade: They encouraged staff to separate in their minds how much the organisation valued each person as an individual from the amount they were paid. While it might actually be healthy to decouple your sense of self-worth from your pay, it's also good to be paid a fair rate for the hard work you are doing. So be aware of the tactics – or we might say 'mind games' – that paymasters will try.

In organisations where everyone expects big bonuses and pay rises every year, this isn't an issue. Your value to the business is explicit in the level of your pay and bonus. It's stark, but it's obvious.

A note here on boosting your status and recognition internally as a precursor to asking for a pay rise: Working to make yourself 'seen' (as discussed in Part II, Chapter 4) is a way to be proactive about the status you attach to yourself and your job. You don't need to wait until you get a new title or more money 'conferred' on you. If you *seem* important, your pay request may land differently.

Start that quest by reducing or removing any 'non promotable tasks' you are seen to do. These are things like taking minutes at meetings, getting the cake for special occasions, circulating the leaving cards, etc. All this is also known as 'office housework', and yes, women do most of it. If you are perennially doing this stuff and it's not part of your core job, then push back and get someone else to step up. I am not saying never do this – I still do lots of it – just don't make yourself the default person for that tasks.

3. Prepare your 'ask'. Storytelling + data = success

The worst thing you can do is impulsively book a meeting with the relevant person and ask for a raise. The best thing you can do is to spend considerable prep time on 'crafting' your story. Yes, I mean that.

Essentially, what you want to develop is a compelling narrative that is memorable – why you should have a pay rise, and why now – and back that up with some data. You need to keep all of this extremely concise. Ideally, you come out of the preparation process with a one-page document, possibly loaded with bullet points and certainly containing a couple of useful graphs or data points, to show your case 'at a glance'.

The main reasons for doing this are:

- It focuses your mind, with laser-like precision, on what you want and your 'ask'. There may be cases where you don't give a precise figure for the pay rise you want, but ideally you have come up with a realistic figure by 'knowing your worth' internally and externally. Get the text as concise as possible and remove anything not related to the pay rise request and the reasoning behind it.

- It makes everything clear to the person handling your request. They may not be the person who makes the decision about your pay rise but a one-page document with all the facts and figures is going to help your case when your boss takes it to the next boss up the chain.

- It shows how much thought and care you have put into it, something that is also very attractive to bosses. This is a world away from the (all too common) tactic of wandering into a pay meeting and saying, 'I deserve a pay rise'.

- It makes you look important and professional. And perception is vital.

Here's Professor Grace Lordan again, giving some detail in the FT on how to structure your pay 'ask'. 'It is worth paying attention to the 'peak-end rule', meaning that the peak and the end of a conversation are the most memorable parts. Pay conversations will go better if they focus mainly on two significant accomplishments.

'When choosing your two accomplishments, one should capture your best performance last year and the second should look to the year ahead. Pay talks need to be polished, memorable and information overload-free. You should also set out your expectations on what the pay rise might be. Setting an early anchor in the conversation provides a mental reference point for your manager to refer to when deciding the award level.'

4. Find the right time to ask for a pay rise
By this I mean the right time of the year, the right month, or even the best time of day. Timing is important.

Is there a pay review timetable at your organisation? More particularly, how does your boss's review work? Is there an incentive for them to give or not give pay rises? Gather as much information as possible about the wider pay system at your organisation. Your boss may not even make the decision about your pay. If that's the case, who does?

Get the meeting in the diary and (a tip I belatedly learned from experts) you don't need to say it's about pay. Clearly your boss may suspect, but you can leave them guessing. An element of surprise may help your case. If this leaves you queasy, and you think the manager will freak out at being surprised, do of course say what it's about when you book the time. Never, ever, stop the boss informally as they are walking out of the office or going to the bathroom. Nobody will pay attention when they are hangry or have a full bladder.

Grace Lordan adds, 'If you can, avoid having the meeting during a period when your boss is suffering from negative emotions. This is where the rapport you have built with their executive assistant can pay dividends: It once saved me from a pay discussion when my manager had just learnt their spouse was filing for divorce.

'If you can, pick Tuesday to have the discussion. The Monday rush is over, but there is plenty of time left in the week for your boss to feel awkward if they reject you. It is easier to reject someone on a Friday, just before the weekend break from work.'

5. Make your pay meeting count
Ros Atkins, the BBC's analysis editor, and the man behind dozens of explainer videos that often go viral, has written a very good book called *The Art of Explanation* about how to achieve clear, concise communication. Ros came on the *Working It* podcast to talk about it. He is a stickler for preparation before any sort of meeting or presentation. The time you spend prepping your pay rise request is going to pay off. His advice on all communication is to pare everything back to the essentials of what you are trying to get across. Lose any extra words or

'nice-to-have' data. Be ruthless with yourself. If possible, get a trusted colleague or friend to look over your one-pager or listen to your pitch.

Once you are in the meeting, Ros gives this advice from his own experience: 'I will try and quickly stop and think, OK, who's going to be in this meeting? What is it that I would like to get across? What is it they might want from me? How can I help them get that? And what is it that we're all hoping to decide to do?

'And if you can be conscious of that, the way those conversations go, you can't guarantee an outcome, but you can give yourself the best chance of having passed on the information you think matters, of trying to get the information you would like in return, and of making sure at least the people you're speaking to know what you would like to happen and why.'

That advice works for any sort of workplace meeting or discussion, not just pay rise conversations. *Always* have a piece of paper to hand and make notes beforehand, even if you only have a minute's notice. Or use your phone, if you prefer that.

Once in the meeting, after the pleasantries, go through what should be a rehearsed pitch, including the two accomplishments that Grace recommends.

The phrases 'I need' or 'I deserve' are red rags for managers. (They need and deserve pay rises too.) Always avoid those.

You'll be nervous, but you have every right to be there. Keep focused, keep it adult-to-adult (try not to slip into needy child-parent dynamics), and above all, do not waffle. Stick to your points, and keep close to what's written on your one-page pay rise explainer.

Note down the main points given to you as they happen, and as you understand them. This can be hard to do if you are nervous or something shocking happens. I know people secretly record meetings but I am not going to advise you to do that. If you know you are going to struggle with taking it all in, you could ask for permission to record. Be open about it, though.

You'll need your notes later . . .

6. Follow up and confirm what happened in writing

Even if the meeting was a disaster and your manager barely heard you out, talked over you, or generally behaved like a jerk, you need to do a follow-up. In writing. And do it while the meeting is still fresh in your head. Keep it neutral, however furious you feel.

'Dear X, Thank you for seeing me today to discuss my pay rise request. I noted the following points from the meeting, and wanted to confirm with you that my takeaways are correct . . . '

Then you go through the points made in the meeting, perhaps as bullet points. If the answer was, 'Yes of course, here's a £10k pay rise', that's great – but you need to have it confirmed in writing. If it wasn't such good news, you can outline what was said and what reason was given, for example, 'You said you would not be offering me a pay rise at this time as my performance has not been judged outstanding. You agreed that we can revisit this decision in Q1 of next year.'

As always in workplaces, there is no such thing as overcommunication. You might bore your boss into submission with your notes and emails, but it will stop anyone relying on faulty human recollection when you come to revisit the pay discussion. Nobody wants a debate about what was or wasn't said.

Scared managers have been known to deny they made or implied any promises once they've been leaned on by someone higher up, and then you'll get into a situation where you feel gaslit. Try to avoid it by setting an example with your clear, timely communication. Replaying the conversation highlights in an email will be good for you and will prevent your boss from wriggling out of what they said.

Make sure to put something on the end, asking them to confirm what you've put in the email, i.e. that you both agree that your version of events is correct.

7. What happens after 'no'?

A lot of pay rise requests get turned down. If it's a 'no' for you, try not to internalise the rejection (hard, I know). Your salary is not a reflection of your personal worth as a human being. Rich people are not more moral, decent, or brilliant than you. They are just richer.

Often, the next step is for us to think, 'When can I ask again?' You may have been fobbed off with a general 'not at the moment' excuse. Jonathan Black, the FT's careers expert, suggests reframing the next step like this: 'The question is, what do I have to do to be eligible for the raise?'

He suggests another meeting with your manager to clarify what they'd want to see before offering you a pay rise. 'I would be turning to them and asking for their advice, their support. What extra skills do I need? I'm obviously eager to get a pay rise or to progress to the next level.

What training can you offer? What projects could I take on? Can I have your support? Can I have a secondment?'

This is where your pay rise conversation turns into something bigger. Maybe you don't (immediately) get more cash, but your enthusiasm is going to be hard to resist. There may be training and skills opportunities opened to you that you hadn't considered. Can the company sponsor you through a part-time business-school course? Do you want to learn more about AI? Is there an executive coaching opportunity internally – and can you join the next cohort?

Think about what you need for the next few years of your career and how your current employer could do more to help you achieve your goals (or help you find those goals in the first place). Something as simple as asking for a title change may help and it won't cost the employer anything. It could help position you better, both internally and to potential employers.

Other tactics, often driven by the cost-of-living crisis, might be to swap the pay rise 'ask' for a more flexible work schedule. Perhaps you're meant to be in the workplace three days a week but on one of those days you just have endless virtual meetings. Why not ask for a formal arrangement to work one extra day at home? You will save commuting time and money and you won't lose out on collaborative work because . . . that's not happening in the office anyway. The money you save on commuting, coffee, lunch (and even childcare) will be valuable.

On the other hand, you may be turned down with no hope of a raise – perhaps the organisation has no cash, or perhaps the bosses are explicitly saving the money to entice new hires rather than encouraging the career development of existing staff (which is a red flag – and a surprisingly common and short-sighted tactic). In those scenarios, you are probably going to want to think about moving internally or to a new employer.

8. Next steps

Here's where you need to think carefully about what drives you at work and what you want from your future career. If you got a pay rise – even if it's not for the amount you wanted – that doesn't mean you should simply park your career ambitions. You've been recognised for what you've already done, and for your potential. Now you can get on with fulfilling your potential and reaching even higher.

If you were asking for a pay rise to help ease the cost of living and your request declined, then asking for more flexible working patterns or taking on a side hustle will be short-term options worth exploring.

You may or may not want to tell the manager about any side hustle. An Etsy shop is one thing but if you are running a personal training business on the side, as one staff member I heard of was doing, then that might start to impact on the working hours of your main job. There have even been recent cases of people working in tech development doing two full-time remote jobs – and each employer didn't know about the other.

If you've been told you need to gain experience or qualifications before you'll get a pay rise, then you also have a clear goal.

But if the whole experience has been demoralising, negative, and made you realise that something needs to change, that's good, too. Time to start looking for a new job or a new start.

Preparing to move on

You'll need to deploy different tactics depending on whether you are in a big organisation and think you can move to a different team or department in search of pay and promotion, or whether you are starting an external job search.

The explicit 'jobs board' method of finding a new post internally is always useful, but don't discount the power of your 'loose ties' – the people you know, but who are not your close friends. Keep an ear out for changes and opportunities internally. Get involved in internal events and employee affinity or resource groups (these include women's groups, parents' groups, LGBTQ+ groups, and groups for people of colour, and there are many more). You may already be involved in cross-team projects, but if that's an option, go for it.

Your search for your next career move is also where your internal mentor/sponsor could come in useful. Ask their advice and see if they can suggest anyone else useful you could speak to. One of the disadvantages of applying for new roles internally is that people may have fixed ideas of what you can do and your skill set. It's up to you to be proactive and shift how others see you.

A secondment or maternity/paternity cover job is often the quickest way to get people to see you differently – you've stepped up or moved across to something new.

If a change isn't on the cards, you could start 'job crafting' immediately. That means working with your current manager to ditch the parts of your role that you like less, or which don't fit your career aspirations, and develop new skills and work areas that will help you progress. (This obviously depends on a good relationship with the boss.) At a time of talent shortages, many companies are starting to be more open-minded about developing staff, so a 'crafting' request may not land negatively.

The external job search is a wholly different experience. Rather than having hiring managers who have fixed perceptions of who you are and what you can do, you will be going into the unknown, and having to prove yourself to strangers.

The recruitment field has changed enormously. Over the past two decades, LinkedIn has been the catalyst for a shift from 'passive' recruitment, where hirers put out job ads and seek out candidates who are explicitly job hunting, to 'active' recruitment, where hiring managers seek out likely candidates and proactively approach people who might not be looking for a job but who would be a good match for an opening or employer. You probably already have chancers and timewasters in your DMs but there may be useful contacts among the messages, and it's very good to get an idea from headhunters of benchmark salaries in your sector once you start the job search.

LinkedIn, with more than 950 million users globally, can also be a great tool for you to seek out potential employers rather than waiting for them to land in your messages. It's worth spending time polishing up your bio and profile if you are about to embark on a job hunt. The platform's managing director for EMEA (Europe, the Middle East, and Africa) and Latin America is Josh Graff, and he talked to me for *Working It* about how a proactive job search can go.

'We launched a job search filter on LinkedIn to help people find companies that share their values. And when I say values, that could be diversity, equity, inclusion, sustainability, employee wellbeing. On the other side, we've encouraged companies to showcase their values on the company page, and since October last year, forty thousand companies have filled out their commitment section on their company page and they're uploading evidence to support those claims.'

What companies say they do in public, and how the corporate culture feels once you are inside, can be very different things. So start to activate your network. Do you know anyone inside a company that interests you? Where do friends of friends or good social media connections work? What do they say 'off the record' about the culture? Have there been big scandals or employment tribunals that suggest all is not quite as 'purpose-driven' as it seems?

The big resource here is Glassdoor, which is a useful website for intel from both current and former employees, and for salary information. Because – and this is something that really doesn't get aired enough – there's no point moving for a £20k pay bump, only to find you are miserable inside a dysfunctional organisation. You might, as my colleague Claer Barrett says, end up 'spending it all on therapy'. So try to scope out as much information as possible about every place you apply. You could also use generative AI to give you an initial answer on the history and salient facts about any potential employer. (Don't rely on it completely, though, these bots do sometimes 'hallucinate' things that aren't real, but it's a good first step.)

Ready to roll on with your job search?
Start with these steps:

1. Perfect your CV – this is your shop window. If you work in marketing or sales you have a head start on how to present yourself. The rest of us have to work harder. A lot of experts stress the 'storytelling' aspect of the CV, the idea that someone reading it should get an idea of what your story is and what you have to offer. There are lots of resources out there to help you. I recommend *Harvard Business Review*'s online guides, and Google searches will give you lots of free online help.

2. You can use ChatGPT or other generative AI platforms to help with a CV and cover letter. Many people do this very effectively already but just check it over and make sure it sounds like you. This is an emerging trend, and only you will know what works, and whether a computer-generated CV and letter is going to give you the best shot at your next job. It might be worth creating an AI-generated bio in tandem with one you do yourself. How do they compare?

   It's worth noting, however, that you may not need to do any of this for much longer. Generative AI is possibly going to end the dominance of the CV. Recruiters already use it to scan through CVs and cover letters, looking for keywords. This is something to bear in mind for the future (and make sure you get those keywords into your CV now).

3. Be prepared for interviews to be in person, on screen, or automated, using AI; there are so many interview models now. For a first round

of recruiting, you may find yourself in a timed interview, being asked set questions. Your performance may be assessed by a human or an algorithm. While these automated interviews do help to prevent bias on the part of hirers, they may not show some candidates at their best. People with some neurodiverse conditions, for example, may struggle. Again, it's all new. It's still more likely you'll be interviewed by real people, online or in person, so prepare well for that and read Part II, Chapter 4, for tips on presence and confidence.

4. Expect frustration, delays, and ghosting. The world of recruitment has become complex, filled with multiple layers of interviews and assessments, and you may be asked to do a lot of preparation. Are you actually ready to start the search? It's going to be worth it in the long run, but be prepared for frustrating weeks and months ahead.

Takeaways

- Asking for a pay rise is the quickest way to find out more about how you are seen internally. It's not just about the money. You may come out with no cash, but with offers of training, secondments, or coaching. It is always worth the ask.

- Preparation is everything. Gather all your facts and data to back up your request. Find out how much others are paid in similar roles, internally and externally. Get it all on one sheet of paper (something that is easy to share with bosses).

- Never say 'I deserve' or 'I need' as part of your pay negotiation. You'll sound needy rather than proactive and it will annoy bosses. They deserve a pay rise too; you aren't special.

- Make the meeting short, well prepared, and full of 'storytelling'. Work out the narrative of why you should have a pay rise.

- If you don't get a pay rise, what else can you get? A simple (and free) change of job title can be transformative in the long run, as it positions you differently, internally and externally.

- No pay rise? Ask what would help you get one next time. Aim for skills training, coaching, more flexible work patterns, etc. See what your employer can give you.

- Really no pay rise, ever? Time to move on. Internally, you can start your own PR campaign, and use your friends and contacts to find opportunities. For an external job hunt, you will need time, patience, and a lot of preparation.

- Do your research on potential employers: They may all say they are 'purpose driven and inclusive' but they probably aren't. Everywhere is dysfunctional, but talk to current and former staff if you can, and see what they say on Glassdoor. A bad corporate culture will wipe out the benefits of a pay bump.

- Generative AI can help you in your job hunt, just as it's already being used in recruitment. It may soon render your CV and cover letter obsolete, but until that happens, take time to craft them well (and if you use AI, do it with care). One cover letter does not fit all. Sadly, you'll have to remake them for different employers.

- Getting a new job is a full time job in itself. Unless you are under siege from headhunters (and even if you are, you'll still have to sift through the offers), build this time commitment into your plans for the next few months.

Chapter 8: Keeping Family and Work on the Road
There's no easy fix, but honesty at home helps

There are now many books aimed at helping women advance in the workplace, and others that specifically highlight practical ways to reach elusive gender equity targets. I've attended and moderated panels at many women's conferences, panels, and networking groups over the years. Yet I do sometimes think . . . isn't there something missing here?

My own answer as to why women aren't doing better overall – and this comes after years of exposure to the issues (heck, actually *living* the issues) and also a fair degree of professional expertise in this area – is that too much of this discourse focuses on women alone.

Men, and a discussion of their 'allyship', usually get a panel session at every conference, but that's it. And it's not just about including men. What I mean is that the hyper-focus on women at work, how they can advance, how to make work more flexible for women, and so on, forgets that the question of how to make work *work* is a question for us all. It's not just for women. It is for everyone who is human.

The real question should be: How can we all shape our work lives into something that can sit alongside spending time nurturing our relationships, caring for our kids and elders, being a good friend, and doing the volunteering and sports and connecting stuff in our communities?

How can we keep ourselves, our families, and our work commitments together, without burning out or feeling generally used up by a rapacious and unforgiving work schedule? They don't call law, consultancy, and investment banking 'greedy jobs' for nothing. This work pays big, but it takes away nearly all of your most limited commodity: time. (As a caveat, other jobs can be just as 'greedy' but for a lot less money.)

This is a huge topic but here I will summarise some ways to start rethinking and future-proofing your work. Just don't think of any of it in isolation. All those corporate attempts at, for example, advancement and promotion for mothers at work are useless unless the structure of the woman's home life offers 'scaffolding' to her ambition. Is there a supportive partner or grandparent around to share the care or is she doing it all alone? Is she earning enough to pay the exorbitant cost of childcare?

Many women, including those with partners, still do all of the 'second shift' at home, once they've finished at work. By looking at how we fit work into our lives in the round, we can think about how best to help ourselves, and eventually pay it forward, and be the kinds of colleagues and managers who enable others to thrive in the workplace and at home.

Dual careers, flexible lives

There's something impossibly '80s and big-shouldered about the phrase 'dual-career couple'. Mostly, the couples I know who fit this description – where both partners have full-on, usually full-time, careers – are just working incredibly hard at everything and don't have time to think about how shiny their lifestyle looks from the outside. Because to keep these shows on the road they need a lot of energy, as well as stellar organisational ability. And, frankly, money.

There's been a lot of academic research on how dual-career couples manage, and how they thrive, or fall apart. The best-known expert in this field is Jennifer Petriglieri. In 2019 she published a book called *Couples That Work*, which came out of many interviews she did with dual-career (or 'power') couples.

As Jennifer wrote of her research in the *Harvard Business Review*, 'Although the 50/50 marriage – in which housework and childcare are divided equally between the partners, and their careers are perfectly synched – may seem like a noble ideal, my research suggests that instead of obsessively trying to maintain an even "score," dual-career couples are better off being relentlessly curious, communicative, and proactive in making choices about combining their lives.'

The 50/50 balance seems like a big thing to give up, but there are times in any relationship when one partner is at home more than the other, or someone steps back from work a bit. The key is to talk about it, and not to let resentments fester (I've done plenty of not talking and actively resenting in my time).

I wish I could write something novel about what works in terms of balancing all the things in our lives while both partners have big jobs, but it all boils down to trust and communication. And also adaptability. I have learned, at an emotional cost, that having a fixed idea of the roles we occupy in the dynamic of our relationships is hopeless. It should actually be constantly under review.

Jennifer's book was published just before the pandemic. It's still a very good primer for anyone embarking on (or trying to improve) any sort of partnership. You don't even need to be a 'power couple' because a lot of the advice is universal. It's useful because most conventional relationship guides don't take into account the effect of work on our personal lives; they focus instead on the romantic and emotional stuff, things like 'love languages' and revitalising tired sex lives.

But we can't live in a bubble at home. Work provides its own tensions and disruptions, and for most of us, a part of that issue is that our partner has no place in our separate work life. We have a different identity there. It's no surprise that in the celebrity psychotherapist Esther Perel's bestselling book *The State of Affairs: Rethinking Infidelity*, plenty of the affairs she describes start at work.

The new focus of work and life: your kitchen table

Since 2020, the rise of working from home and flexible work has really shifted how we manage our working lives. The 2023 McKinsey Women in the Workplace report finds that 'women are more ambitious than before the pandemic, and flexibility is fuelling that ambition.' Around one in five women say that flexibility has allowed them to stay in their job or avoid reducing their hours.

The report focuses on women, who are 'defying the outdated notion that work and life are incompatible, and that one comes at the expense of the other'. But the findings are also important for men. The debate is still raging about whether flexible and remote work is holding back anyone who isn't 'visible' in the workplace.

This was on the mind of Janine Chamberlin, a senior LinkedIn executive, when she came on *Working It* to talk about returning from maternity leave. Janine (who was about to go on mat leave herself) talked to me about some research that LinkedIn had done.

'More than a third of employees [surveyed] would actually quit their job if they were asked to return to the office full-time. And I think this is where companies need to look at how does the system work? So in what way does a manager, for example, assign a stretch project to someone? In what way does a manager consider promotions and pay increases? And if that is only based on whomever is nearest to them or whomever is the best at speaking up, then, ultimately, proximity bias is going to become a real big problem.'

Ah, proximity bias. The scourge of the post-pandemic workplace. Its relevance here, for those who are trying to find a way to balance all the elements of their lives, is to be aware of it. Does it actually hold women back? I don't think so, but I have yet to see statistics.

Ultimately, all you can do is what's right for your circumstances. If you can spot that opportunities are going to people who are more present in the workplace than you are, then you can take a decision on how to play it. You may feel you want to 'cruise' in your work for a while. You may also want to push back on any opportunities that have been lost.

Recognising that proximity bias is real, and perhaps affects managers in your workplace, is the first step you can make. Then you can judge how it might affect you if you make the choice to work more at home than in the workplace. People go through so many different life stages that there may well be times in yours when the payoff from being able to work flexibly is worth any career setback or stagnancy. Not everything goes upwards in a straight line, including our careers, and anyone who suggests that 'the only way is up' is giving you old-fashioned BS.

Paternity leave – the new key to workplace equality

Recently, the people who have been talking most about career setbacks, or proximity bias, have been men. Extended paid paternity leave is a brilliant benefit and many more companies are offering it, including some law and City firms.

But for those men in corporate jobs who do take up extended paternity leave, there's sometimes a cost. That's because there's often a disconnect between policy and reality. One lawyer quoted in the *Financial Times* found that he'd been passed over for partnership because of taking time off. Men are finding that absence from the workplace for family reasons can lead to career detriment, something that has affected women for decades.

But as more men take longer leave periods, this should ease. And the experience of men finding they are subject to bias and discrimination may help advance everyone in the workplace. Struggle creates solidarity.

In the UK, statutory paternity leave is two weeks, and not all men take that (almost a third take no leave after the birth of a child). Only a few men (estimates hover around 2–3 per cent) are taking up their legal right to longer shared parental leave, which offers up to fifty weeks between parents. In many jobs it's only paid at a very low statutory rate. But if and when more parents start to take up their full shared parental leave – and this shift is likely to be led by big employers who are paying for it as a benefit for their staff – then attitudes will change, too.

Longer paternity leave is one of the biggest workplace shifts in recent decades, and in coming years its impact will start to be felt more fully. If you are thinking ahead to having children, then this development is likely to change how *everyone* works.

And looking at the rest of our lives, taking time off from work to bond with babies, whoever is doing it, creates a link that's far more important and enduring than the short-termism of office promotion. When it comes to balancing work and family life, sometimes you have to play the long game.

Letting go of guilt and presenteeism

These are pervasive barriers that can prevent you from making all areas of your life work in harmony. The pandemic, and all the working change it brought with it, has ended a lot of the presenteeism that was common in workplaces, and which prevented many people, not just mothers, from leading more balanced lives. Even after tech advances made working from home easy, it didn't take off until the enforced shift of 2020. And for those frontline workers who can't work from home, the pandemic also brought with it more understanding of how our work and home lives blur.

That's not to say it's easy to leave the office early or absent yourself from the perma-busy Slack channel. But it's reassuring to realise that colleagues still at their desks may be performing work, rather than doing anything useful. Slack's global State of Work report found employees spend 32 per cent of their time on work that gives the appearance of productivity, rather than on actually useful activity. A lot of this effort, it seems, goes into impressing bosses.

You don't need to buy into that, although peer and manager pressure is very real. If you are serious about making your work fit into your life, rather than vice versa, you do have to make some hard trade-offs about what to prioritise in the limited time available to you.

The 'limited time' point here is key when you are trying to keep all the parts of your life in some kind of synchronicity. If you haven't read Oliver Burkeman's bestselling *Four Thousand Weeks*, I recommend you do. He's written about productivity but he starts from the rarely-spoken-about reality that we are all going to die and we need to get real about how we spend our time. (Work can be a massive displacement activity, after all.)

You can make a choice either to leave at 5 p.m. to visit your parents and cook them a meal, or to stay at work until after that long-hours manager leaves. Nobody can do both on the same night.

Nothing is easy. There are no trade-offs that will please everyone. You can buy into the performative working system to appease your own guilt, or you can work towards letting go of it.

Talking to colleagues and friends, joining an employee group, becoming part of a sector-wide network – all of these will help you manage your career and family and create connection with others who are going through the same things as you, or who have done so in the past. If you don't do that, and you are isolated, it is going to leave you exposed and vulnerable to anxiety and spiralling thoughts. It is your workplace friends and supportive mentors who will boost you when you face that kind of dilemma between work and life, and the feelings of inadequacy that may follow.

And, finally, you are not 'letting down' others by not staying late, nor do you need to appear on Slack at all hours of the night, rather than taking a break in the evening. There are few jobs where this sort of urgency is needed – and if you are in one, you will know about it.

Reassuringly, younger people coming into the workplace are changing norms and expectations. Many Gen Z workers refuse to overload themselves with tasks. They prioritise balance, and they aren't going to stick around in toxic work cultures. Older people can learn from them (one of the best free resources for seeing how demographics are changing workplace culture is the Edelman Trust Barometer).

Can I say that I've ditched all the bad habits of my presenteeist past? No. But I am working on it, and so can you.

<u>Takeaways</u>

- Women's advancement at work is ongoing but if we want a future that creates more balance for everyone, we need everyone on board. Men too often get left out of conferences and networking events.

- Being part of a working couple is hard (although not as hard as working while being a single parent). The challenge is to adapt your relationship to the changing demands of both people's work lives. It requires a lot of honesty and talk. And compromises. Remember, nobody likes a compromise, as it means giving something up.

- Flexible work has boosted women's ambition. It's kept more women in work. If it helps you and your family keep your lives on track alongside your work, then that's another great outcome. Many employers talk a big game about getting more people back in the office for more days a week, but they know that some of those workers will leave if forced back. The future is flexible.

- Not every career needs to be on an upwards trajectory all the time. This gets forgotten. Sometimes workplaces can put pressure on us to go for promotions or management roles. But when you are trying to play many roles in your life, there are times when you can put the career on cruise control. It's okay.

- Extended paid paternity leave has the potential to be the biggest transformation in workplace culture we've ever seen. Done right, and taken up by more men, it may help solve a lot of the inequity around women's and men's relative career progression and recognition, speed up change, and allow people to balance their lives. That's the hope, anyway.

- The dreaded proximity bias is something to watch out for when you are balancing home and work life. If you are not in the office, the boss may not notice you. This may not matter, your company may be more enlightened than that . . . or you may not care. But don't let the mere existence of this bias stop you from doing what is right for your circumstances.

- Work can be a great source of fulfilment and identity. It is also not your family or your friend (although we can have friends there). Don't lose sight of this.

- We are all going to die. That's the sad truth behind every single thing we do. Little of what we do at work matters when we put it into this context. Don't use it as a displacement activity to fend off engaging with the rest of your life. Time passes alarmingly quickly (I have found).

- Guilt and presenteeism have been our constant companions. We can do plenty to try to change how we react in future, but the biggest shift may be systemic. Gen Z is entering the workforce in big numbers and their relationship to work and balance is very different. They have high expectations of their employer. Let's hope the employers step up.

Chapter 9: Late Career Blooming
How to deal with the extremes of mid-life, and come through it (sort of) okay

I have lingered over far too many Instagram posts about the exciting possibilities of mid-life. Improbably wrinkle-free women stare at me from empowering wellness retreats or mountain streams. I scroll through in a daze but never lose sight of this grim fact: We are all racing towards retirement, irrelevance, or the grave – pick your outcome. None of them are good.

And shit happens. As we age, so do our families, friends, and colleagues. I can't think of anyone who hasn't faced serious illness, divorce, bereavement, or some other crisis. One gloomy friend described our lives from the late-forties to late-fifties as a 'snipers' alley'. People get picked off, seemingly at random.

So far, so miserable. And yet, reframing later mid-life as a time for reflection, reinvention, and a new zest for life and work is very possible – and indeed desirable. This chapter is about potential because, once any children you have are (semi) independent and you have accumulated decades of experience of being alive, what remains is a tasting menu of possibilities.

You probably have more time, more emotional bandwidth, and certainly more wisdom than you did in your twenties and thirties. Use it.

Why bad mid-life things can have good outcomes
While it may sound counterintuitive, the traumatic events in your life might in fact be the starting point for a reconsideration of what it means to flourish in our careers – and lives – as we age. Experts call this 'post-traumatic growth', and researchers find that it's common in people who have had life-threatening illness or profound loss.

Let's be clear that this positive spin is not always possible. Loss, grief, the end of relationships and of lives, not having enough money, life-changing illness – these have huge and negative impacts on our lives and everyone's experience is different.

But a life-changing event did change everything, in dramatic fashion, for Jonathan Frostick. The British financial services professional had a heart attack in his mid-forties and then blogged about it on LinkedIn from his hospital bed. And the fact that he used LinkedIn, a *work-focused* social platform, to talk about a critical life event – rather than, say, Facebook – is interesting.

By using LinkedIn, Jonathan's post connected with other work-oriented people to tell them not to neglect their personal lives, even when they think busyness at work is the most pressing problem.

Jonathan's posts went viral, with tens of millions of views and hundreds of thousands of likes. Commenters shared their own, often very moving, stories. He had struck a global chord with his openness about the chance that this crisis had given him to rethink the rest of his working life – and his actual life.

Because those two things are not separate.

Jonathan came on the podcast to talk about that moment of crisis. 'I was lying there faced with my own mortality. There was no blinding white light, no angels, no anything. I was lying there thinking, "Oh my God, is this it? I am going to die."'

Many of us will recognise Jonathan's attempts to impose some kind of normality onto that extraordinary moment. And his instinct was to think about work first. 'I had sat down at my desk. It was the weekend, and like most people do, I set out the week ahead. And the first thing that struck me was that I had this meeting with my manager – I really wanted to have this conversation; I had some key points I wanted to cover off. And that was the first thing that came into my mind.'

Thankfully, Jonathan made a full recovery. But at the time of his heart attack, he had to face mortality for the first time, and he thought he needed to capture that, and to 'highlight where I've got this wrong, so other people can learn. So I just wrote down what was on my mind.'

Here's what Jonathan wrote from his hospital bed. It's – of course – raw but I haven't seen a better summation of what our priorities should be in mid-life and onwards.

1. I'm not spending all day on Zoom anymore

2. I'm restructuring my approach to work

3. I'm really not going to be putting up with any s#%t at work ever again – life literally is too short

4. I'm losing 15kg

5. I want every day to count for something at work else I'm changing my role

6. I want to spend more time with my family

Jonathan did change his life. He left his corporate job. His LinkedIn profile now describes him as a 'speaker, mentor, advisor, transformation leader'. He was relaxed when he came into the FT audio studio a few months after his collapse. 'I can say with absolute certainty that having a heart attack quite possibly was the best thing that could have happened to me,' he says.

Jonathan made some promises from his hospital bed, and he's kept them. What's interesting about them all is that they are achievable and pragmatic. He doesn't say he's going to uproot his life, sell all his possessions, and buy a yacht.

And that, let's call it, 'reasonableness test' is key. As someone who has recently been through a totally unexpected life trauma, my only hard-won advice is not to decide to change anything dramatic in your life – quitting your job, for example – while you are in trauma or still processing difficult or painful events.

I was helped in this 'delay' process by a very understanding manager at the FT, and I am going to name check her: Alice Fishburn. I was able to work flexibly, often out of sight, and she arranged for an experienced journalist to cover the management part of my job because I had no capacity to think beyond myself.

Even so, I came very close to making life-altering decisions for myself and my family while in a months-long fugue state of anger and misery. Only a very patient therapist stood between me and what I would now characterise as catastrophically bad judgement.

Whenever you think you will 'never change your mind', or that you need to escape, make a big statement, or go on social media to really piss off your ex . . . don't do it.

I am not saying I didn't do anything crazy. I did. I paid £2.5k for a very luxurious and intensive wellbeing and therapy weekend that I scuppered by catching Covid the day before – and there was no refund. The resulting four days alone at home was actually the recharge I needed. (Expensive) lesson learned.

Focus first on recovery and rebuilding – there's no time limit. Change can wait, even in mid-life.

How to prepare yourself for later career happiness

Even if you are at the top of your game personally and professionally, the good times are going to end. Humans are very, very averse to thinking about or preparing for this. I hope this chapter helps you to start that process – I am finding my own way on this as I go along, too.

My favourite commentator on age and the search for a good life and happiness is Arthur C. Brooks, who I mentioned in the introduction. Arthur is an *Atlantic* magazine columnist, Harvard professor, and a former president of a right-wing US thinktank. (Don't let that put you off – I was resistant at first, but surely part of getting older is about learning to listen to, and understand, different viewpoints?)

His book *From Strength to Strength* is one I'd recommend to anyone seeking an overview of why we have to change our attitudes to work, and to the idea of status and success, as we age.

Arthur offers this observation, from his own field of economics: 'We have something called Stein's Law, named after the famous economist Herbert Stein from the 1970s. "If something cannot go on forever, it will stop." Obvious, right? Well, when it comes to their own lives, people ignore it all the time. But you ignore this about your professional success at your peril. It will leave you falling further and further behind, shaking your fist at the heavens.'

Key to Arthur's viewpoint – and one that I've since tried to bring into my own understanding of the arc of professional working life – is that we need to switch from striving for worldly success to 'to adopt[ing] parts of life that will make you happy, even if they don't make you feel special.'

According to Brooks (who credits British psychologist Raymond Cattell for the following analysis), as we age, our 'fluid intelligence' declines and our 'crystallised intelligence' rises. Essentially, this is the difference between 'the ability to reason, think decisively and solve novel problems,' which declines with age; and the subsequent rise of our 'ability to use a stock of knowledge learned in the past,' wisdom, in other words.

You don't have to agree entirely with this thesis to find it a useful way to take your career forward. Teaching, mentoring, a life of using and distilling your accumulated knowledge – all of these are great ways to think about heading into the future. The concepts of service and 'giving back' also loom large here – both give great satisfaction and can help take the edge off of fading status and (horror!) the idea that soon we will be irrelevant.

Anyone who's ever left a job they've poured their heart, health, and soul into will know how irrelevance feels. When you meet up with your old work colleagues, you realise that it's as if you were never there. Your contributions were welcome, but are now invisible. Life, and work, always goes on. If you were a senior manager or the CEO, imagine that magnified a hundred times. That's what irrelevance feels like.

Once you've processed how different being over 50 is from your younger self, then you can start to look outwards at your current work situation – how you might like that to change (or not), and also what your employer is doing to nurture its older workforce.

Next steps and next acts

Preparing for your 'next act' at work and beyond is key. A new-ish jargon word, 'pretirement', actually sums this up pretty well, as it fits those who are thinking ahead to the next phase of their lives and doing something different.

For a far larger number of people, though, 'pretirement' is a luxury they can't afford. They need to keep working – or even re-enter the workforce – for financial reasons.

All this movement for change is not to ignore the fact that many people in their late fifties, sixties, and beyond are still very happy in their current role for professional and personal fulfilment reasons – we don't see many CEOs or senior leaders stepping down early. And when it's your own business, that desire to hold on to power is even more pronounced: In 2023, Rupert Murdoch stepped down from Fox and News Corp, his media empire, aged 92.

Stick or switch?

If you are keen to use your institutional knowledge and hard-won life wisdom within your current employment setting, then you may find your employer is happy for you to move out of leadership (for example) and into a mentoring-focused or training role. Management expert Stefan Stern wrote in the FT about 'third age' opportunities in 2021. This emerging idea of a 'third age' (another term for this is 'middlescence') refers to the time after age 50, which can be considered as the third quarter of a life that might last into our nineties or beyond. In the 'third age' many people are physically well and want to explore options in their lives beyond a full-on career.

Stefan interviewed CJ (Chris) Barton, a former drama teacher turned actor and executive coach, who points out that employers have a duty of care to staff in preparing them to move to the next step in their lives. 'Jobs will come to an end, do you want them to come to an end with everybody tetchy and uncomfortable and miserable, or as a positive move? Perhaps organisations need a kind of "succession advocate".'

I love that idea, although I have yet to find evidence of an organisation that has one. Many, though, are starting to offer part-time work to older staff (the FT does this) to allow them the flexibility to retrain for a new career, pursue voluntary work or other interests, or perhaps for caring responsibilities. It's a stepping stone or bridge between full-on professional work and thinking about moving to the next phase of our working lives.

Is a coach right for me?

You may also want to think about seeing a career coach between different jobs or phases of your working life. Many coaches are specialists in 'transitions', and there is a growing niche who focus on older people and the transition that comes from stepping back after going full-tilt at your career.

Julian Mack is one of these people. His coaching business is called There's More To Life, and is part of the Haddon Coaching group, the UK's first B Corp-certified coaching company. He and fellow coaches, he says, are incredibly busy in this post-pandemic time. 'It feels as if Covid gave Generation X, in particular, a ticket to live the life they always wanted to live but never had the guts to do before. In a nutshell, the process means they are shifting from the "ought" self, closer to the "ideal" self.' I asked Julian to sell me the benefits of mid-life coaching and what it can do.

'I see us as thinking companions, creating time and space for people to listen to themselves and feel seen and heard. I know "thinking companion" is unlikely to catch on!'

Julian's probably right on that last point, but I like where he's going with this, and asked him to expand.

'A good coach illuminates a path while allowing the thinker [the client] to choose the direction. It's self-generated insights and agency rather than "ought to" and "should". Advice is always rubbish (in my humble opinion).'

So a good coach is essentially an expert sounding board, companion, and guide. And they can be a boosting presence at a time when your confidence may be low. Julian sees common patterns of feelings and behaviour when clients are just starting to think about the changes they want to make (or which are being forced on them through redundancy, ill health, or retirement). He says, 'People use the words "foggy" and "stuck". Awareness of mortality comes up frequently. Self-belief is an issue. We are perhaps less bold in our fifties – I know I am.'

The ideal outcome from your work with a coach at this time would be to help you to outline or articulate, and then start working towards your personal vision of the future. Once this happens, Julian says, 'you tend to witness a big shift,' and people get moving quickly.

Some companies are starting to provide coaches as a perk for senior staff as they approach agreed exits from employment. Realistically, however, you aren't going to get a small employer to pay for your coaching.

The blight of workplace ageism

I won't write another optimistic word about mid-life transition and blooming until we have acknowledged the breathtaking amount of ageism that still persists in workplaces. A 2022 poll by the UK's Chartered Management Institute found that just four in ten managers were, to a 'large or moderate' extent, open to employing those aged 50–64.

In an FT article by my colleague Jane Croft about the rising number of age discrimination cases being brought in the UK, she includes a startling quote from Stuart Lewis, chief executive of Rest Less, a digital community and advocacy group for the over-fifties.

He says, 'Age discrimination is very widespread and people talk about age as the last socially acceptable form of prejudice. Language we would not dream of hearing about ethnicity or gender is routinely used about age.'

This discrimination is happening while many countries have shortages of skilled workers, and the UK government is trying to tempt people off the golf course (as one politician put it) and back into the workplace.

In reality, some older people have long-term health issues and/or are carers, and both of those factors limit them to working fewer hours, if at all.

After decades of overt ageism in workplaces, older people are fighting back. The employment tribunal in England and Wales recorded 15,366 age discrimination cases logged in 2020–1, the highest annual figure since 2007–8.

Thankfully some employers are (finally) starting to realise what a goldmine of talent and experience sits within older workers. It's just taking a very, very long time.

Menopause and other life changes

Jane Croft, in an FT feature about discrimination, heard from one woman who won her case against a former employer, having been told in a meeting to 'Calm down…don't let the hormones get out of control.'

I am speechless.

This manager was talking about menopause. The effects of the perimenopause, which begins in women's early forties, or even earlier, and the later menopause, with its attendant symptoms, had until recently been rarely mentioned at work (or elsewhere). That stigma is slowly eroding, thankfully; it's one aspect of ageism that has been ignored for far too long. An estimated 900,000 women have left the UK workforce because of their symptoms, and three in five women report being 'negatively affected' at work.

It's heartbreaking because it's almost always preventable – women can thrive in mid-life and beyond, and many of the changes can be positive ones.

Rising awareness of menopause treatment options, thanks in the main to campaigners, including TV presenter Davina McCall, have created a surge in demand for hormone replacement therapy (HRT), and the conversation about supporting women through this stage of their lives is now happening in many workplaces.

When I interviewed Davina on stage at an FT event in London, she talked about how perimenopausal symptoms had first affected her work and her life. 'I'm on this commercial, I've got to look amazing, and I looked like I'd aged thirty years overnight. My skin was so dry and I just looked so tired. I was flatlining through life. I couldn't remember the last time I'd felt joy.'

After realising what was happening, Davina started on HRT and things improved. But so many others still aren't able to get the help they need. Her message to other women? 'I think the most important thing is that there are solutions and there are ways out and there are ways to feel better. But you need support! I didn't do this on my own.'

As Davina also points out, menopause and ageing are not all bad. There are huge upsides. 'I feel very lucky to be a woman because we go through all the pain. And the difficulty of being working mothers and the difficulty of the gender gap and the difficulty of the menopause makes us stronger. It's all going to be okay.'

Workplaces have a big role to play. Liv Garfield, CEO of Severn Trent Water, was one of the first senior leaders to go public and talk about the menopause – and bring in a formal policy for the workplace. When I interviewed her at an FT Women in Business Forum event in May 2023, she said she started off by talking openly about menopause in dedicated meetings to break the taboo about it. 'Everybody who was there would try to drop in the word "menopause" at least once a week. Within a few days it was coming into conversation.'

Then Severn Trent Water started to offer training to managers. 'If you're going to lead people, then you need to be trained up on things that could affect [those who] work for you,' she said. After that, the company introduced an official policy. Severn Trent's menopause policy offers 'time off if you need it, a support package and access to a private GP, and flexible work if you need it.'

If your workplace doesn't have a menopause policy yet, Channel 4 television in the UK (one of the first companies to introduce one) makes theirs freely available for others to use as a template or starting point – you can find it on Google.

Talking more openly about the menopause, and about ageing more generally, as well as being supportive and offering flexibility to accommodate the caring responsibilities that many women – and some men – have to undertake, are two easy ways to improve things at work for older staff.

I understand why anyone would be reticent about talking about the menopause in public, because I felt that way too – although I am now happier to talk about it. My only regret is not beginning HRT years earlier than I did. Like many women, I had been fobbed off by a GP and put up with mild but niggling symptoms, many of which I didn't realise were perimenopausal – and then menopausal – until I read Davina's book, *Menopausing*.

The problem with men

I don't want to end this chapter without including the particular problems facing older men as they approach change and transition – or as they decide to carry on full-tilt with a corporate career or self-employment. Either brings its own issues that need to be traversed.

Because – especially for boomer and Gen X men – there have always been expectations around masculinity, earning power, status, and so on. What does the actual or potential loss of any of these do to a high-earning, high-status man?

Julian Mack, the mid-life coach, knows the issues well. He had a big corporate job that he left to start his own business, just as the financial crisis hit in 2008.

He lists the common problems in order of relevance and prevalence:

• What peers/friends/relatives will think

• Change in lifestyle

• Loss of relevance

• Fear of vulnerability

• Loss of autonomy

• Belief that retirement is managed decline

All of these will take time, a lot of consideration, and possibly coaching and therapy to resolve or at least settle. But if the imminent end of full-time work is looming for you, the first step is to make sure you start to redefine success for *yourself*, not for society at large.

Easy next steps

Julian recommends reading *The Modern Maverick* by Ed Haddon as a good first step for men (and women) looking at redefining success. I'd also recommend Lynda Gratton and Andrew Scott's enduringly popular book, *The 100 Year Life: Living and Working in an Age of Longevity*, as well as Arthur C. Brooks's columns in the *Atlantic* (and his book *From Strength to Strength*, which I've already mentioned), to start thinking about transition or ageing more generally.

In addition, for women, and men who want to be informed, Davina McCall's *Menopausing* won a UK book of the year award in 2023. It's a groundbreaking read, and she's also a great follow on Instagram.

Takeaways

- Mid-life can sometimes feel like a series of unfortunate events. It's possible to reframe them as prompts for change in your life. There's no need to be upbeat or hyped about it – realism and compassion are the keys to success in later life.

- Never make a big decision, or even a medium-impact one, when you are in a state of trauma or emotional turmoil. Wait, think, get some outside counsel.

- As we age, areas of our cognitive ability decline but our ability to synthesise and make sense of huge volumes of information – plus our accumulated wisdom and the post-traumatic growth we've experienced – makes the over fifties ideal employees in a multigenerational workforce. Not enough organisations recognise the strengths of older workers so be your own advocate.

- Try to let go of the addiction to success and status that come with a high-level job. It's transient. What matters long term are the real connections you make, your family and friends, and the things that make you happy.

- Mid-life brings particular physical and emotional challenges for many (but not all) women as they enter the perimenopause and menopause. Don't suffer in silence. Explore treatment options and get informed (some GPs can be reluctant to prescribe HRT). It's a complex subject. Always ask for adjustments at work if you need them.

- A coach may be a worthwhile investment at this stage in your career, not to tell you what to do, but to help you find your way to a new path.

- Men who are moving on from senior and high-status positions can be especially prone to negative feelings around transition. To begin to overcome these – and it's a slow process – reframe success to mean something personal to you, not something seen through the lens of what conventional measures of success mean, such as money or status.

FOR THE

MAN

AGERS

Chapter 1: New and Returning Managers Start Here
You'll wish they really did pay you the big bucks

Congratulations! You're reading this because you have just been made a manager. Or you are likely to become one soon. Or perhaps you have been a manager for a while, but want to go over the basics. Management is a bit like yoga: Going back over the core moves (asanas, for those who like a workplace joke) is never time wasted, however advanced we may be in our practice.

I am advanced in neither yoga nor management but I am self-aware and know where I need to improve in both areas, and that's the key to success.

Too often, discussions about management skip over the basics to talk about performance management, productivity analysis, and other by-products of a manager's role. But the first question to ask yourself about your role as a manager is this: What is the point of management? What am I doing here?

At its most basic, I have always used a definition of management that is about making sure that the people who report to you have the space and opportunity to do their best work, to be effective as a team and as part of the wider organisation, and eventually to progress in their careers and move on, or up. That's it.

If you want to expand on that, and think about the other essentials of the role, then focus on the fact that you are, in any half-decent organisation, there to help your team thrive. You will know more about their lives and backstories than most other people. You probably saw their kitchen/cat/kid in the background of team video calls every day during lockdowns. You can advocate for them and you can communicate strategic decisions to them; to them, you are the voice of the company.

Obviously, there are tougher aspects to management. Noticing, flagging, and dealing with below-par performance or toxic dynamics can be very stressful. That's why you, as the manager, need to be trained and supported. Any management position that leaves you hanging or exposed is not worth clinging to. It will likely wring you out mentally, or your bad bosses will make you the scapegoat for their poor leadership – or both.

You may be called on to create specific goals for someone who is falling short at work, meaning you will be keeping a close eye on them. You may even have to fire a team member for misconduct or failure to meet targets. You won't be popular, ever. (I was once lucky enough to have a colleague who had been a peace negotiator in a previous career. They taught me how to fire someone with dignity, clarity, and minimum drama. But I still wasn't popular.)

Feedback, when given carefully and thoughtfully, is a career booster and something everyone should learn to accept. But it's an art, not something to be done lightly. Clumsy, biased, or angry feedback from a manager causes damage to the person hearing it, and that damage can be permanent.

You may feel, having read this far, that taking on a management position is a no-win. Plenty of people say no to this sort of promotion, even though it's likely to mean a higher salary. It's certainly not for everyone. You will be required to be the adult in the room. Your team probably won't thank you, and they probably won't invite you for drinks, unless you are paying. It is, to be honest, lonely at the top.

And managers have an overall image problem, too. The manager is the filling in the sandwich between senior leaders above and the staff below. They are stuck there in all senses.

So why would anyone want to be a manager – let alone enjoy it and find it, as I did, managing a small team at the FT throughout the pandemic – very rewarding?

I hope this chapter persuades you to come over to my way of thinking, there's a lot of satisfaction, both personal and career-wise, in helping others reach their full potential and in creating a happy, productive, and inclusive team culture where everyone feels they belong.

The middle manager – nobody likes us but we don't care
Back in 2001, INSEAD business school professor Quy Huy wrote a *Harvard Business Review* article called 'In praise of middle managers'

that has become very famous (well, famous in management circles at least).

It begins: 'The very phrase "middle managers" evokes mediocrity: a person who stubbornly defends the status quo because he's too unimaginative to dream up anything better – or, worse, someone who sabotages others' attempts to change the organization for the better.'

That opinion – that middle managers clog up systems with their bureaucratic ways and lack of imagination – is still widespread. The article, which goes into detail about all the ways middle managers are, basically, heroes, still reads really well now. Because the responsibility of managing others is, at risk of sounding a bit dramatic, a noble and important calling.

While the term 'middle manager' is less than flattering, you can defuse it by using 'team leader'. My wonderful FT colleague Andrew Hill, who was the management editor for eleven years, and knows more than I do about almost everything, offers a very clear explanation of why team leaders became so important during the pandemic, and why they are likely to become more so in future.

'You need to know when to encourage warmth and loyalty in your team and when to step back,' Andrew says. During the early pandemic, a lot of managers were essentially being therapists, making sure their teams were okay physically and mentally. (If this was your situation, I commend you. Far too little praise and attention has been given to managers who gave so much of themselves to support teams during the pandemic, often at great mental cost to themselves.)

Now, as the global economy hits tougher economic times, Andrew says a change of focus may be needed. 'Are you able to know when to calibrate that warmth and "I'm a friend to all" into a slightly harder [attitude]: "Look, if we're going to meet our performance targets or indeed keep this company alive, we're going to have to take some tough decisions."'

Andrew is now senior business writer for the FT, but before he handed over the management editor baton he wrote a valedictory column that I think offers some of the best advice I've ever seen on why good management matters, and why it matters that we all try to be the best managers we can be. I won't go into too much detail here. I urge you to look it up but here's my favourite bit:

'Extensive research, both before and during the pandemic has shown that good management pays off. Unsurprisingly, better managed companies managed better during the crisis, switching more quickly to remote working and online sales. Given that the tools for improvement are simple – target setting, performance reviews, training programmes – it is astonishing that more companies fail to apply them, relying instead on what the Chartered Management Institute has called "accidental managers".'

Part of the future challenge for managers is that technology is transforming the world of work almost as quickly as I can type this. So it's likely that tracking performance and progress will get much easier (we have the tools to do it now) and the human side of management will come to the fore. Managers with good listening and communication skills will be the ones who succeed.

What has not changed over the years, and is unlikely to change in future, is that people overwhelmingly leave bad managers, not bad jobs. That in itself should worry us as managers. But the good news is that few managers are truly terrible. A big piece of research by Amanda Goodall, a professor at Bayes Business School, found that only 13 per cent of European workers rated their boss as 'bad'.

Mediocre managers, though, are everywhere. You might be one yourself, not because you are a terrible person, or empathy free, but because not enough organisations invest in management training. 'Accidental managers', who have had no training at all, are everywhere. You may recognise yourself here.

The epidemic of 'accidental managers'

Ann Francke, CEO of the Chartered Management Institute (CMI), is someone I follow assiduously and listen to. She speaks plainly in a world full of jargon, and makes a lot of sense. (Ann had a long career in blue-chip companies before this job – she's done all the management and leadership things she now talks about, which counts for a lot.)

Her organisation, the CMI, coined the term 'accidental manager' to mean 'individuals who have been given management responsibilities due to their functional expertise and performance.'

So someone is good at their job and gets promoted. It happens all the time. But the flipside is that in the new role, 'they lack the necessary skills and training to manage people, teams and resources effectively. A great salesperson, for example, will be promoted to become a sales manager. But they will not be trained to manage the team and left to "get on with it" with no support.'

If this is your experience, being thrown into management because of your talent at doing other things, with little to no training, then you are not alone. CMI data suggests that there are eight million managers in the UK alone – one in four working people – and yet *80 per cent of them have not received any formal management training.* In italics because that is a truly shocking figure.

It's a problem on every level, right up to a macro one. The persistent productivity problem that the UK has compared to many other countries (we work hard, but are inefficient; we are simply not making as much *stuff*, or getting as much done) is partly a result of our terrible management practices. According to Ann, 'The World Management Survey suggests that more than half of the productivity gap between the UK and America can be attributed to poor management practice. Bad management also contributes to individuals' workplace stress and poor organisational skills.'

Some of the workplace stress may be your own, as it's grim to be out of your depth at work, especially with others depending on you for guidance and direction.

'Great managers are made, not born,' says Ann, and that's important to remember. We are not innately talented at management and leadership. Some people have better interpersonal skills than others, but that isn't enough to make you a good manager. It can actually count against you. For example, if you are massively concerned with making sure others think well of you, the team will love having you in charge – but how will you also be a manager who tells them hard truths? The 'people pleaser' is a joy around the office but may stumble in managing a team, where relationships necessarily include friction and disapproval. This is one of the issues I am aware of about myself. It's an ongoing struggle to overcome it, but I am trying.

If you identify as 'accidental manager', here's how you can start to develop yourself as a much more intentional manager:

Accept the need to train yourself

You shouldn't have to be doing this alone, but here we are. By training yourself in basic management principles, you'll be getting a valuable set of skills for your own future. Ignore the mediocre leaders of your organisation who have left you floundering, and instead tilt towards what might come next for you. It's too easy to focus all our resentments and anger on inadequate bosses.

I like to repurpose a tactic we have to deploy in our personal lives when unimportant or destructive people try to muscle in and drain us: Centre yourself in your own narrative – not theirs.

Let's start with where you are now. Do you recognise any of the following common pitfalls that happen to accidental managers? (And with thanks to Ann Francke for setting this list out so clearly for me.)

Poor communication

This includes avoidance or lack of communication. You might be overwhelmed and hiding out in your own office with the door shut, or at home where you can filter the calls. Or you might be too vague in your messaging, which leads to delays and misunderstandings. If you haven't been trained in giving good feedback, you will probably avoid it. That may be one problem to delay acting on until you can get good training. Bad feedback is, IMO, worse than no feedback at all, but it's such a key skill to gain that you'll need to work on it.

For the moment, aim for brevity and clarity, and frequency in your team communications.

Remember, there is no such thing as too much communication with your team, and everything you say, write, or do will help avoid misunderstanding and resentment.

We need to be aware of the downsides, though. Be careful in how you express yourself to the team. You may pride yourself on being super-honest, or 'calling it as you see it'. That can go badly wrong.

One good example of how not to do it was the badly misjudged comment on a video 'town hall' of a US office furniture company, which went viral in April 2023. In a Q and A session, MillerKnoll CEO, Andi Owen, told staff who were worried about their bonus payments to, 'Stop worrying what you are going to do if you don't get a bonus,' and to leave 'pity city'. The story follows a familiar pattern: First came a 'sorry not sorry' apology, as a damage limitation exercise, in which the company said her words were taken out of context. All journalists are familiar with this tactic. People say things they later regret in interviews and then sometimes try to backtrack by pretending they didn't say what was quoted, i.e. that the reporter lied or they were 'taken out of context'.

Anyway, Owen herself later wrote an email to staff. 'I feel terrible that my rallying cry seemed insensitive. What I'd hoped would energize the team to meet a challenge we've met many times before landed in a way that I did not intend and for that I am sorry.'

I don't want to spook anyone into not communicating well, and often, with their staff. This cautionary tale is just a reminder to be aware of your own peeves and biases. Though maybe don't go all-in by giving away to the team exactly what those are. Especially when you are a manager, not a CEO, and haven't got a protective string of zeroes in your salary.

Micromanaging and bullying

This is essentially telling staff what to do and exerting control over them rather than allowing trust and autonomy. As Ann Francke puts it, 'It's control over coaching.' It's also a very common behaviour pattern for inexperienced or insecure managers.

If you are in an organisation where you, as the manager, are micromanaged by those above you – meaning you will be heavily criticised if someone on your team gets something wrong, with the implication that you should be controlling everything that happens in your own department – then it would be no surprise if you started to try to micromanage everything and everyone.

Remember that anything like this is poor management from above. The fact that these leaders have offered you no management training in the first place is the clue that the organisation is badly run. It's not you; it's them.

So if you are not a natural micromanager, and want to trust and empower your team, while also accepting the risk that things may go wrong, then there are things you can do to fix it. You can liberate your team to learn more, to innovate, and to enjoy their work. All the studies suggest that giving people freedom and trust does improve performance. 'By fostering an environment in which employees feel valued and respected, managers can build a thriving team that is motivated to do their best work,' Ann says.

Caveats apply. This is the real world and it's imperfect. If you have an underperformer on the team, and whether or not that person's weakness has been noted more widely, you and the team will know all about it. And so you may need to exert more control, especially in a situation where there is no support for performance management, structured feedback, or even an HR department.

It may even be your sole responsibility to deal with it, not only to keep damage to productivity and morale to a minimum, but also to signal to the other team members that you are aware, and are supporting their efforts, which might well include increased workloads as they 'carry' the underperformer.

This instance might be one where a degree of micromanagement is needed, although you will have to be careful how you go about it. And first think about other potential causes. Mental health problems and burnout can manifest at work through making more mistakes, getting anxious, or behaviour changes, such as mood swings or getting stressed about something that was perfectly manageable before. Physical symptoms and increased absences can also be an indication of mental distress.

Be compassionate and take your time finding out what has happened. This may be something to refer to your occupational health department (if you have one) or get advice from someone in HR.

If you have a colleague outside the team, a mentor, or a good contact (remember, a 'weak tie' is often better than a close friend for workplace dilemmas, as friends often tell you what you want to hear, not what you need to hear), ask their advice on how to handle things. Most experienced managers will have been in your position at some point in their careers.

Never let your management descend into bullying. You may be panicking inside about dealing with the team, but there's a fine line between control through micromanagement and actual destructive behaviours which deny people agency, and can destroy their wellbeing. Two-thirds of people in the UK say they have been bullied at some point. Bullying in adulthood had a major impact on those affected: 35 per cent said it impacted their life 'a great deal' and 39 per cent said 'a fair amount'. That's a lot of long-lasting misery, and the onus is on us not to create more of it.

If you are wondering exactly where 'firm but fair' moves into bullying, well, it's subjective, of course. However, a 2023 report into alleged bullying of staff by a UK politician, Dominic Raab, is a useful benchmark. The senior barrister who investigated the claims used a common non-legal definition of bullying, as 'offensive, intimidating, malicious or insulting behaviour' or 'an abuse or misuse of power through means intended to undermine, humiliate, denigrate or injure the recipient'.

That could include a very wide range of behaviours. Ultimately, the reason not to be a jerk at work is only obvious to those who are, fundamentally, not jerks. Which I hope is almost all of us. If you have a scrap of self-awareness you will know, as Ann says, 'How managers behave towards colleagues has a huge influence in setting culture, and the culture a manager cultivates within their team is critical to enabling success.'

Bad vibes = less productivity and engagement = bad outcomes for you, the manager, and your team.

Staying in your comfort zone

Seeking the safety of working with people who look like us, or who have similar upbringings and educational backgrounds, is a time-honoured tradition. That approach summed up most of British business until the last couple of decades, as women, non-white people, and anyone from a disadvantaged background found it very hard or even impossible to progress up corporate ladders.

It's also an approach that is very appealing to inexperienced managers. We all like the comfort of familiarity, and you will know there is a 'cultural fit' with these people that acts as a sort of shorthand and saves you time and energy. Building a team of people who don't look or think like you is hard and time-consuming – but it pays off. As Ann says, 'Companies that are diverse in terms of ethnicity and culture financially outperform their least diverse counterparts by 36 per cent.'

That's impressive, but the work of building diverse teams is exactly that – work. And it can be uncomfortable. Diversity expert Grace Lordan, wrote in the FT on what works in terms of building and maintaining diverse teams. 'One often-overlooked point is that diverse talent [staff members] should not be forced to conform to the perspectives already held by their colleagues. If they are not listened to – or even actively shouted down – the firm is losing crucial insights.

'The endless drive to consensus-based decision-making is a scourge on innovation, which only happens when outlier ideas are allowed to breathe. Consensus-based decision making is also the thing that most often silences under-represented talent. Endless battles to be heard require mental muscle that most humans find hard to develop.'

There is, especially in the US, a huge amount of heat around corporate diversity goals and practices. And this can be a very polarised and polarising subject. New, time-pressed, and untrained managers may feel harried or pressurised by the pace of change in workplaces, or even miserable and threatened. The extreme 'manosphere' influencers like Andrew Tate didn't come out of nowhere. Plenty of people want to hear what they are saying about the 'marginalisation' and denigration – as they see it – of white men.

It's my belief that some of that anger comes from the recent success of DEI. As it becomes well embedded in corporate life, being responsible for building a diverse team is increasingly part of every manager's job, rather than being siloed off in a 'nice-to-have' department, probably attached to HR, and signalling the CEO's commitment to change without them having to do anything about it.

The quickest shortcut to better management of diverse teams, or simply to understanding how and why they are a great thing, is to read about it and understand how to build a better culture. Your time is short, and I've read plenty of these books. If you read one book, my top recommendation, without hesitation, is *The Conversation: How Talking Honestly About Racism Can Transform Individuals and Organizations*, by Robert Livingston, a Black American social psychologist.

The book was shortlisted for the FT/McKinsey Book of the Year Award in 2021, which shows its depth and rigour. It is one of the few that has stayed on my shelves. (I get so many business and management books sent to me that I have to rotate most of them out to the charity bookshop.)

For a second recommendation, I'd go back to the topic of gender diversity. It's an old fight, but one that still isn't won in terms of managers routinely recognising and promoting women, and unblocking the pipeline that has kept too many women from reaching the top, or even the higher management positions, in their professions. Some 80 per cent of UK companies still pay women on average less than they pay men, mainly because not enough women are in senior roles. The gender pay gap is still 12 per cent.

In Iris Bohnet's 2016 book, *What Works: Gender Equality by Design*, the Harvard behavioural economist calls out the uselessness of most diversity training and then gives examples of how to change processes in order to make lasting change. By changing how systems and processes operate, we can change the outcomes without having to rely on people's biases and opinions being shifted.

One example Iris gives is the shift to blind auditions in American orchestras from the 1970s onwards. At the time, women made up fewer than 10 per cent of players. Once the audition was held behind a curtain, making the individual anonymous, the numbers of women hired started to climb. As Iris told the *Harvard Business Review*, 'My

Harvard colleague Claudia Goldin and Cecilia Rouse of Princeton showed that this simple change played an important role in increasing the fraction of women in orchestras to almost 40 per cent today. Note that this didn't result from changing mindsets. In fact, some of the most famous orchestra directors at the time were convinced that they didn't need curtains because they, of all people, certainly focused on the quality of the music and not whether somebody looked the part. The evidence told a different story.'

I haven't read anything better on the subject since Iris's book. A lot of books rehash the same ground on gender equity. If you can't persuade the leaders in your workplace to change the structures that prevent women from advancing, then it's probably time for you to move on.

If you prefer video, there are some great TED Talks on these topics. The organisation helpfully curates collections of some of its most popular talks. Try 'A Blueprint for Diversity in the Workplace', for example. I've only recently come to appreciate the power of a quick video to supercharge my thinking. If you are flagging, then watching an enthusiastic person on stage really works as a quick boost. (As a bonus, you might get lost down a rabbit hole of other fascinating talks on obscure topics.)

Where next?

Finally, for general information on becoming a better manager, the CMI has a lot of free resources. Your employer may well have a corporate FT subscription, which will allow you to make the most of the enormous back catalogue of articles and resources online at FT.com. And if you can swing a subscription to the *Harvard Business Review*, you will be winning. This magazine and online resource is my go-to and will help you develop yourself as a manager, regardless of how badly run your organisation is.

I can't leave without plugging the FT's *Working It* podcast. We've built up a big back catalogue of episodes, so chances are that a short burst on the topic you want to know more about is already on Apple or Spotify.

Once you have the bug for better management, you may find that you want to undertake some formal education. Business schools offer a huge range of courses, from short online subject-specific modules to full-time one- or two-year MBAs that cost a fortune in the most prestigious schools. An MBA at Stanford in California, which feeds many of its alumni into Silicon Valley jobs, costs more than $150,000.

What else is on offer? Here's Leo Cremonezi, one of the FT's top statistical journalists. Leo manages our business education rankings of the world's top schools and courses and is an expert in the management skills sector.

He's seen a change in business education since the pandemic. 'I have been talking a lot with [business] schools recently. I noticed that after Covid, most of the schools participating in our rankings are offering the blended mode [a mix of online and in-person teaching] and students want that. This is different for executive education courses [non-degree programmes with a short duration], where participants prefer to attend them in person. MBA programmes are full-time and demand long hours of commitment from students, so they usually do not work. EMBA [Executive MBA] programmes are part-time, and students usually work and study at the same time.'

The internet has brought in a massive democratisation of online management and skills development. Companies such as Coursera offer their own online modules known as MOOCs – massive open online courses – and sometimes go into partnership with established universities. Leo says of MOOCs, 'They also have international recognition and the courses are flexible, affordable and recognised by future employers.

'However, some students prefer to use it for learning specific topics – such as leadership, sustainability or data science – rather than an entire degree. There is still a concern among students that for some of the courses, there are no teachers available to give personalised feedback.'

So a course that fits around your work is possible, and if you can persuade your employer to pay, so much the better.

How to be a very modern manager: A quick summary

You may not have seen this happen – yet – in your workplace, but there has been a profound shift during and after the pandemic in terms of how many good managers, right up to senior leaders, approach their jobs.

If you want to future-proof your career as a manager, one of the most important mindset shifts you can make is to think of your role as that of a communicator and a listener.

- Clear communication is key in terms of passing down strategic messages from senior leadership to your team.

- Clarity and frequency of communication – however you like to do it – is vital in terms of making sure your team know what is expected of them across workload, productivity, hours, corporate culture, and beyond.

- As a manager or leader, you can never overcommunicate. We all know that communication is absolutely key in the workplace, especially between managers and their teams. Yet far too few people learn from it. I count myself among them. Communicating is time consuming. Factoring in the time for a one-on-one meeting with each staff member, every week or every other week, becomes hard in a big team. Find out what works for you and then stick to it.

- Listening is hard to do. Don't interrupt your team members when they want to vent. They need to be heard, and often problems melt away once people feel they have said what they need to say. Don't think about what you are going to say next. Instead, focus on what *they* are saying. This trick is at the heart of active listening and it's incredibly hard to practise well. You don't have to go on a training course to learn it (although do jump at the chance if offered). It doesn't even matter if there is a pause while you gather your thoughts in response to what your team member has told you. A bit of awkwardness is fine. The important thing is to remain attentive to what the other person is saying, even if it is unreasonable, a rant, or just plain boring.

- The bonus from learning to listen properly is that you, in turn, can learn things that may be to your advantage. Team members may well have great ideas for improving the workflow, for a new product, or for how you, the manager, can do your job. For anyone wanting to learn more about why listening works as a management tool, and in life more generally, I recommend Kate Murphy's *You're Not Listening: What you are Missing and Why it Matters*. It's an easy read (i.e. it's not a straight-up business book) and also fun. There are lots of resources for premium members on LinkedIn, too.

The future of management involves less authority (yours)

Boundaries are being broken down across the world of work, and structural hierarchies are being challenged. One I pay particular attention to is the so-called 'boundaryless world' of work and workplaces. This is a phrase used by the consultants Deloitte in their big

2023 Global Human Capital Trends report – and it suggests a not-too-distant world where the specific jobs of one person will be replaced by a range of workers with skills, who can use their particular expertise, turbocharged with technology and data, to work across different areas of the business.

That would be a huge shift for us all, although we have seen many businesses starting to hire people based on their skills, their practical ability to do the work, rather than by looking at their potential via educational background.

The implications of this loss of control for the traditional role of manager are profound, but also exciting. As workers become more independent, they will make more decisions themselves. Though it's clear that worker autonomy and agency is seen as a threat by some organisations.

As tech advances, so surveillance and micromanagement can increase. But in enlightened organisations, the future might be liberated and liberating. The role of managers may shift to a purely motivational and humane one.

All the more reason to communicate well, and often.

From 'entitled millennials' to 'bombastic boomers': How to manage intergenerational tension at work and not get cancelled

I am a member of Gen X, the so-called 'forgotten' cohort born between 1965 and 1980. The internet wasn't invented early enough for us to get our own memes, or to share online memories and a love of Instagram, or to date online rather than meeting people IRL. (So as not to generalise too much, I love Instagram and have a corrosive online shopping habit – the algorithm sees me coming.)

Gen X number about one billion globally, against 1.8 billion millennials worldwide, and no one cares about our love of John Hughes movies and the original Raleigh Chopper and Grifter bikes. So I will move swiftly along to the wider point, that for the first time in history there are now four age-based cohorts in workplaces: baby boomers (born 1946–64), often now just called boomers, named for the birth surge after World War II, and the only 'official' generation designated by the US census bureau; then Gen X (1965–80); millennials (1981–96); and Gen Z (1997–2012). Anyone reading this with children born after 2013, they are part of Generation Alpha.

In a few workplaces, which are often family-run businesses where people don't retire, there may still be workers from the so-called Silent Generation (born 1928–45). So those could be five-generation workforces.

The ways in which every generational cohort brings its quirks and smarts into the workplace has recently become the subject of much debate, probably because it is a new topic. Back when I started work and the people in charge were all what we now call boomers, it was very much a case of being 'seen and not heard' for younger workers. Nobody asked us what we wanted, or thought. We were just expected to be grateful for having a job.

We also had no way of knowing – beyond whatever common sense we had, and I had very little – what was and was not acceptable from the people who were our elders, managers, and leaders.

I did not realise that the older colleague who told us at the team Christmas dinner (date: hazy, but very early 1990s) that he could 'jiggle women's breasts without actually touching them' was not behaving in a workplace-appropriate way. And especially not when he proceeded to, yes, jiggle women's breasts (though not mine) by touching them with a £1 coin. Nowadays, both readily available coins and that sort of behaviour are rarities. And if someone tried that today, I'd bet a video clip would be online within twenty minutes and the colleague would be visiting HR.

Gen Z – or Zoomers – entering workforces have a clear expectation of what they want from a job or a career. And thankfully, they know what is, and is not, acceptable at work from years of seeing other people's experiences reflected online. I wish I had had this sort of clarity.

Whether you are 20, 30, 40, 50, or older, there are some universal tips for making sure your team management is age-appropriate for everyone. And the terrifying reality that everyone has access to the internet to make public their complaints about their managers is perhaps the greatest unspoken tension that exists between generations. Do I worry all the time about saying the 'wrong' thing, committing a microaggression, misgendering someone, or using the wrong pronouns? Yes, of course I do. I am Gen X.

Every time I chair an event, I make a mental note *not* to call on 'the lady on the third row' or 'the gentleman in the back'. What if the people I am calling on don't identify that way? I keep doing it because it's hardwired and I haven't sorted myself out to say 'person in the back row' or whatever. (Anyone who has a better idea, tell me.)

But I don't spend my life worrying about being cancelled. I try to do what I think is the right thing, and I sometimes blunder. (We all have to hope we don't get captured on viral video doing it, though.)

My kids are Gen Z and are constantly telling me where I go wrong. It is a long list that starts, I am afraid to say, with the perfectly normal yet now problematic and passive aggressive use of a full stop at the end of WhatsApp messages.

This digital culture gap is huge and potentially explosive. It's so important to communicate well with anyone that there's a whole chapter on it – Part I, Chapter 5.

I also worry – and this is a well-founded worry because I have done it – about simply wording something clumsily so it comes off as crass, ageist, mean, or whatever. Snark doesn't work at work, and especially not in digital work.

Managing intergenerational workforces

Wherever you are on the demographic spectrum, here are some basics on managing people effectively across different age groups:

Understand differences – don't dismiss or belittle

While a lot of people get annoyed at generalisations about people based on age, there are some common themes and it helps to be aware of them. Research from IMD business school, aimed at people who manage millennials showed that 'millennials have a more significant informational need than their predecessors. They clearly like to be kept in the loop, finding an ongoing flow of information reassuring as well as informative.'

That's a polite way of saying that millennial workers – and the same applies to younger generations coming into the workforce – have specific expectations around communication (lots of it) and support (lots of it) from their managers.

We have all heard about the 'entitled millennial' at work, but I asked Shelley Johnson, the millennial host of the *My Millennial Career* podcast, whether there is any truth to this assumption. 'When it comes to entitlement,' she says, 'it's not an attitude problem with millennials, it's actually an expectations problem.

'So when you think about entitlement, often it comes down to a different expectation between an employee and an employer. And what millennials and Gen Z expect of their employer has lifted because they have a different expectation to what some of those generations have gone before them.'

Reframing 'entitlement' as 'expectation' worked wonders for my understanding of dealing with different people, and it's not just age based.

It's tempting to try to mould or force colleagues to conform with your expectations of how people behave or even why they work. In the case of older managers with younger teams, our learned approach after decades in the workplace might not take account of the biggest drivers of why younger people work, including meaningful work with social impact. The word 'purpose' is often used. (I don't like it as a catch-all as it's become shorthand jargon for companies trying to convince others that they are doing good in the world. But if you are a manager, it may be obvious what it means in your own organisation – or why it is missing.)

More than just tech geniuses – managing Gen Z

If you are any way thoughtful as a manager or leader, you will want to learn more about what Gen Z workers actually want, rather than what you think they want. And try to stop worrying about what they don't want, and about yourself getting cancelled.

The positive and exciting way to frame this moment in workplaces is to know that understanding Gen Z is key to working out where workplace culture and norms are going next. Rather than focusing on what we – as older (definitely) and wiser (hmmm) people – can teach our new young colleagues in terms of institutional knowledge and workplace culture, the forward-looking manager will flip that and be curious about what we can learn from Gen Z.

Too many of us are convinced we have the 'right' way to do things, or that's how it's always been done. (My least favourite workplace phrase is, 'If it ain't broke, don't fix it.')

I am challenging myself to challenge everything I think I know about Gen Z (mostly off TikTok and from my kids). Research from Edelman, a global consultancy, throws up some findings that have already surprised me. Interviews with nearly 10,000 Gen Z people in six countries show the gap between accepted beliefs, such as 'Gen Z mobilises cancel culture', and the finding that what Gen Z actually wants is accountability. 'One in three want brands to take responsibility for wrongdoing.'

The consultancy has developed a Gen Z Lab, offering advice for corporate leaders, even appointing an age-appropriate 'ZEO' as the lab's cultural and creative adviser.

Cydney Roach, Edelman's global chair of employee experience, told me, 'Gen Z can be your best advocates on behalf of your company.' They are, she says, 'not out to disrupt for negative reasons.'

This, then, is the key to managing the young people coming through onto your teams. See them as a force for good, but know that they will hold you, and your attitudes, to account. Expect to be challenged, in a good way. As Cydney says, Gen Z is influencing older generations profoundly. They have 'gravitational pull'. So it can't be business as usual for you, as a manager.

Beyond acknowledging a profound societal shift in outlook, there are more practical ways in which managers can get the most from young workers, and keep them on board.

The FT's careers agony uncle, Jonathan Black, is also head of the careers service at Oxford University and talks to hundreds of graduates and their employers every year. He writes about what helps to retain those young staff. 'Flexible and hybrid work offers are now expected as standard by Gen Z staff. In a May 2023 survey of 647 Oxford students, "Good work/life balance" was the most important attribute of a job, edging out "Intellectually challenging" from the number one position for the first time. Any professional employer that is demanding five days a week in the office is likely to find its pool of candidates shrinking.'

Rejecting hustle and burnout culture is a good thing

Older cohorts were brought up to do whatever it took (long hours, putting up with creepy or bullying bosses, sucking up unfairness) to succeed in professional workplaces. Millennials, in particular, have worked incredibly hard and found themselves unable to move up career ladders (too many older people above them), as well as being largely unable to afford to buy a property or start a family.

If you are someone who has taken extreme workload for granted and expects the same of others, there is something very liberating about making changes after listening to, and learning from, people we manage who have different aspirations.

According to Shelley Johnson, host of the *My Millennial Career* podcast, 'Through conversations with Gen Z employees, one of the things that I am seeing from them is, they don't want to opt in to what the millennials have done, which is hustle and burnout culture. They are understanding that they need to have healthier boundaries than I think our generation has done. And so, that's a really healthy thing.'

Learn from everyone and think 'horizontally'

Anything you do to improve your network of influence, with as wide a range of people as possible, in terms of outlook and background as well as demographically, is going to help educate and develop you as a person and as a manager.

As the old hierarchies and boundaries erode, your position as a manager may seem insecure and uncertain. There are ways to boost your own confidence and knowledge, and the easiest and most effective is to be curious. Learn from others, wherever they sit in the org chart.

I have always been a fan of the 'horizontal network' – developing connections with colleagues in different departments or functions. Information travels in a limited way through organisational structures; the vertical path from the CEO down to the workers is constrained by how communications are managed at every level.

Now think about the smokers' corner outside your building. There would be – perhaps still is – a random collection of people there, from many different departments. Smoking created chance encounters with colleagues one might never normally meet, and information flowed across departments, horizontally.

You can use this model to create your own horizontal network without having to develop a nicotine addiction. In a larger organisation, there will be ways to meet people via joining employee affinity groups (EAGs), such as a women's group or an LGBTQ+ group. Collaborative cross-team projects are also a way to meet new colleagues, as are sports, social, or other events.

Lots of organisations are keen to foster social ties at the office and will put on lunchtime or evening talks. Can you get involved? The kinds of contacts you make in this way are likely to be what are known as 'weak ties', which is a terrible name for a very good thing. If we think of 'strong ties' as being our close family and friends, the weak ties are people who are in our lives but not close, such as team members, professional contacts, friends of friends, people you meet at a regular yoga class, those who attend the same place of worship, and so on.

The original research that suggested weak ties are a vital source of new information (and happiness) in our lives dates back to a 1973 paper by sociologist Mark Granovetter, then at Johns Hopkins University. Since then, a lot of time and academic effort has gone into showing that, in short, we should invest in the people at the edges of our lives because they will bring us new information and different job opportunities. In turn, we are more likely to recommend weak links for jobs than our close friends. (Why? One reason is that we worry it will reflect badly on us if it doesn't work out with someone we are close to. That makes perfect sense.)

Author and startup founder Elizabeth Uviebiné wrote in the FT about what she did after learning that new ideas, relationships, or opportunities come from weak ties. 'This framing changed my mindset and approach to such relationships. It has served me well and has allowed me to do things I naturally find uncomfortable, such as striking up conversations with strangers, attending events alone or contacting someone I admire. The people I meet this way always have fresh insights and information.'

Elizabeth is a Black woman and her perspective has always informed and enlightened me. I was her editor when she was an FT columnist for some years, and I know I don't have enough non-white people in my networks, or indeed people with any sort of perspective beyond the middle-class, white, English one. I was clueless and didn't start to build my networks of contacts until quite late in my career.

Don't make that mistake. The internet is there for exactly this reason! (Sometimes I struggle to love the toxic online world, but building contacts and networks, via LinkedIn, live event follow-ups, and beyond, is all good.)

One of the biggest barriers to advancement for people of colour is that many of them are not in the same traditional networks as the hiring managers and people with influence. We could all widen our range of people who count as our weak ties.

I first learned about this network-widening idea from Pamela Newkirk, an NYU professor, in her eye-opening book about the failings of the diversity and inclusion industry, *Diversity, Inc.* I asked her to expand on why building a different outlook matters. She writes, 'The rigidly segregated worlds in which most of us live is reproduced in homogeneous workplaces and the acute under-representation of non-white professionals. This problem, whether stemming from human nature or discomfort with people whose experiences and world views fall outside of the white cultural mainstream, requires intentional interventions if institutions are to conquer the systemic lack of diversity.'

As a manager, you may not need weak ties in your day-to-day life, but exploring the world beyond your team and learning from others is going to help you – and those you manage – thrive in the long term.

Reverse mentorship as a way to connect, learn, and develop

We've all heard of mentoring, and I cover it elsewhere in the book, but the concept of reverse mentoring is also gaining popularity. That's when an older, more senior, person is paired in a mentoring scheme with a younger, more junior colleague. They learn from each other, and within the partnership the usual hierarchy is reversed.

When I first came across this trend a few years ago, it was mentioned as a way for the younger mentor to show their older colleague how to use social media or workplace tech more effectively. It's evolved very quickly into a much richer type of relationship.

On the podcast I talked to a reverse-mentoring pair from a high-street bank, who were both enthusiastic about the trust element. Once confidentiality had been established, 'the trust flows very naturally,' said the younger partner. In this pairing, the younger partner valued the problem-solving that her senior mentee could help with, while the senior mentee enjoyed hearing what was going on among less senior colleagues and in different parts of the business. It's a form of information exchange, after all.

If you have been in the business a long time, reverse mentoring is one way to pass on institutional knowledge to younger staff, and to learn from them how things could be done better.

The downsides to reverse mentoring might be less obvious but could include lack of openness and fear of being called out or 'cancelled' on both sides. And I'd have some residual worry about very young staff being given such proximity to power. A misstep could blight their careers.

These are minor quibbles. I am convinced reverse mentoring is a great way to harness intergenerational energy and cross-pollinate knowledge, so if your workplace has a reasonably large workforce distributed across age ranges, and doesn't have reverse mentoring in place, think about suggesting it – whether you are on the older or younger side. There are plenty of online resources to help with this, including the HR professionals' umbrella body, the CIPD, which is one of the best-stocked and up to date, with free access.

Failure happens. Expect it and 'pre-mortem' it

As managers we get paid more than others on our teams (we hope), but in return take on more responsibility. And when things go wrong, you have to get through it, see if anything can be done to make sure it doesn't happen again, and then move on. I realise this is far, far easier to say than to do. When I've been leading a team and there is failure, it's been a sledgehammer to my self-esteem.

The first hard thing is that in the heat of the moment, a good team leader absorbs the hit from the leadership above. Our reactions in these crises often reflect our wider values or approaches as people. During my career at a variety of magazines and newspapers I have seen some team leaders take all the criticism, essentially standing between the boss and the team member(s) who effed up. A media environment is one with very obvious mistakes; you might get a name or number wrong, for example.

My worst moment was about twenty years ago, after I wrote an interview with a prominent woman working in finance (there weren't very many of them back then). I mentioned in passing that her father was a famous banker, 'the late Sir XX'. Next morning, that very much alive and very rich man phoned the FT editor in a rage. My manager at the time, to their great credit, saved me from the worst of it from above. I apologised, moved on, and learned to check my sources more carefully. In that case, I had found someone who had described Sir XX as 'the late' in another paper, and I just copied what they'd written, without checking. I never did that again.

We have probably all seen managers, in their own panicked state, hanging their team out to dry and getting out of the way while the big boss offers their unvarnished thoughts to the unlucky team member(s) who blundered. It's brutal. Don't be that boss. Nobody will respect you afterwards – and you won't respect yourself.

Once a failure has happened, a project has been cancelled, or whatever ails your work life, the trick is to accept it. And also to separate the event from your sense of wellbeing and of a healthy self-esteem. *You* are not a failure. I asked performance specialist and executive coach Olivia James, who works with CEOs and many leaders, about the best way to deal with actual failure (or being told by an angry boss or client that you have failed).

'Just because a project failed doesn't mean you are a failure, easier said than done, I know. Too many people outsource their self-esteem to their professional achievements. Build an identity outside of work. This will serve you well if you get made redundant or when you retire.

'I recommend having a mentor who is older and more experienced to help give you perspective and look at the big picture. My mentor once told me, "If you've never had a bad session you haven't done enough sessions."'

One of the best things on failure that I have ever read is a post on Substack by Farrah Storr. Farrah was a senior and very successful magazine journalist for many years, and is now a senior staff member at Substack. In her post 'What Goes On Behind a CV?' she lays out the jobs she really wanted but didn't get (relatable) and is also very honest about her failures from when she was in senior management posts. Of one job, she writes, 'I failed big time here. The job was simply too big for me and I made a hash of it. Every piece of copy I used to put through came back covered in red marks. And I was the features director! I was so embarrassed. Though I'm sure it's not true, I started to feel like the bad smell in the room that no one wants to be near. I spent many teary nights over this job.'

I loved this post so much that we asked Farrah on the *Working It* podcast to talk about why she has decided to be so open about failure, and what others can learn from her example.

'I definitely would urge other leaders and people who are in a place of success to absolutely share . . . some of the jobs and how it didn't work out because it's going be such a sort of burning beacon of light for those coming behind you, who can look at you on the top-of-mountain of success and go, "Well, how am I going to get from here to there?"

'If you tell them actually, well, the path is littered with rejections and failures, and a little bit of misery, it just makes it all so much more doable for those coming behind you.'

Can you predict or pre-empt failure?

Probably not, but you can act to reduce risk and reassure yourself by going through a pre-mortem process. This is helpful as a pre-emptive strike against the inevitable failures we will all experience, and it has its roots in solid psychological research. The 'pre-mortem' was invented by experimental psychologist Gary Klein in the early '90s, for use in his own consulting company, and later popularised by Daniel Kahneman and Richard Thaler, two leading psychologists and bestselling authors.

We've all heard of the post-mortem, but a pre-mortem, as developed by Gary Klein, is a simple check-in before any organisation goes ahead with a plan or new scheme or product. Everyone is asked to imagine that they are in the future, and the plan has gone horribly wrong. Each has two minutes to write down all the reasons why it went wrong. Then, starting with the team leader, everyone gives their top reason for why the plan failed and someone writes them down, preferably so everyone can see it (on a whiteboard, for example).

By the end, it should be clear what is emerging as the biggest perceived risks to the plan. And because everyone has been asked to take part, there is less worry about speaking up. (Plus – it's imaginary!)

This is a simple idea and one with wide-ranging implications. Executive coach Olivia James is also a fan of the pre-mortem and suggests managers and leaders can use it in all sorts of ways, both public and private.

(As a demonstration of the power of weak ties – see page 141 – Olivia is someone I know because we often have interesting exchanges on LinkedIn. She is now part of my network and has helped me by answering some questions for this book.)

If you are an anxious manager and very worried about failing, the pre-mortem is a good way to prepare before you take a risk. And, as Olivia wisely points out, don't make the mistake of believing that negative thinking will impact you in some way (we really don't have to 'manifest' positivity all the time). 'There's a lot of shame about anxiety. Proponents of positive thinking feel there's something wrong with even thinking about what may go wrong.

'In my view, this is delusional and counterproductive. How many companies and grandiose individuals believe they are too big to fail?

'You need to be realistic, and an anxious manager can be an asset because they are acutely aware of all the risks. You could say being anxious is a superpower.'

Be prepared for failure – it will happen. But also do everything you can to make sure it doesn't.

A world without managers is a reality, not fiction

I can't write this chapter without making the point that not only is your status and role as a manager likely to be less strictly delineated in that 'boundaryless', and perhaps AI-driven, future, but there are companies that have already radically changed what it means to be a manager in the first place.

Some of them have done away with management structures altogether. One early model of this is called a 'holacracy', a word that comes from the Greek for 'whole' and 'rule'. It was tried out at big American companies, such as Amazon-owned shoe company Zappos. (Anyone fascinated by unorthodox business models might like to know that the late founder and CEO of Zappos, Tony Hsieh, is the subject of a 2023 biography, *Wonder Boy*.)

Holacracy is a word for a particular process: It has a set of rules and offers users a constitution to refer to, on an open source document. It is just one form of what's known as flat hierarchy. This sort of structure is the opposite of the traditional 'organigrams' (usually known as org charts, and which date back to the nineteenth century) that show who reports in to which manager, and where the vertical power lines lie. In flat businesses, teams may self-organise into small groups, or group around a leader they choose to follow. Power and information may flow horizontally rather than vertically.

In a truly flat hierarchy, the idea is not to do away with managers altogether but to have hierarchies based on skill levels instead of status levels. It's a bold concept and one I really like. As AI advances into our workplaces, skills-based clusters are likely to become far more common as the admin or data analysis parts of our jobs are handed over to computers. What is left behind will be the humanity we all share and how we relate to each other. Do we still need to be told what tasks to perform by a manager? Probably not.

Until AI arrives big time on the work scene, flat hierarchies are still a niche idea, but they can work well, and I mention them here as a model that some readers may encounter in their career – or want to implement in their own business. Exciting as they sound, I'd suggest that in many instances, no-management workplaces may be a case of 'be careful what you wish for'. To illustrate why this may be so, consider companies that offer unlimited holidays to staff. It sounds as if it would be amazing to work in a company like that, but it has many limitations in practice. Not least because many people actually end up taking less holiday because they are so diligent and don't want to be seen to be slacking off.

However, there are very successful companies that operate without managers at all. Jellyfish is one of them. I heard its co-founder and CEO, Rob Pierre, give a fascinating talk at an event organised by the Amazing If workplace consultancy and its co-founders Sarah Ellis and Helen

Tupper. (Their podcast, *Squiggly Careers*, is a must-listen for anyone who cares about their career development, i.e. anyone reading this book.)

Later, I asked Rob (who has since stepped down as CEO) to explain to me how Jellyfish, a digital marketing company that has more than 2,000 employees in thirty-eight offices, set up its unusual workplace structure. Rob told me that he and his team felt that 'traditional hierarchy was stifling people's career prospects and stunting business growth. We decided to dismantle the system and rebuild it from the ground up. At Jellyfish, we implemented a radical new organisational infrastructure that includes the end of line management and 'heads of department' roles, and the introduction of individual support networks and global steering groups.'

At Jellyfish there is career progression, within a system designed to eliminate bias. 'To progress, employees have the opportunity to submit a business case, which is reviewed anonymously by a rotating panel, thus eliminating unconscious bias.' Everyone, Rob says, has the freedom to make decisions that have a direct impact on business success.

And because nobody has to do any line management, it frees them up to 'focus on and share the expertise that they were originally hired for.' Staff can still be leaders in their areas – they are just not line-managing anyone.

Rob's last point is interesting. His version of a workplace allows people to be good at the things they were hired to do, rather than making them spend many hours a week in people management (which they probably *weren't* hired to do).

And as we will see in the next section, being good at the job you were hired for can also make you an exceptional manager, assuming you are (like most employees) working in a traditional hierarchy.

Why your hard-earned skills will make you an expert manager

Too little is written about the value of being a manager with a specialism. And the idea of it is too little valued. Think of it this way: If you have spent years building up expertise in a particular area, and then someone is brought in from outside to run your department or the whole company, and that person has precisely zero specialist skills, would you be annoyed?

You'd have a right to be. While companies frequently parachute in outsiders to turn around a troubled business, it often doesn't work.

Knowledge matters. I'd always thought this was the case but my nagging feeling was confirmed recently, in a new book called *Credible: The Power of Expert Leaders* by Amanda Goodall, a professor at Bayes Business School, London.

Amanda is a former model who took an unconventional path into academia, and you won't forget her if you meet her in person, as her personal style is unique. What I like about her thinking is that she focuses on what successful managers do, so others can learn. And on what bad management does to staff (in short, it makes them leave).

Amanda's work is also very practical. Far too little of the $4 billion annual spend on the business-school research industry ever makes it off the page and into practical applications in workplaces.

Amanda explained to me what she'd discovered to back up her claim that being an expert in a sector is a good basis for management success. 'Expert line managers lead by example, because they have already walked the proverbial walk, and importantly to a high standard. Because of this they can motivate employees through shared values and communicate goals clearly, which can empower and encourage their staff.

'We know that those who have an expert line manager report they feel supported in their career development. If you think about it, having a line manager that we can look up to in terms of their core talent (a great lawyer, chef or technologist) instils confidence in us that they will understand the best path for us to follow in our careers. They can point out where we should focus on or improve.'

So if you have those job-specific skills, you are well placed to become a good manager. The issue often comes in workplaces where senior leadership look outside, rather than internally, for management- and leadership-level new hires, who may come from outside your specialism.

In medicine, for example, where Amanda has done a lot of research, 'It is often assumed that experts either do not want to go into leadership or management, or they are told "You stick to your expertise".'

If you want to go into management, and not be outrun by newcomers and non-specialists, Amanda's advice is, 'Ask to be included on a leadership development programme – as a first step. This is important because they will receive the right training and it signals to the organisation an intention to lead.'

As an aside, I recently couldn't get funding to go on a leadership course from my employer, so I paid for it myself. Your needs may not match their funding priorities (as mine didn't). If you are serious about investing in yourself and your development, you are the only person for whom that is going to be a number one priority.

Where can you improve?

What qualities make someone a good expert leader? I think this is a great list from Amanda; it makes a handy benchmark for all sorts of management and leadership 'wishlists' of the qualities we should cultivate, whether we are experts, generalists, or somewhere in between.

- Self-awareness and commitment to personal growth. Essentially, working on your self-awareness and managing yourself in relation to others.

- Effective interpersonal communication skills. This includes listening and motivational skills.

- Speaking the truth. Trust and credibility are painstakingly built but easy to lose. 'Speak fearlessly and honestly,' Amanda advises.

- Navigating diverse stakeholders and systems. A stakeholder is anyone or any group with an interest in your organisation. Your staff are the most immediate stakeholders. Don't just talk to other leaders or manage upwards and internally – look around and outwards, as well.

- Continuous learning and flexibility. This speaks for itself but is harder than we think because it's time consuming. People with specialist expertise, Amanda says, 'must learn to put the curiosity and hard work that initially made them an expert to use in areas that might not greatly interest them.'

Takeaways

- Management is hard, lonely, and often thankless. Why would you want to lead a team? To earn more money, to help you get to the next level in your career, and – last importantly – to help others thrive. Your work has purpose and will make a difference. (If it doesn't, or you aren't supported as manager, discount the above and sort out a different future for yourself.)

- Middle managers are often denigrated or even removed in corporate reshuffles. That's short sighted. Be proud of what you do. Evidence shows that middle managers and team leaders, the 'filling' in any organisational sandwich, are doing vital work in terms of communication, motivation, and innovation.

- Accidental managers, people who have been promoted without any training, are way too common and haven't been given the tools to do the job. If that's your situation, demand training. Management skills are learned; nobody has an innate idea of how to do it.

- You can manage some of your own development. There's loads of material out there. I like the *Harvard Business Review* and its podcasts, the *Squiggly Careers* podcast is great, and of course *Working It* from the FT. TED Talks, books, and short courses are everywhere. LinkedIn is a good place to look for education and training. Ask your employer to pay for LinkedIn premium as a very bare-minimum perk to help in your management career. (And if it doesn't work out, you can start looking there for your next job.)

- Don't bully. Trust staff, behave with care, and offer dignity to everyone. This helps enormously (especially) with intergenerational tensions, though there are still bound to be issues when you are working with people who have very different upbringings and outlooks. Remember, age is another aspect of diversity, so be curious and learn more about your colleagues.

- It's normal to be anxious when you take on more responsibility. And accept that failure is inevitable. You can learn techniques to try to pre-empt obvious bad decisions. They all involve listening to other people, another reason why 'active listening' is a key skill.

- Some companies work well without managers. This is hard to achieve but we can all learn useful lessons about trust, autonomy, and what motivates human beings by studying the examples of those who run without a management layer. Remember, no line managers doesn't mean people aren't accountable. These sorts of set-ups actually demand a very high level of personal accountability, and they don't suit everyone.

- Were you appointed as a manager because you are an expert in your profession or sector? The good news is that that expertise should help you become a better leader. Use your insider knowledge to communicate and innovate with your team.

Chapter 2: How to Manage Anyone, Especially People You Don't Like
And learn to deal with the full range of messy emotions

I wanted to put the issue of 'managing anyone' at the top of this chapter because it is a far, far trickier – but potentially more rewarding – process than usually gets aired. The combination of your own background and emotional make-up, in a close working relationship with someone else bringing totally different experiences and outlooks, can be incredibly fruitful.

It can also be explosive, damaging, energy sapping, and ultimately lead to stress, bullying, and burnout. Your impact as a manager is vital, both positive and negative. You might be a great manager to the highly engaged and appealing person who is always ready to take on extra work and bakes a mean brownie. You might be less great for the lacklustre colleague who has been in their job too long (and now you're irritated because you've discovered they earn a higher salary than your favoured staff).

A lot of articles and seminars focus on the positives of management, or seem to assume that if we were 'better people' then we wouldn't be so negative or have bad thoughts. Sometimes, after a long session among the earnest 'thought leaders' of LinkedIn or after listening to too many uplifting podcasts, I start to believe that I could really change. Ha.

The truth, as we all know at heart, is that we are all flawed. We can, though, aim to do better, day by day. Half a century after the famous maxim of the 'good enough parent' that originated with Donald Winnicott in the early 1970s, we now know we also just have to be a 'good enough' manager and colleague.

Am I proud of feeling irked when people I find annoying take up my time? No, I'm not. But it still happens. Don't dwell on your imperfections. Instead, here's how to handle unruly emotions in the workplace, and how to be 'good enough' for everyone on your team, as well as those you interact with internally and externally, without burning yourself out.

Crying, shouting, and all the messy things

There was a time many years ago when I would go into a particular set of lavatories in my then-workplace and often hear someone sobbing in a cubicle. We all knew that one manager was to blame. I didn't know these people, and pretended it was not happening, fingers metaphorically in my ears, not even stopping to comfort a fellow worker in distress. It was just accepted that their department was toxic – and that it was somehow sealed off from the rest of us.

Would I act in the same way now? I hope not. Life, with its inevitable griefs, miseries, and setbacks has come between me and my youthful embarrassment at encountering any sort of emotional outburst. I rarely cried in my twenties. Now, I often do, and it's usually because I am furious or frustrated, or suddenly touched by an act of kindness, not because I am sad. As we age, we learn our own triggers for tears and that can be helpful in averting them if the timing is awkward. But don't ever worry about being 'too emotional'. Those days are gone.

Tears can actually be a powerful tool. One friend in a senior corporate job would often cry in frustration or anger when talking to even more senior people about her career, or when arguing for more resources for her team. She powered through the tears, acting as if it wasn't happening. This can be a good tactic. Her tears signalled that she cared deeply about what she was talking about, but powering through them showed she would not be derailed by emotions. Also, many of the people in those meetings were older men, for whom overt or acknowledged displays of emotion were hard to handle.

They, just like me, were more comfortable pretending it wasn't happening, even while seeing plainly what was going on. This is the kind of cognitive dissonance that once came easily in workplaces built to be 'professional', which I often think was a synonym for 'not built for humans'. Things are changing. Gen Z workers are far more open about their emotions and expect to be respected for that. Your future management style will need to adapt accordingly.

Another tactic, though, can be to acknowledge what's happening and then move on. If you are the person with the strong emotions, you can frame it around feeling passionate about what you are discussing. And if you are the person who is expected to react, you can acknowledge without fuss the strength of the other person's feeling and either offer to postpone the rest of the meeting or, with their permission, carry on.

As a manager, you will almost certainly have to deal with crying in the workplace – and the tears may even be your own. The boundaries have blurred between our work and home lives, and more people are willing to be open about their stress, problems at home, or mental health struggles. This has inevitably brought more extreme emotions to the workplace.

A good tip when you are the listening party – and one I've found useful in many situations, inside and outside of work – is to be thoughtful and curious, and allow time for the colleague's tears to subside. Do not, and I can't stress this enough, try to find a solution to their problem, or try to make it all better. Obviously this is impossible for situations such as grief for a dead parent. That simply requires expressing sympathy and giving your colleague space, time, and support for their own emotions. I am referring here to crying triggered by a workplace problem, conflict, or disappointment. Your job in these cases is to listen, not to fix. If there is something that needs following up, then do it. You are not the all-knowing fixer and it's not your job to make people happy. It's your job to create a good working environment where people can thrive. And being a good listener is part of that. I realise how hollow this sounds when most of us are so busy we can't spare thirty minutes between meetings, but it's what you have to do.

Anger – the roadblock you must not ignore

We are all getting angrier at work. A 2023 Gallup survey of more than 120,000 workers globally found that almost one in five UK professionals (19 per cent) report feeling angry at work. UK workers are angrier than the average European (14 per cent). The data is based on how people experienced emotion the previous day, so it's a snapshot, not a long study.

Gallup's principal partner, Anna Sawyer, told me that negative emotions have been on the rise among workers for about a decade. One big factor influencing how we feel at work is how we feel in the rest of our lives. Anna said, 'We don't experience our work in a vacuum – so our life and work intersect highly.' High cost of living, personal problems, political polarisation – all of these are likely to affect you and your team, and it's a wise first step to think about what is behind the anger that you are witnessing in the workplace. Anger, as anyone who has been in therapy will know, is a symptom, not a cause.

Anger at work can hit out of nowhere. If it's your own, take five minutes to step away from the situation. Turn off the camera in the video meeting, walk around the block, take the heat from the moment. This useful advice also works in your romantic relationships and with teenage children who are driving you to the limit.

So how *do* you deal with anger in the workplace? If you are a manager and one of your team displays anger or even aggression, whether in a one to one or in another setting, that's something you are going to have to deal with head on. The first point to note is that if you feel unsafe, personally attacked, or that the level of the person's rage is not going to lead to anything productive, just walk away and say that you can return to the encounter when your colleague is calmer.

Frontline workers (hospitality staff, medical staff, or any customer- or patient-facing employees) have particular issues to deal with around anger, because it can tip into outright aggression and even violence. A recent survey of US frontline workers showed that aggression is on the rise. Nearly seven out of ten healthcare workers reported erratic or aggressive behaviour from patients, and, across all occupations, Gen Z workers were far more worried about their safety than older, boomer staff.

In the workplace of the future, personal safety concerns are likely to rise up the agenda. Something has shifted. Post pandemic, we've seen reports of all sorts of social codes and rules being broken, from people at concerts and festivals to children at school.

It's shocking to witness someone's rage at work, even if it's not directed at you. I've seen a few items kicked and thrown over the years, not in my direction, but this sort of cosmic rage always comes, in my experience, from men.

I have had some fascinating conversations with senior women in workplaces, many of them since the #MeToo movement began, during which we acknowledged that men will always have an element of physical intimidation and power. To try to ignore this, as if workplaces are somehow pure and equal, and free of the reality of women's physical weakness against men's – and the threat of violence that shadows all women's lives – is just wilful blindness.

You don't have to report it if you see someone shouting in the workplace. It happens. People get angry. Take the time to find out what's happened and what's behind the anger before you do anything on your own behalf or anyone else's.

Do not, though, accept any personal abuse or physically or verbally threatening behaviour, or let it pass if you see it happening to someone else. That wilful ignoring of something bad going on is called the 'bystander effect'. We all have a desire not to get involved but we all need to be braver about calling things out or reporting them. Amy Cuddy, a well-known social psychologist, is calling for us all to display what she calls 'social bravery' against the bullies and by standers at work, and her new book, *Bullies, Bystanders and Bravehearts*, explains this.

There's definitely a shift in the air – but it's in its earliest days.

Nobody should be intimidated at work. I think this is one area where workplace boundaries have, thank God, tightened considerably in recent years. It's not 'woke' or weak, or whatever pejorative term gets thrown at people, to expect to be treated courteously and with respect in a workplace.

And if you have to have a meeting with someone who makes you uncomfortable, or who is known to be volatile, then make sure there is a third person there who you can trust.

How to manage people you really, really dislike

This is such a hard thing to talk about without sounding really mean, yet it's totally normal. Having struggled to keep feelings to myself in the past, I don't think this is something I can say I am on top of, so I turned for advice to Naomi Shragai, psychotherapist, FT contributor, and author of the book *Work Therapy*, which I mentioned in Part I, Chapter 4.

When I told her about my dilemmas around feeling annoyed for no reason, Naomi urged me to think about 'sitting with the discomfort'. That's a phrase anyone in therapy will be familiar with, but it's not one I'd thought about bringing to work. Sometimes you don't have to act, you can just be, and this is one of those occasions. As Naomi explains, 'You may have strong feelings, but you can keep them to yourself by simply acknowledging you have them and sit with the discomfort.'

Step two in dealing with people you can't stand is to examine why you feel that way. Take a deep breath. These feelings will date back to your childhood. In fact, once you accept that many things that happen in workplaces are simply the various players acting out scenes from their early lives, or reacting to stresses using tactics they learned long ago, and which don't serve them well as adults . . . well, you have the workplace sussed.

Naomi says, 'Does this person irritate you because they remind you of someone from your past? Perhaps an irritating younger sibling, a suffocating mother or dismissive father? You may be reacting to your historic relationships rather than the current one. Or, they may be reminding you of a trait in yourself that you find difficult to acknowledge.

'Perhaps their neediness, or weakness, reminds you of these traits in yourself that you despise. By locating them in other people, you can convince yourself you are rid of them, but of course, you are not, you have merely accused the other of carrying these unwanted traits.'

Naomi is reminding us of the core issue with any workplace friction – it often makes us feel uncomfortable because sometimes we realise we are not perfect (horror!).

Dealing with those who are actively unpleasant at work requires even more tact. Usually, they won't even be aware that their actions are viewed as rude, angry, or toxic. As Naomi says, 'Unconsciously they are repeating an experience from the past where they might have been neglected or abused. Knowing this should help you develop more compassion towards them. By not engaging in their process, by being kind and interested in them, interrupts this dynamic and they may respond differently.'

Being kind to a jerk at work is probably the last thing you want to do, but it might short-circuit their stressful (to you) ways. The important thing to remember in all these dealings is not to personalise it. Getting a trusted colleague (not someone who is also on the team) or a therapist, coach, or trusted outside mentor to hear you out and help you work through your feelings would be a good way to stop yourself from reacting hastily 'in the moment'. Allowing your own frustration and rage to build up is also a Bad Idea because this stuff always comes out, usually at a terrible moment.

'Thank you' gets results

Moving away from the darkness to light, there is immense power in thanking people in the workplace. It might be for a job well done, for handling a difficult assignment, or simply for an act of kindness or concern to another colleague. As manager, you can leverage goodwill towards you in a (frankly) extraordinary way simply by noticing and thanking team members, or indeed anyone. It's such an easy win. Recent research by Sara Algoe, a professor at the University of North Carolina at Chapel Hill, suggests that saying thank you can 'increase productivity, enhance collaboration among employees, make managers more effective and improve corporate performance.'

The key to success in this area – and this is something that had never struck me before – is to thank the other person, rather than making it all about how we feel. 'Put the "you" in thank you,' as Sara says. (She attributes this excellent tip to her colleague, Barbara Fredrickson.)

Emailing a team member who stood up to an overly assertive client could easily read like this: 'I was really proud to see how you handled that situation.' Instead, turn it around and write, 'You did very well in that difficult meeting and handled it with aplomb.' Another point to remember is to make notes genuine, specific, and timely.

Public notes are also a good idea. Put messages on Slack or whatever communication channel you use to thank team members publicly.

I have too often failed to thank people. The thought occurs to me and then something gets in the way. Having read this research, I will do better. Small things mean a lot in workplaces; it's not all about the big stuff. It builds goodwill and, like all good deeds, it also makes you feel better. Win win.

Managing the dream team

Talking about managing people who are great performers and who you may also like is easy, but there are some pitfalls. The two biggest ones are bias and complacency.

We all let our own preferences get in the way of fair practice, usually in small ways. The hardest thing in the world is to acknowledge our own weird unfairnesses, but being aware that humans are hardwired towards 'affinity bias' – a preference for people like ourselves – is the first step to checking ourselves before this stuff gets out of control and you risk treating colleagues unfairly.

Focusing on the 'process' and the job in hand, rather than on how much you like or dislike the ideas and opinions of the person doing the job, is the best way to keep your feelings under control. And it's okay to feel liberated and excited by having team members who are stellar performers, who are being noticed, and for whom you are responsible. It reflects well on you.

One of the joys of management (and we have probably covered too few in this chapter) is that you are responsible for helping people do well at work, for seeing them develop and shine. There's a parental analogy here, however much we choose to ignore it. When your children become independent and don't need you anymore (except for cash injections, obviously), it's bittersweet. We've done our jobs and launched adults into the world, but we feel bereft and possibly a bit lacking in purpose.

At work you are never an empty nester. There's always a new recruit on the horizon, or someone for you to focus your laser-beam management skills upon. (At home, a lot of empty nesters . . . get dogs.)

Allowing your star performers to blossom may inevitably mean allowing them to move up or on. A bigger person lets that happen, however hard it is, rather than blocking a move or guilting the individual into staying because it helps you out. Don't be that manager. That way staff exits lie. Talented staff who are being blocked do not stay.

The other major pitfall happens when solid team members stay in the job a long while, and you rely on them to do your own job. Be aware of how much you depend on them and tell them how valued they are. The situation, though, can be a recipe for complacency – yours. There's an old phrase that nobody is indispensable at work. Yes, but also no, because there are instances where there is a person who has developed a unique skill set, who holds the 'knowledge keys'.

Never let yourself rely too much on one person. People leave, get ill, want to move sideways. I've heard about cases where businesses allowed themselves to develop a serious 'key person' problem, where only one trusted long-term staffer could build a particular dataset, for example, because the software hasn't been updated in so long. What happens when that person falls ill or leaves?

Think beyond the present and work out what skills you'll need to replenish on the team so it's still running smoothly in a year, or five years (yes, even when you probably won't be there anymore).

Don't let the person you all rely on become someone who asserts power by hoarding their expertise. When we feel threatened by newcomers or new technology, it's common for humans to be obstructive or refuse to share knowledge. We've all seen that happen at work. When someone with exceptional experience and knowledge feels threatened, they may well protect the only thing of value they have against the incursion.

Sometimes it can appear easier for managers to let things slide and not to poke at the problem. That means it is kicked down the road, while the 'key person' is given the green light to refuse to share their skills and institutional knowledge with others on the team. They are likely doing it out of fear, because they think they'll be left obsolete.

That can be catastrophic. It doesn't take much for a dream team to collapse. Reassurance of your key staff is important, but beyond a certain point you, as the manager, will have to take charge to keep things running smoothly. Even the calmest of workplace waters get choppy sometimes.

Talent and troublemakers

We've all worked with people who are seemingly untouchable because they are so successful at what they do. They are also absolute jerks. Or they fit some other descriptive phrase that we all understand as a kind of shorthand – bully, takes all the credit, diva, twat. I could go on.

None of this is easy to prove officially but if you find yourself managing someone who fits the organisation just fine in one way (the productive or financial one) but is hated by everyone else on the team, then the onus is going to be on you, and it's going to be hard.

To rewind, how has it got to this stage? A bit of excavation is worthwhile before you launch into a management strategy. Talk to anyone who has managed said Problematic Asset before. Talk to former colleagues. Talk to clients and anyone else who might have a view on how things have developed. Was this person given free rein to behave in ways that are against the organisation's mission statement and goals? If so, why?

It often, depressingly, comes down to money. Many (most?) organisations will tolerate a pain in the arse, sexually harassing, or otherwise #problematic employee if they are the boss, or are making a lot of money for the company. There is some evidence this is changing, but slowly.

Every so often a story gets reported about senior people (almost all, but not exclusively, men) who have resigned or been sacked because of bullying or other workplace conduct accusations, or because internal complaints about a person's behaviour haven't been taken seriously enough.

A 2019 case at KPMG in the UK saw two of its senior women partners resign because they felt that 'KPMG had failed to respond adequately to concerns raised last year about alleged bullying by a senior male partner.' A few days later, the FT reported that the man in question had left the partnership.

This story follows a typical pattern. People try to raise concerns about a senior leader's behaviour, those concerns are apparently minimised or not followed up, and then some public fallout happens and the person leaves anyway.

The most dramatic recent case of this pattern is that of Crispin Odey. The FT reported in May 2023 that thirteen women claimed he had abused or harassed them in different incidents, over decades. Odey, one of the UK's richest figures in finance, ran an eponymous hedge-fund firm (that's power for you). Odey has strenuously disputed all the allegations against him from these women.

The initial FT investigation (by Madison Marriage, Antonia Cundy, and Paul Caruana Galizia – which is free to access and very much worth your time as a case study in abuse of workplace power) was followed by Odey's removal and a swift unravelling of the company fortunes.

But many women had tried to raise the alarm over the years; one even took Odey to court, where in 2021 he was found not guilty by a judge who told him he left 'with his good character intact'.

Internally, women were allegedly told by senior staff not to get into lifts with Odey or go shopping or to lunch with him. A blind eye was turned for decades. One woman said she 'felt unable to report Odey's behaviour internally because one of the HR managers was his former personal assistant'. That lack of independence within HR is a massive red flag.

These stories focus on senior managers, but they are worth noting for their patterns. Humans often behave in similar ways, and if you are managing a star performer with a bad reputation, you are likely to face resistance to change.

If that's the case, start by keeping a written note of every interaction you have. Keep all the emails and notes the tricky team member sends. Make it your business to be on top of the admin around this person. Don't antagonise them. Make sure the rest of the team knows that you have their backs.

A top expert in this area is Tessa West, psychology professor at NYU and author of a book actually called *Jerks at Work: Toxic Co-Workers and What to Do About Them*. It's a wise investment for anyone managing (or working with) a jerk.

She breaks down jerks into different categories, so you can work out which one you are dealing with, and act accordingly. You may even have a 'kiss up' on your hands, someone who sucks up to power while behaving appallingly to those beneath them in the workplace pecking order. Make sure you are alert. Listen to what the rest of the team is saying. Does this person's behaviour not make sense in some ways? Don't, in other words, fall for their wiles because they are flattering you and perhaps making your life easier.

When she came on the *Working It* podcast, Tessa outlined what to do if you or a colleague is faced with unacceptable behaviour from jerks in the workplace. 'I think the first thing you want to do before you complain or you go to HR is document, document, document. Every detail matters, from the time it occurred to who also was present. Write it down as soon as it happens because memories are fallible; you're going to forget the details.

'The biggest reason why people fail to get support for these types of things in the workplace is because when people ask them for those details, when they say, "Okay, you're telling me this person bullied you, what exactly happened?", they get fuzzy on the details and that's when credibility falls apart. So the more you can document, the sooner in time from when it actually happened, the better off you'll be.'

Underperformance – real and imagined

You may have a different problem, lacklustre, clock-watching, or 'quiet quitting' staff. There are many terms around the practices of not-working-very-hard, most of which were first identified on TikTok, as an antidote to the relentless and exhausting 'hustle culture' that was long held up as something to aspire to but now . . . isn't.

Let's consider first that these quiet quitters may in fact have the right idea. Most of them aren't actually quitting, but simply doing what used to be called 'working to rule' and which might now be called 'common sense'. In essence, they are simply not doing extras or overtime.

If we want to avoid work ruling our lives and stealing our free time, then you may need to step into their shoes for a moment and see the workplace as *they* do, rather than through a manager's perspective. Ask yourself if the team member(s) who tell you that they are clocking off at the exact time are triggering you for some reason other than that they aren't working as long hours as you'd like. I've felt this discomfort myself. Someone who gets up to leave at exactly the same time every day, regardless of how their workload is progressing, really annoys the manager in me. But that's my problem, not theirs.

The bigger issue with quiet quitting is when your staff are disengaged from work overall. According to Gallup's giant global workforce survey, only about one in four employees (23 per cent) are – by their own estimation – 'thriving at work'. Another 59 per cent are 'quiet quitting', which means, in this instance, 'not engaged'. And the rest – 18 per cent – are 'loud quitting', meaning they are actively disengaged at work and probably not working at anything like their best.

While it's not up to you as a manager to solve everyone's engagement issues, you could probably get some traction by delving into the causes of disengagement, and another big issue at work, anger. As Gallup's principal partner, Anna Sawyer, told me, 'An interesting fact we found out through our engagement research is that only half of us say we have clarity about what is expected of us in the workplace. So half of us pitch up at work every day and are not clear on what is expected of us. That's unnecessarily stressful for people and you can imagine how, over time, that plays out in creating a less than positive relationship with the workplace.'

So, instead of getting worked up and cross, make sure that your team knows what they are meant to be doing. Are the processes and priorities clear? Is everyone's job description up to date? Have you given appraisals or feedback regularly? Feedback, if you have it in your organisation, should be regular, positive where possible, and freely given. A big session once a year is likely even worse than nothing.

A side note here: You are probably stuck with delivering your employer's feedback system. But be questioning about both the process and the outcomes it seeks. Many organisations have developed feedback systems that are outdated and 'just how things are'. You may be stuck in the system as a manager, but try to be aware of your own biases and irrational impulses.

Bonuses may be awarded for easy-to-spot metrics like sales levels. They may also be awarded for rather more nebulous things like 'going above and beyond'. Question that, even if you can't immediately change it. Is there someone on your team who gets overlooked because they are not a 'value creating' person? Or perhaps they are not a people pleaser and may be prickly personally. But should the value they create be rewarded as much as a big sales target reached? Do they keep everyone on the team on track, with all the right data and charts ready in time for big meetings? Look beyond the obvious.

I am not a massive fan of feedback, generally, as most of us are terrible at both giving and receiving it. I once spent a hideous lunch hour in a well-known fast-food chain, attempting to eat while being berated by a manager who was giving me an annual appraisal that consisted of telling me that I was not confident enough (no evidence given) and my work was not good enough (no evidence given).

Feedback takes tact and expertise. It also takes an organisation-wide, robust, non-biased and data-driven mechanism for any sort of feedback process to be impartial. Anything less than this and you are probably wasting your time, and may be doing more harm than good.

Communications expert Matt Abrahams gave me some golden tips on feedback and difficult conversations that I use often, and want to pass on. Number one is to separate the people from the problem. This goes back to the point about having to manage people we don't much like.

Matt says, 'A lot of the time we blame the people or we get emotional about the people. I like to see feedback situations as opportunities to problem solve – it is really about inviting the other person to help solve the problem.'

Once you have identified what it is you want to change, in the case of having to give negative feedback, then you can focus on that thing, rather than on personal feelings. And you can stop a difficult conversation from snowballing into confrontation and drama.

There are times when no feedback is preferable. You don't always have to be honest. 'Sometimes, if you are in the midst of a crunch time, trying to get something out of the door, giving the feedback could derail things,' says Matt.

Is feedback pointless anyway?

My former FT colleague Esther Bintliff wrote a brilliant long-read article in 2022 (do look it up) about the history of feedback, and why it's such a hard thing to get right. Some research suggests that feedback may not work, and can even backfire. So don't feel bad about hating it.

Esther spoke to one of the biggest names in the feedback field, Avi Kluger. His research led him to conclude that feedback is useful for some situations. The example given is of a construction worker walking around a site without a hard hat. That person needs immediate feedback to put a hat on. In other situations, however, it's much more nuanced, as the article went on to explain: 'The formula for good feedback includes too many variables: the personality of the recipient, their motivations, whether they believe they are capable of implementing change, the abilities of the manager. Kluger now calls himself a researcher of listening. Instead of managers giving top-down feedback, he argues they should spend more time listening to their direct reports. In the process of talking in depth about their work, the subordinate will often recognise issues and decide to correct them on their own.'

Avi worked with Esther to show her an alternative: Good listening from the manager, in what he calls 'the feed-forward interview'. In this process, it is the staff member who is leading; the manager's role is to help guide them. He asks Esther to talk about a time when she felt full of life at work. She outlines a reporting trip when she realised a source was telling her something important. The exercise, which draws on techniques therapists use, led her to realise she wanted, among other things, autonomy at work in order to flourish.

Esther concludes that 'being truly listened to is exhilarating. As Kluger intended, I end up seeing work from a new perspective and giving myself some critical feedback about my priorities. But I'm not sure all managers would want their employees to go on a similar journey, one which is potentially unsettling and could lead them to rethink their choices. And it's not exactly feedback. Of course that's the point.'

This extract makes me realise that so much at work – and in the future of work – comes down to better listening, whether you are a manager or a team member. Most people in corporate settings have to follow a set path in terms of appraisals and feedback, but if we can learn to listen better, both to team members and to ourselves, we can perhaps forge something better from flawed practices and structures.

When you need to take action to manage team members

If you have persistent underperformance, and you've ruled out personal problems, mental or physical health issues, and anything else that temporarily stalls people, then seek help and guidance from the HR department, your line manager, and even trusted outside mentors. And do this first, before you do anything rash.

I say this because, in the age of iPhone recordings, viral clips (to go for the more dramatic end of the spectrum) and, more commonly, assertive staff who know their rights and are not afraid to complain or leave, you need to be on solid ground before you have any difficult conversations. Fail to do this and you may see yourself shamed on social media.

And when you have a difficult or underperforming team member, that's not the best of times. Every workplace will have its own performance management system, so I won't go into detail here, as they vary so widely. But if yours doesn't have a formal structure in place to address underperformance, that's a big issue in itself.

Get help, explain the situation to the HR team or whoever is supporting you, and work out what initial outcome you seek for this team member. Are they basically great but lacking in skills, confidence, or application? Do they need close mentoring? Is there, in short, hope for improvement?

Take a step back and think about your own role. Might this person perform better for someone else? We all get stuck in our behaviour patterns. Ask good questions and listen to what your staff member is telling you. It might be worth raising the idea of a move for them to another department, if possible. Yes, it gets you off the hook, but it would also give them a fresh start. I've heard of this tactic working well in many situations.

Or are you – if you are being honest – trying to manage them out? If the latter, there may be a short cut, such as a redundancy package, that will save you, the team member, and the company a huge amount of stress. Never, ever raise this type of offer without first getting advice from HR or, if necessary, an employment lawyer.

If the staff member has any self-awareness, they will know they aren't up to the job. But sadly, not everyone is self-aware, so you may have to be prepared for months of marking their homework and close supervision. It's crap, and not what you signed up for when you went into management.

On a related note, my favourite new workplace term is 'resenteeism', when staff are pissed off and just don't bother anymore. I think we've all been there, but don't be the manager they resent.

Takeaways

- Everyone has biases. Accept you will like/respect/want to praise some team members more than others. Keep yourself in check by focusing on the quality of the work they do, not on your feelings.

- Communication – make it regular, make time for one-on-ones, be in touch even when people are remote. This is the way to keep on top of team management. That's hard when you have no slack in your workday, and doubly hard if those things are not valued in your workplace. But it's the key to everything.

- Crying and extreme emotions are on the rise at work, partly because we've all blurred our work and home lives, partly because of generational change, as people become more open. Listen to staff, take time, don't rush to 'fix' anything, and it's fine to acknowledge the tears.

- If you are the emotional one, work out what's happening. Why are you crying? Take time out or plough on, as you wish. There are no fixed rules for the new emotional landscape of the workplace.

- Anger is a symptom of an underlying problem. Don't ever engage with someone in that state. Give them time to cool off and return. Listen and learn; you may not be able to change anything, but you can hear them out.

- Feedback is an imperfect practice, beset with bias and outdated assumptions. Do what you have to do within the system you have in your workplace, but remember that it's probably not doing much good. The future of work may not include old-fashioned feedback. (We can only hope.)

- Supplement outdated practices by trying to find time to ask team members to focus on what they want from their careers. Ask them to look ahead and become self-aware of their own ambitions and strengths. Listen.

- Dealing with underperformance can become very personal, so keep focused on the job and not the person. Is there an underlying problem you can join forces to solve? (Or is your staff member struggling with something they aren't telling you about?)

- Managing great staff is a gift. Enjoy it, bask in their success, and let them fly when they want to move on.

- Force yourself to reduce reliance on super-competent and long-standing staff members. Train other people to understand their roles so the institutional knowledge is shared.

- Complacency is the enemy of good management. When things are good, be on the alert.

- When anything 'weird, off, or bad' happens – write it down. Make a note. Keep making notes. If you are managing toxic people, they often start small and work up. A record of it will help enormously when (deep breath) you have to tackle it.

- Always get HR or a senior staff member involved before you have any sort of tricky or potentially confrontational meeting. They will guide you. You don't want to be the bad guy, either internally or on the world's social feeds.

- Say thank you more often than you think you need to. (Remembering that almost nobody will thank you, as the manager. Ever.)

Chapter 3: Making Sure You Run an Inclusive Team
Diverse teams can be great teams – but they take work

Everything I read about workplaces states and restates the importance of having 'diverse teams' that foster inclusion and belonging for all. But what exactly does this mean? It might be helpful to put some context in to try to understand that even when leaders express an apparent desire for change ('We strive to create diverse teams'), they can actually use the mere mention of diversity to get away with papering over the cracks, and prevent meaningful change.

If your workplace makes a big deal of diversity in the workforce without ever saying what it means, or doing anything concrete about it, you may have a paper-over situation.

So, here's what I mean by a diverse team. It's one that shows a range of differences in its members, ranging from LGBTQ+ identities and others to having people of colour and from minority backgrounds. A massive and not often talked about aspect of diversity is ensuring that people from disadvantaged socio-economic backgrounds get a fairer chance of recruitment and advancement in what used to be called 'white collar' areas – now known as knowledge-based or professional workplaces. For decades, people at the top of elite employers (law, media, accountancy, financial services, etc.) sought to recruit in their own image: graduates from what they perceived as the 'right' backgrounds, meaning fee-paying schools and top universities.

A shift away from screening candidates to make sure they have a degree-level education is one encouraging sign that things are changing for the better for people from lower socio-economic backgrounds. Many more good jobs are now available to school leavers and older people with excellent skills but no degree.

Also 'diverse' are people with visible and invisible disabilities, those with neurodiverse conditions, and older people – who frequently get discriminated against at work. And then also think about diversity of thought, cognitive approach, and political outlook.

This latter area has sadly got caught up in the culture war discourse over the past few years, especially in the UK, where the divisive Brexit vote polarised families and workplaces, and in the US, where political divides are a live issue.

To take one example, Florida governor Ron DeSantis's very public dispute with Disney over the latter's championing of liberal (or as DeSantis would say, 'woke') causes, neatly sums up the American culture wars.

You probably already work in a diverse team. It's just that many of the differences and outlooks I've cited above haven't been noted and celebrated in the past, so it was diverse but not inclusive. That's because people who were 'different' in any way from the majority 'in group' in the workplace generally kept quiet and probably felt they didn't belong there. One phrase I often heard around workplaces, until about five years ago, was 'cultural fit'. This was usually used in a negative way, for example, 'They just weren't a good cultural fit for the team,' when someone was turned down for a job.

It's shorthand for, 'That person is not someone who looks or behaves like us or went to the same university.' We've come a long way in just a few years, and whenever I get depressed about the state of politics or the polarisation of workplaces, it's good to refocus on the fact that nobody says 'they're a good fit' anymore. Not in my hearing, anyway.

Why bother with all this?

Across any organisation, this sort of focus on improving the mix of people in the workforce better serves customers, society, the planet, and the greater good. As a manager, all this is useful grounding for you. It will, I hope, encourage you to think about expanding your thoughts on what is 'included' in terms of building a diverse team.

And a diverse workforce is not incompatible with maximising shareholder returns (in public companies). The best research I've seen on this comes from the giant consultancy McKinsey, who in 2019 showed that companies with the most gender-diverse executive teams were 25 per cent more likely to have above-average profitability than companies with the least gender-diverse leadership teams. And companies with the most ethnically and culturally diverse leadership groups were 36 per cent more likely to have above-average profitability than those with the least diverse senior teams.

One practical example of how building internal workforce diversity can help customers and the greater good is period products. Until well into the twenty-first century, the big sanitary product manufacturers often had marketing teams largely led by men. Traditional advertising for pads and tampons often showed them being filled with blue liquid. At the time I didn't even think about how absolutely bizarre this was. I'd grown up with it.

Think about how pads and tampons and the eco-friendly menstrual cups are marketed now that more women are on these teams. The targeting is far more relevant. Much of the innovation in the femtech area (startups that focus on women's health) is driven by new women-led period product companies, using Instagram and other social media to get their messages across, offering sustainable products and doing social good by donating to charities that alleviate 'period poverty', for example.

In 2014, Apple came in for criticism after it launched a health app to 'monitor all the metrics you are most interested in', but it didn't include menstrual tracking. The issue was quickly fixed, but as many pointed out at the time, this sort of omission was a classic example of what happens when male-dominated tech people doesn't listen to other perspectives.

When you bring in people with diverse backgrounds and perspectives, they won't just enhance team performance. They could bring about profound shifts for the better in wider business and society.

In 2018, when I commissioned an article in the FT on the 'periodpreneurs' getting venture capital money to back their businesses, it was the first time (I think) that anyone had covered the topic in the paper. All this change is very recent. There is still so much scope to shift attitudes, products, and perceptions across all sorts of areas. Think of tampons as the starting point. The big 'but' is that it's not easy to run a diverse team. When you all think and maybe even look the same, things go smoothly and discomfort is minimised. As a manager, you'll need to be aware of why people think and react differently. Something that has stuck in my mind since the pandemic is the startling gap between the number of white knowledge workers who are happy to go back to their offices full time (21 per cent) and their Black colleagues (3 per cent). That's 2021 data from Slack's Future Forum, but I'm sure things haven't changed. Remote work freed many people of colour and other minority groups from the confrontations and microaggressions of a workplace. As a manager, inclusion is on you.

This chapter will help you to navigate your shift to putting diversity first, and to introduce changes that will outlast you. The best legacy you can leave when you move on from your job is that you have recruited and promoted people fairly, and managed them well.

Work towards giving your team members the freedom and confidence to stay with your organisation as they grow professionally, or to move on to their next career goal or personal ambition. There's no better or worthier goal in management.

Why diverse teams are hard work – and that's not a bad thing

Most of us prefer an easy life at work, but bringing diverse groups of people together causes discomfort. That's a given, so as the manager you need to be prepared for this.

Research in 2019 on ethnic diversity in teams found that its presence increased discomfort but enhanced performance. As sociologist Robert Livingston points out in his book, *The Conversation: How Talking Honestly about Racism Can Transform Individuals and Organizations*, it's 'worth bearing in mind that the extra effort and challenge associated with diversity are front-loaded. In the long-run, the advantages of diversity far outweigh the disadvantages, as people learn to co-operate.'

Learning to co-operate is essentially creating a team that is greater than the sum of its parts. That's what you are aiming for. Interpersonal tensions in teams will thwart innovation and stifle what's called 'psychological safety', the feeling that you can speak up about problems and be heard, and believing that your views will be acknowledged. (Read more about psychological safety and why you really need to create it for your team on page 34.

As the manager, you need to be aware of the potential tensions in any team, but they can be especially pronounced in diverse ones. The biggest issue for many people is not being heard, or struggling to join in conversations, whether that's in meetings or more informal settings. Anyone who doesn't feel part of the 'in group' may feel excluded.

Some companies give training to managers on how to read visual clues so you can see where people would like to speak up, but aren't doing so. You can do it yourself by reading the room, watching for cues, watching facial expressions, and, if you do nothing else, make sure you prevent the loudest and most dominant people from hogging the conversation. As ever, we can boil all this advice down to one word: listen. (And, we may add here: observe.)

Be aware that the bias towards consensus and agreement in your attempts to build a harmonious team may be papering over the cracks that need to be seen, and the differences that need to be heard. Colleagues from diverse backgrounds may find it hard to speak up. If you've been shouted down or crowded out enough times, you stop trying. For managers, losing these different viewpoints will lose them fresh thinking. Groupthink is the scourge of teams and, at its most extreme, can lead to terrible errors of judgement, business disaster, and even death.

Want to read more on this? There are many papers and books about the Space Shuttle *Challenger* disaster of 1986, which has become something of a benchmark for this sort of analysis. The deaths of seven astronauts were preventable; many processes and management decisions along the way contributed to a launch that was too high-risk.

Things to do now

There are some simple things you can do to boost the diversity of your team. An easy (and visible) one is to work towards gender balance, if that's still lacking, or be more aware of the benefits of the team you have created if you have already reached gender parity.

When there are more women on teams, there is likely to be more turn-taking in meetings. People feel more able to speak up. Even more strikingly, research led by Anita Woolley at Carnegie Mellon University found that 'there's little correlation between a group's collective intelligence and the IQs of its individual members. But if a group includes more women, its collective intelligence rises.' That's right, teams with more women are smarter.

The other great tip I've learned here comes from Professor Grace Lordan, who is doing groundbreaking work at the LSE's Inclusion Initiative to work out exactly what works in terms of creating and maintaining inclusive workplaces. Writing in the FT, Grace says, 'I see again and again that the battle that still needs to be won internally in organisations is that of eliminating favouritism.'

Grace goes on, 'In practice, this means those with closest affinity to their manager get the biggest share of opportunities, visibility and voice. Winning the favouritism battle will close unexplained pay gaps and boost senior leadership roles for under-represented talent.'

Are you, even unconsciously, giving more opportunities to those you favour? It's a hard question to ask ourselves but it's key if you are to make progress in building an inclusive team. And as a team leader, you will be judged by your actions, not by what you say you believe.

Managing people with neurodiverse conditions

For way too long, neurodiversity has been seen as a problem in workplaces. Countless people have been managed out of teams over the decades because they don't 'fit', and many of them probably had no diagnosis and no idea what had happened. The term 'neurodiverse' was only coined in 1998, by the academic Judy Singer in her doctoral thesis. It covers autism spectrum disorder (ASD) but also includes ADHD, dyspraxia, dyslexia, dyscalculia, dysgraphia, and Tourette's syndrome.

Even now, only about three in ten people with an autism diagnosis aged 16–64 are in employment in the UK. We have a long way to go to become an inclusive society for people who have differently wired brains, but we can all do our part as managers, on a human level, to help 'neuro minority' people feel they truly belong in our workplaces.

With greater numbers of diagnoses and more awareness in society that an estimated 15–20 per cent of people have brains that function differently from the 'neurotypical' among us, the benefits of diversity of cognitive approach are finally starting to be celebrated.

As a manager, you'll need to set clear expectations for your neurodiverse (ND) colleagues and everyone else. You may need to be extremely explicit about how you expect the team to interact with each other. Some ND conditions, especially people with ASD, may have difficulty 'reading' social and workplace situations and so you need to set the parameters and expectations. It requires thought and a lot of very open communication.

As an example of how to do this in practice, I talked on the *Working It* podcast to Nancy Doyle, neurodiverse herself, and a professor of organisational psychology at Birkbeck, University of London. Nancy is the founder of Genius Within, a consultancy that works with organisations to create better workplaces for neurodivergent staff.

Nancy advises on what employers (and you, the managers) can do in the first instance. 'If you are employing people, you are employing neurodivergent people already. So start with the neurodivergent people you already have. Find out how to make your onboarding more neuro-inclusive. How to manage performance in more concrete and explainable ways and how to do wellbeing in a neurodivergent-friendly style. Think about your environment, the sensory input that people are getting. Is it too overwhelming? That's where you start the whole business.'

I enlisted Genius Within's help again in my *Office Therapy* advice column to advise a reader who was struggling to get along with a team member who has autism. 'They have strong opinions and shoot down others' ideas. They debate logically and do not consider "emotional" responses in their words.' The reader worried that they were conflating the team member's personality with their neurodivergence. Plus, these matters of social niceties in meetings are complex to address.

This sort of communication gap is common where neurodiversity is involved, and as a manager you may find this an uncomfortable situation to be in. How to sort things out?

Genius Within experts confirmed that 'this situation is something we see regularly. This is an excellent example of when information is interpreted in different ways.' The answer for this question, and for many other similar scenarios, is to learn and use something called 'clean feedback'. It's a way to unpack behaviours and reactions and then work out what would work better, in a way that is neutral and practical for both you and your ND colleagues. Genius Within's website has resources on this, as well as on other aspects of ND awareness for managers.

As an example in this case, the consultancy said that, what would work better in the future for this manager and their team might include 'setting out boundaries for new team members, providing background on the project, the objectives of the project and guidance on contributing to discussions'.

As ever, this boils down to clear communication and proactive behaviour on the part of managers.

There are big benefits inside teams that embrace ND colleagues and their skills. A 2023 report from tech training agency Sparta Global interviewed 500 staff at different levels across the digital businesses it serves, and gathered data on the benefits of recruiting and retaining ND teams across different workplace functions. It found that 'neurodiverse teams show higher adaptability levels. This is because they leverage diverse perspectives and problem-solving approaches to address complex issues both quickly and efficiently. In areas such as AI and machine learning, these competencies can drive new solutions.'

Artificial intelligence is coming for us at work, whether we are ready for it or not. An adaptable and skilled team is perhaps your only worthwhile preparation for the next few years, and people with ND conditions are in a position to help.

Physical and invisible disabilities

People with disabilities are the world's biggest minority, around one billion people globally. As a manager, the most important thing you can do is be aware of the barriers facing people with disabilities at work and make sure they have the right accommodations, in terms of both the physical workspace and flexibility in working patterns. It's mysterious to me why disability is so low down the agenda for many companies when they roll out diversity plans. This is a huge group of people with so much untapped potential.

What can managers and leaders do to make a difference and include more people with disabilities in their teams (and keep them there)? I asked Caroline Casey, a disability campaigner and founder of the Valuable 500, an alliance of 500 CEOs committed to disability inclusion. She told me on the *Working It* podcast that the 'most important thing any company can do now is to say, "You know what, we don't know. Help us, teach us, what is your experience?"'

By asking team members about their experience of disability, you will be getting the help you need to make the team more inclusive. As one former colleague with a neurodiverse condition told me, 'My manager doesn't have to do anything. I tell them what I need.'

The personal angle – to declare at work or 'mask' your differences?

And what about if you have a neurodiverse condition or disability yourself but are unsure whether to declare it at work?

Many, many people go to work and 'mask' the fact that they are different from the majority (or think they are). Some 80 per cent of disability is invisible, so it can be relatively easy for people to cover up. In the past, the consequences of coming clean were often dire. The rise in adult diagnoses of neurodiverse conditions, for example, has mirrored a shift in perceptions. Most famously, Elon Musk has declared himself to be a person with ASD. According to Caroline Casey, when a senior leader like Elon Musk goes public, 'it's signalling that "it's okay". But we have a lot of uncovering still to do.'

The higher up within an organisation you are, or if you run your own business, the easier it may be for you to be open about your differences. If you work in an organisation where you don't feel comfortable being open about your condition or your identity, then consider, is that the right place for you?

A note on the endless debates around differences of opinion

Running an inclusive team also covers the issue of managing team members who disagree. Nobody should want a team that agrees on everything, so that's really not a bad thing in itself.

It's when people start to get political that things can get heated. In the past few years we've had a far more progressive attitude in most workplaces. DEI policies have become mainstream and that's alienated some groups. When we did an episode of the *Working It* podcast about how to create diversity strategies that work, someone (a man) commented on my LinkedIn thread about the episode that he thought diversity was aiming at eroding 'western lifestyles'. And LinkedIn is the polite platform.

The best advice I've seen on bridging political divides among your team is not to actively encourage debate on contentious issues. People may 'bring their whole selves to work', and it's important that managers allow that, but that doesn't mean your team meetings need to descend into a points-scoring debate about them.

On the *Working It* podcast I wanted to drill down on the best ways to stay respectful of all views, while managing disagreement and political divides at work. MindGym, a consultancy that uses behavioural psychology to change workplace culture, has some good advice for managers on its website, so I spoke to MindGym co-founder and CEO, Octavius Black, who told me that staying work-focused is the key.

'We should be really careful about forcing people to debate issues that aren't work-related, but really encourage them to debate different views that are work-related. "Should we launch this product? Should we move ahead with this investment in this bit of technology?"'

He continues, 'What we want to do is to create workplaces that are safe spaces. And by that I mean that you don't end up having to have conversations that might cause offence to you or to somebody else, or you just say something you might later regret. So this is perfectly fine to have walking in the park after on the way home from work or wherever else you might happen to be. But it is not right to have it in the workplace.'

Finally . . . trust in yourself and be trustworthy

You'll make mistakes, even as you try to do your best. Building and maintaining a truly diverse team is a really hard task, and I can only hope you have plenty of support from your own managers, HR and recruitment people internally, and from your personal and professional networks. If you find yourself lonely and alone in your aim to run an inclusive team, that's not a great place to be. It might even be time to rethink the future.

Swimming against the corporate tide is exhausting. If you or your team members are from a minority, they will know this. When leaders say they want change to happen (as many did after the Black Lives Matter protests following George Floyd's murder in 2020), that isn't the same thing as those same leaders actually following through, or changing corporate structures to be more inclusive. You may be on your own.

Black colleagues have always known this. They've borne the brunt of what's known as 'cultural taxation' – being asked over and over again to relive racist experiences for the benefit of co-workers who want to 'understand more', being given all the 'diversity' events to organise, being told by white people about that white person's own reactions and sorrow. I could go on. I've made masses of mistakes in terms of how I, as a white manager, understand and approach colleagues' experiences of race and racism.

To move forward, I've tried to become more open in how I approach matters of race, discrimination, and bias. Name the uncomfortable thing, don't shy away from it. (My other tip is to read around the subject. LinkedIn has some very good voices to follow on race, and *The Conversation* by Robert Livingston is my go-to book.)

The best advice I've ever had as a manager is to behave in a trustworthy way. Your reputation is what other people think of you, professionally or personally. But you can't rely on what other people do, think, or say. Personal grudges and unfair biases plague all of us at one time or another and you can't control that. Your career path and promotions probably aren't fair. The best candidates often don't get the job.

All you can do is show who you are by your actions. Try to do the right thing. Sometimes the path may not be clear, but by focusing on what you can control – your own actions and behaviour – you can become a manager who is trusted and considered trustworthy by all members of the team. And when your team knows you will treat everyone fairly, that's inclusive management.

Takeaways

- Diverse teams are stronger, make better decisions, and avoid groupthink. They are also often hard to manage and full of dissenting voices and experiences.

- Ask yourself what sort of inclusive management you are trying to achieve. Who do you have already on the team? If it is not visibly diverse, that's something to change, but you will likely already have colleagues who are neurodiverse, identify as LGBTQ+, or who have visible or invisible disabilities.

- Building a team reflective of different ages and socio-economic backgrounds is another challenge. You'll need to be hyper-observant to see where people do or do not fit into the wider team. Can you help change that? 'Belonging' is a buzzword right now, but it's there for a reason and we all want to belong.

- You aren't responsible for your team's happiness. But you can help to create the conditions for their wellbeing, trust, and psychological safety, so everyone feels able to speak up about problems and issues – and that can prevent mistakes.

- Encourage openness and 'being oneself' at work. Don't encourage antagonistic political debate. Leave that outside the workplace. Focus productive disagreement on work-related things: workflow, product design, who gets to be on the cool new project team, who has to deal with the terrible client.

- Listen, observe, communicate. Overcommunicate. Make clear your expectations. You want a disparate group of people to work together – it doesn't come naturally but you are the glue holding it all together.

- Model trustworthy and open behaviour. All you can control are your own actions. You can't stop people judging you, being biased against you, or gossiping about you (and they will). But you can show that you are trustworthy.

Chapter 4: How to Talk to a CEO or Senior Leader and Be Heard
Get over yourself, your nerves, and your imposter syndrome

One thing to note before we go any further is that far too often, senior leaders are Not Actually Listening To You. They will call you in and talk *at* you. Or worse, shout at you. (I've been on the receiving end of pretty much the full range of Boss Monologues over the years.) That's because they want to impart, not listen.

When (or if) you get a turn to talk, they'll probably not be giving you their attention because they will be thinking about what they are going to say next. Or about the next meeting. They might even be on their phone throughout. I've heard of a few instances of this and can't think of anything more disrespectful.

To be fair, the 'waiting for their turn to talk' non-listening trait isn't confined to leaders. We all do it, it's just that the more powerful the person, the less likely they are to be called out on it. Nobody accuses a CEO of not listening. (Nobody at work, anyway. I am sure their families do.)

But why aren't they listening?

Michael Skapinker, my former boss and now a counsellor to many senior people, wrote in the FT that 'listening is not an attribute many leaders think is important. They think leaders should lead and set out a vision. They're at the top because they have the answers. Those who educate leaders often don't think listening is important either. A 2015 study of US undergraduate business programmes found that 76 per cent included oral presentation and 22 per cent some aspect of conversation. Just 11 per cent focused on listening.'

If your upwards trajectory at work depends on the favour of someone who doesn't listen, please do read this chapter, but you'll have to be realistic about your situation. You can use your communication skills elsewhere, to work the rooms, lifts, and coffee shops to your advantage, by making yourself known and building your network of 'weak ties' – aka useful people, who you like but who are not close friends, but who might help your career.

The other sort of leader, one who actually listens, offers more opportunity for you to be noticed, and for your ideas to be seen and heard. In these cases, the chances are that the executive has had coaching to help them to become a 'curious listener'. Yes, that's a real thing. (Or they might just be freakishly empathetic.)

Intentionally paying attention to what a subordinate says makes them feel listened to and that they matter. It's also useful intelligence gathering for leaders, helping them remain relevant and not cut off from the day-to-day goings-on in the organisation. Listening can, at its most extreme, help prevent corporate disaster.

That's the upside of having a boss who listens. The downside is that it puts pressure on the worker, as you'll need to decide how honest you should be about that internal dysfunction or your terrible team members. The balance is a delicate one.

And have you got a few positive facts or ideas at your fingertips? My FT colleague, Claer Barrett, who hosts the very successful *Money Clinic* podcast, once gave me the tip that she always holds a piece of good news or a number in her head – either something about her own work, or amplifying that of a colleague – in case she happens across a senior leader in a lift. (More on 'elevator pitches' later in this chapter.)

Nothing works all the time. It's fine to be awkward, miserable, or anxious about speaking honestly to a superior. I'm often far too preoccupied about what other people think about me (the perils of a people-pleasing Gen X childhood) and have developed world-class conflict-avoidance skills over the years. If you also have this trait, you will know it can leave you feeling wrung out and, when dealing with people who are offhand or rude, sullied.

But the other thing is that . . . leaders are just people. Like me and you. Try to overcome your nerves, and approach interaction with cautious openness. (Easier said than done, I know.)

Who should I be when I talk to the boss?

The ideal approach to communicating upwards is 'mediated authenticity'. You don't have to bring your whole self to the boss-charming party, but drawing out the best parts of yourself is the thing to aim for.

It's what the brilliant stand-up and author Viv Groskop calls 'Happy High Status' (HHS). She's written a whole book about it, and it's the most useful book I've read on confidence. It helps you find your 'best self' in a practical, individual, and non-cheesy, manner.

On the *Working It* podcast, Viv outlined the concept of HHS, which originates in comedy and theatre training. 'I came across the idea of Happy High Status when I was first training in stand-up comedy, when I was moving from journalism to stand-up, and it was the one concept that completely unlocked everything for me in terms of being more relaxed on stage, being more relaxed when being scrutinised and judged by people, and being more open to criticism or more able to let things bounce off me. It's a really relaxed and magnanimous way of thinking about yourself, where you can lead if called upon, but equally you can follow if called upon.

'I think it allows you to take a step back and ask, who am I when I'm feeling at my most comfortable? Who am I when I'm not trying too hard? . . . We are human beings, and we're all weird and different and individual, and that's what we need to embrace.'

All of this is a lot, and your nerves may not allow you to shine and be your truest self because let's be real, these situations are stressful. You never need to be the loudest, funniest, and most 'memorable' person in the room. Those people are generally none of those things.

How do I become more visible to the senior people at work?

That sounds worse than the reality. You don't have to be a cringey self-publicist to read on.

When US personal branding expert Aliza Licht, author of *On Brand*, talked to me on the podcast, she was careful to suggest that nuance is the key to 'good' visibility. Nobody likes a self-aggrandising bragger. Or a humblebragger.

Aliza explains, 'We all know those people who are constantly talking about their wins online, in person, and, you know, essentially you kind of just want to mute those people, right? I want people to learn how to shine a light on themselves and become, in a sense, their own hero, but not to the extent that they become the villain.

'I think a good ratio is for every one time that you are talking about an accomplishment or a win – either in person, on email, or online – proactively go out and amplify five other people so that the ratio between how often you're talking about yourself versus helping to promote other people is one to five.'

I love her tip about amplifying other people while boosting your own visibility. It makes the whole thing a lot less cringe, and you can frame it as actually worthwhile (because it is).

I am trying to amplify others more often. I do forget sometimes because I am as self-obsessed as the next person (and probably more so – an expert told me that journalists and people in creative industry work tend to have higher narcissistic traits because a lot of our work is about the 'self').

Whatever your natural inclination, making sure that others are heard in meetings and, as the manager, praising your team and colleagues when talking to more senior people is a very good start on your 'amplification' campaign.

Being visible means, at its most basic level, actually showing up to the workplace. Obviously this is tricky in an age of hybrid work, and there are many reasons why you may not want to be in the office or workplace very often or at all. There's no point showing up and finding the place empty. But – and this is a slightly controversial stance for those who believe the workplace is an optional part of life – if your leaders are physically in the office, and you know when that is, then you have the chance to make yourself visible in a very real way. By being seen.

Even before you think about asking for a meeting, or even talking to a senior leader, your presence in the office will be noted. This is 'proximity bias' and it's hardwired into humans. It means that we see and prioritise the people in front of us. So a 'hello' by the water fountain could be your first step in a plan to be noticed, picked for a new project team, or selected for a training scheme. Whatever your goal is, start small. And however socially awkward you are (or, more likely, feel), this type of interaction or micro-interaction is going to be fine.

The boss may even make some awkward small talk with you, while perhaps not knowing your name. An advanced micro-interaction at this point would have you dreaming up a reason to tell the boss your name. Go for it, if you can.

Is this a bit cynical? Yes, yes it is. Are you going to fret about it? I really wouldn't. If you don't intend to continue your career with your current employer, none of this advice applies. Boss-whispering is for people who think they might want to advance, or at least stick around for a year or two.

Remote visibility is harder to achieve, but doable. It helps if you work for an organisation that has really worked on getting hybrid right. By this I mean by being careful about inclusion for people who are not physically in the office and by giving managers (like you) training in how to run a hybrid team, so you know what best practice is.

My favourite tip on that best hybrid practice, by the way, is to take charge of video meetings as if you are a talk-show host. Make sure you are running things, and don't let one or two voices take over. Allow the quieter people to have their turns or to use the chat function if that feels more comfortable for them. And encourage everyone to overcommunicate about what they are doing during the work week. This last point will allow the team to know, for example, that Sue is working hard even though she can't come to the office as much as everyone else because of her caring responsibilities.

Sue, for her part, should be letting everyone know what her priorities are, what she's working on, amplify her own successes and those of teammates and colleagues, and so on. There might also be an email or social media aspect to that.

And let's be real about the consequences if you don't embrace a bit of proactive visibility building. Aliza says, 'I think it's essential to understand that if you are not being proactive in your communication, you can become invisible. And we all know, out of sight is out of mind. So it is actually everyone's responsibility to think about, God, what do I want to be known for in my circles, and how do I make sure other people see me that way?' This advice is useful for every aspect of your work life, not just impressing the boss.

Don't sweat the networking

If you want to find the bosses in their natural habitat, you will probably have to attend some awkward events. That's the reality. You can, though, minimise your misery by paying attention to:

Preparation. This is easy. What sort of event are you attending and who might be there? Think of some general and relevant topics that are not controversial. Do a bit of preparation on the guest list, if you have it.

If there's someone you especially want to speak to, have a conversation opener ready for them, should the chance arise. Avoid the usual things: politics, religion, today's spat on social media. (Unless the event is specifically about any of those things.)

One of my favourite communication experts is Matt Abrahams, who teaches organisational behaviour at Stanford Graduate School of Business. His book *Think Faster, Talk Smarter* is a great resource for anyone who wants to become a better communicator at work and in life.

Matt explains why event prep is important, and it's probably not why you think. 'A lot of us, especially when we're nervous or anxious, get very self-focused, and being audience-focused, other-focused can help. So I might go into a room thinking about a few things to talk about.'

Conversation. This means taking turns and listening. I love this advice from Stephen Bush, FT columnist and someone who attends a lot of drinks events with important and, often, famous people. 'When I'm at an event, I model myself after a CEO I once sat next to who did not talk once about themselves and they just asked loads of "Why, why" and bathed the other person in attention. And this person was so indiscreet because they just felt so loved. And so my approach is always just to ask people a lot of questions about themselves, and be very effusive. "How interesting, I don't know very much about x," tends to be my go-to.'

By focusing outwards (as Matt advised earlier) you can take the pressure off yourself. The other thing that's useful to remember is that conversations need turn-taking, but it has to be a particular type of turn-taking.

Matt explains, 'There are two really different types of turns that can be taken. They're those that are "shifting" and those that are "supporting". So imagine you share with me that you've returned from your holiday in Suffolk. A shifting response would be: "Oh, I just got back from my trip to the Galápagos". I shifted the topic. It's still travel, but I took it away from your trip to be about my trip. That's a shifting turn.

'A supporting turn is one where I say, "Oh, tell me about Suffolk, how was the weather? What did you enjoy?" That's a supporting comment. And what research suggests is, if you want to keep conversation going, that your percentage of supporting responses should be higher than your percentage of shifting responses. It's not that you want one over the other, but you want to balance them out and make sure that you're doing slightly more supporting responses.'

I had never consciously thought about this shifting/supporting angle in small-talk conversations before, but it matches up to a concept my colleague, FT columnist Pilita Clark, has written about: radiators and drains. As she told me, '"Radiators" are people who literally radiate energy and people want to be around them because they exude interest in whoever it is they're talking to. "Drains", on the other hand, are people who . . . just continually draw the conversation back to themselves.'

When networking (and in life) always be a radiator, not a drain.

How to exit a conversation, without mentioning your bladder. Because I am slightly too easy-going, or lazy, in the past I spent most of my time at networking events sticking with the first group I had managed to inveigle my way into. I find people fascinating. It's my aim to find something unusual or a point of connection with everyone I meet at events. I do actually believe humans are endlessly interesting, so it's not exactly a trick.

The issue with sticking with one group is that there is a whole room of people, and you have only met two or three of them. If you are trying to maximise your visibility and impact, you need to move around more.

So, whether you've had a good 'supporting' conversation with the one or two people in your group, or you have been on the end of someone else's teeth-grindingly tedious monologue, or you've met a 'shifter' who makes everything about them, it's time to move on.

At this point you probably make an excuse about needing the bathroom or getting a refill of your cheap corporate Prosecco. STOP. Nobody needs to know about your drink or your bladder status.

Here's what to do instead. You 'white flag' the situation. It's a signal that you will leave the group in a moment, but you don't exit abruptly. Here's Matt again, crediting someone else for this genius tip (which is a great example of amplifying, as discussed earlier in this chapter).

'My favourite exiting strategy comes from a friend and colleague. Her name is Rachel Greenwald. She calls this the white flag approach. A white flag in terms of car racing is they will wave a white flag before the last lap. When you want to exit a conversation, you signal that you're going to exit. You can say, "Oh, you know, I really want to go talk to the people over there, but before I leave . . ." and then you ask one question. So it's that final lap.'

This tactic allows you to finish the conversation gracefully and, we hope, leave a good impression on the bosses or other important people you've been charming with your small talk. So you might say, as Matt continues with his holiday analogy, '"I've really enjoyed our conversation about travel and I'm curious about your upcoming trip to Suffolk." So I signal I'm leaving, but I engage the conversation a little bit more and then when it's done, I exit.'

This is the single greatest tip I have ever had on networking events, and weirdly, after I learned about it, I realised that the most socially agile people I know have done this to me, many, many times.

Don't drink too much alcohol. Or any at all. If you are trying to speak to a particular important person, that extra glass of wine might give you more courage, but it might also convert you into a wreck who spouts nonsense. Remember, workplace and career networking is not part of your social life. Treat it like work because that's what it is, and drink accordingly. Also, they always serve terrible wine at networking events. Save your units for a more fitting occasion.

A note on interacting with the staff at an event – don't be an a-hole. On that topic, the FT's Stephen Bush says, 'Obviously, one ought to be nice to the waitstaff because they're human beings, too. But people do notice, "Oh, so-and-so was very rude with the person about the canapés, weren't they? Oh, so-and-so was very sharp on the phone to their junior staffer."'

Stephen's advice is spot on. Always be polite. I once worked for a boss who was famous and often on TV. They were staggeringly rude to everyone below them in the office hierarchy, including me, but most particularly to the PAs in the office. I have never forgotten it, and every time I saw them being charming on TV after that, I knew the truth. Don't forget to manage your reputation and visibility 360 degrees – people who only schmooze upwards are the worst, and we all know it.

Anyway, I'll give Stephen the last word on how to schmooze at networking events. 'I do think in some ways treating it [networking] like dating is actually a good way of thinking about it, because I think most people, if they are honest, don't particularly enjoy their first date. But you prepare for it, you try and put your best foot forward, and that's generally a good approach to it, right?'

So there you have it. Treat everyone with respect, treat it like a date or a work meeting, and prepare in advance. Simple!

Prepare for your 'elevator pitch' moment

Think about what you would do if you actually got to put your amazing idea to the CEO or that VC funder you've been trying to meet. Perhaps it's in the lift, waiting for a coffee, or at some other unexpected moment. This kind of chance encounter (albeit one you might be able to engineer in part, by being in the office when you know the boss is there) is the ultimate test of how to talk to people with influence – and it's your chance to be heard.

If you haven't got a pitch, remember FT *Money Clinic* host Claer Barrett's tip of always having a nugget of 'good news' about your work or your team's results, ready to mention to the boss. Everyone likes to hear a positive story, especially bosses.

I have no idea how an actual elevator pitch should work, so I asked Matt Abrahams for advice. He recommends a four-part structure, so it's something you'll have to remember. It works across all sorts of situations, including ordinary meetings and pitching sessions.

You could even keep a note of the four parts on your phone or in your notebook (old school!) just in case your moment comes. Here they are:

What if you could . . . ? 'This paints a picture of the potential future and gets people to see the benefits.'

So that . . . 'Drives relevance home.'

For example . . . 'Gives a concrete story.'

That's not all . . . 'Paints what is possible.'

Matt gave me an example of how that might work in action, with an idea for starting up a new department in your company. 'What if we could delight our customers and really understand their needs so that we could use proactive support instead of being reactive? For example, we are trying this out with one of our customers and we are seeing their satisfaction increase and the number of support cases logged, decrease. And that's not all – once we have this data across our customers we can proactively apply this to our sales organisations using this data to help them win more deals.'

I love the simplicity of this.

The reality is that many of us get tongue-tied in social situations where we know our place, and where that place is low down in the pecking order. Reassuringly, this has happened to humans since the dawn of time. You can't get past your hardwiring, but you can get past the self-sabotage, learn to talk (relatively) fluently to a senior leader, and be heard.

(Unless they never listen, and that's their problem, not yours.)

Takeaways

- Talking to bosses and making yourself 'visible' at work is a key skill for those navigating the corporate ladder. If you plan on leaving your employer anytime soon, don't bother. But use smart communication and networking skills to build momentum and contacts for your next job or self-employment.

- It's easier to be visible in a hybrid workplace if you physically go in to that workplace. Anyone who is fully remote while their colleagues are in the office has got more work to do on their visibility. 'Proximity bias' is hardwired. Out of sight, out of mind, unless you keep communication frequent, and keep telling your boss what it is you are doing. And doing well.

- Amplify your team members and colleagues. Celebrate them when you communicate upwards as the manager. Don't be a limelight hogger.

- In any situation, aim to be the person who 'supports' what others say. Keep the focus on them; talk less about yourself. Treat networking events like work events (which they are) or like dates (which they sort of also are). Present a better version of yourself than the one who slumps watching Netflix at home, and don't drink too much.

- Exit any schmoozing situation smoothly using the 'white flag' tactic: 'It's been lovely talking to you, and I just wanted to ask you about X (insert final question) before I head off to see Y (insert name), who I've been wanting to catch up with, over there . . . '

- Don't be a jerk. Always acknowledge and thank the people serving you at networking events. Nobody forgets an act of extreme kindness or consideration, nor do we forget it when we witness people being rude to those with less power than them.

- Stay prepared for the impromptu elevator, coffee queue, or even planned encounter with a boss. Have your idea in mind and ready to impart. Or just keep a 'good news' statistic to hand about the great work of your team.

- Some bosses never listen, they just talk at you. There's nothing you can do about it. It's a neat shorthand for you, though. Only bad leaders ignore smart employees with good ideas, or those who warn about problems. If you feel unheard, it might be time to move or leave.

Chapter 5: Up, Across, or Out?
Where do you go next?

So, you've been a manager for a while. It's time to think about moving on, but where? And how? The linear progression would be from management into leadership. I have often been shocked by how little many of us understand about the differences between management and leadership. While academics in business schools write entire books about leadership, and many CEOs spend time pondering their own 'style' of leadership – usually with a very expensive coach by their side – the average person hasn't got time for that sort of deep-dive diversion.

Here's the best and most succinct definition I've yet seen of the difference between management and leadership. It comes from Karren Brady, now a baroness, but more familiar as a senior leader in football management (she's currently CEO of West Ham) and from *The Apprentice* TV series, where her acerbic asides are the best thing about the show.

She says, 'You should never confuse leadership with management. Management is about setting out a series of goals and managing people to deliver them. It's very important but that's not leadership. Leadership is about vision. And sometimes it's only a vision you can see. And your art as a leader is to persuade people to believe in your vision and help you deliver it.'

If you think you have the 'art', as Karren puts it, to persuade people to follow your vision, then go for it. To think more structurally about it, in business, the world of startups is full of founders who do just this – they create, and believe in, a new product or service. They then have to inspire funders to put up the money to get the project off the ground, and then entice people to take a risk and join the staff team. This is leadership at its most raw and immediate as there is a close connection between the vision of the founder and their business. The business is the embodiment of that vision.

In legacy businesses, by which I mean older organisations such as professional services, big retailers, charities, and cultural organisations – indeed anywhere where the agenda is not being driven by a single founder or visionary – leaders have to develop and implement their own goals and ideals. They often have to do this within a culture where there is a very fixed idea of what is or is not the right thing, or there's a sense of 'This is how we do things.'

This can be frustrating for the innovation-minded person, but there are advantages. If you decide to step up into leadership in these organisations, the corporate traditions and established teams should act as support and scaffolding while you start to develop your own vision of what your leadership style will be. Efficient colleagues with lots of internal experience, or 'institutional knowledge', can also be a gift to the newbie leader. (However, they can also be blockers who try to quash your enthusiasm. We've all worked with the kinds of people for whom 'No' or 'We've done that before and it didn't work' is their default reaction.)

Leadership style is probably going to be something you grow into as you spend time at or near the top. At this stage, while you are just thinking about moving upwards, be aware that there are different ways to 'be' as a leader. These include authoritarian, empathetic, listening, empowering. Obviously you can't be all of those, but you will probably find that your style emerges naturally out of your own strengths and inclinations. An executive coach can help you draw your 'inner leader' out, and there's more on that later in this chapter (see page 201).

There are many aspects of leadership that work across sectors, nations, and personality types. The first step to thinking more structurally about leadership and what it might mean for you might be to follow leaders you think make sense on social media, or to listen to their podcasts.

The quote I cited earlier from Karren Brady, for example, was shared on LinkedIn by Steven Bartlett, an entrepreneur, leadership expert, and also the host of one of the most popular podcasts in the world, *The Diary of a CEO* (you should definitely listen to this one).

Steven inspires people to follow him. His staff follows his lead within the business, and external people follow him on social media for his outlook and advice. When I interviewed him on stage in London, his fans bought every ticket within minutes, and I see why. Steven was a delight to interview, an 'active listener' and confident and clear in what he said. He's someone with a leadership vision, who articulates it clearly.

Unfortunately, that talk isn't available in full, but here's a taste of what Steven said on stage that day, and it has stuck with me. 'As a leader, two things can be true at the same time. Clarity with your teams is essential, saying exactly who you are, how you work, the dynamics and characteristics of your expectations. But on the other hand, being as flexible as you can be within the clarity, which means that people are in different phases of life. Some of them are 18 and some of them are 48, and at different phases of life they need different things. It's freedom within parameters.' Steven makes it sound simple, but he's exceptionally eloquent.

Leadership is alluring of course – the power and the status and the fact that people look up to you. Most of us muddle through things, but when senior leadership goes wrong, we can see from the outside how vulnerable organisations are to bad decision making and strategic mistakes.

An increasing number of leadership failures in workplaces come from allowing toxic colleagues to flourish – with catastrophic results like public #MeToo or bullying scandals. These people are allowed to ruin others' lives, and the organisation's reputation, once it becomes public, because it has been too hard to tackle them (or because they generate a lot of money for the business). I wrote more on this topic back in Part II, Chapter 2.

Institutional reputation and trust is very hard to build and very easy to destroy. One bad boss can do it. (And, then having trashed their employer, these disgraced leaders have their enormous payoffs to console them when they are fired, and many of them pop up again elsewhere.)

The single most important thing to ask yourself before you begin the process of stepping up to a genuine leadership role is: 'Do I have the self-awareness for this?'

And, a follow-up question: 'Am I ready for the scrutiny and the pressure?'

There's a hidden aspect to leadership, in that many CEOs and senior leaders have mental health issues and stress that we don't hear about. A 2023 survey by Deloitte found that 81 per cent of C-suite leaders said that improving their wellbeing was more important than advancing their career.

The FT's *HTSI* luxury magazine ran an article peeking into the secret world of leadership burnout, recharge retreats, and coaching (I wish I'd thought of commissioning that). It quotes Chris Connors, a meditation teacher and 'embodiment coach' (I know it's 'out there' but bear with me) who has worked with many senior corporate leaders.

'[Chris] believes what is defining this next generation of leaders is not a big cheque, not only physical and emotional intelligence, but spiritual intelligence. This doesn't mean acting like a yogi – but having high levels of self-awareness. Because then you're able to understand what your ego is doing, what your unconscious is doing, what's driving you into difficult things and what can get you out of them. It's about knowing yourself.'

That self-awareness piece is key here. Think of this as the first part of the decision-making process as you decide whether to move upwards into leadership. And don't confuse your own life goals and vision for those of the company or organisation – self-actualisation and your corporate vision as a leader are two linked but separate things.

So, don't link your entire self-worth to external validation, including getting that next promotion. That way both professional disappointment and a personal crash-landing lie.

Moving sideways, a bit down, across, and up – the wiggly line

Moving beyond the rather tired yet entrenched aspiration of an ever-upwards corporate career path, I really like the idea of a 'squiggly career' which has been popularised by Sarah Ellis and Helen Tupper, founders of career consultancy Amazing If and hosts of the *Squiggly Careers* podcast. They were the first people, I think, to bring into the mainstream work-world the idea that a non-linear career is not just okay but probably desirable.

In terms of future-proofing your career, thinking of it as a very uneven line on a graph, rather than a relentless upwards one, is helpful. Because that non-stop career trajectory represents the ideal for a mid-twentieth-century white man in a professional job. Most of us don't fit that mould anymore, including a lot of white men in professional jobs. Many of them are (thank goodness) no longer so hung up on the status that comes from having a job that is considered important by others but which might be killing an individual's sense of self or purpose.

A squiggly career is an especially appealing vision for women coming back from maternity leave, or for anyone trying to juggle impossible family and caring demands, or their own ill health. It is a simple concept that reframes the long term with our own changing needs and skills.

Let's say it together: Not All Career Moves Need to be Upwards. And That's More Than Okay.

One other reason for not moving upwards in a never-ending straight line is that in a fast-changing workplace, you may need to do something different to acquire new skills for the long term, or to test out what you are good at. And some of those jobs are not going to be 'senior' to what you do now. You may, in fact, need to take a step downwards or sideways status-wise to future-proof your career. Or you may decide to change directions, or skip out of your current employer and become self-employed.

There are many resources online and in print dedicated to career change and direction changes, not least Helen and Sarah's work for Amazing If. (Their latest book is called *You Coach You* and it's a great resource for those thinking of taking 'the next step' career-wise.)

In this chapter, I just want to get you 'thinking about thinking about' your next move. And about widening the possibilities beyond a straight line.

One simple way to shake things up in the short term might be to get yourself onto an internal committee or project team, or to undertake a placement in another department. Without committing yourself to long-term change, you are moving outside your comfort zone, and that will enable fresh perspectives and fresh thinking.

A big advantage of opting into new projects, teams, and departments is the chance to meet people you don't normally come into contact with. This sort of 'horizontal' networking is not talked about enough. And it can be very effective. By finding new ways to connect 'horizontally' at work, your eyes will be opened to new people, new ideas, and possibly new career options. Even being the seller at the charity bake sale, talking to the people who come by, is a way to expand your network.

You might also find wider networking groups to join, either virtual or IRL. The FT has several membership 'forums', for example, which companies pay to join and then offer their staff entry to the forum events as part of their professional development. I've met amazing people at FT Women in Business Forum events (they also run online workshops). Could your employer sponsor you to join a network or go on a short course? Big employers will have a large learning and development budget, but even if your employer is small, your local university or business school will have short courses management or leadership available.

And what if you don't want to move jobs just yet? After one presentation I gave to FT readers about career development, a participant asked what advice I had for someone who had chosen to stay in their role rather than looking for any change. They enjoyed their job, and wanted to carry on. How could they persuade their manager, who was keen for them to seek a promotion, that they didn't lack ambition, but just wanted to stay where they were for a while?

My advice to them, and to anyone in this position, is to remind the manager how good they are at the job, and also about the potential for them to be a creative force within the team.

After the first rollercoaster six months, we are usually adequate in our roles, but after more time – a year or two – a lot of the tasks and thought processes that initially require enormous effort to master become second nature.

That mastery gives us time and headspace, so we have time to do other things. It allows us to go into a precious 'flow state' where we often make breakthroughs in our thinking. The easiest way I find to describe 'flow' is when time seems to disappear. Here's a good definition from Stephen Kotler, an expert on the subject, writing in the *Harvard Business Review*: 'Technically defined as an "optimal state of consciousness where we feel our best and perform our best," the term takes its name from the sensation it confers. In flow, every action, every decision, arises seamlessly from the last. In this state, we are so focused on the task at hand that all else falls away. Action and awareness merge. Our sense of self vanishes. Our sense of time distorts. And performance goes through the roof.'

Use those extra years in the job, and your flow state, to learn new skills or to dedicate some time to creative thinking. Consider new opportunities for your team, revenue-generating ideas, or forward-looking business ideas. That's what you can sell to the manager.

The other advantage of staying put (and you will have to decide whether or not to be explicit about this to your boss) is that you can start 'job crafting'. I love this term – it conjures up a wholesome air of creative activity involving scissors and glue. In fact, what it means is that you are bending the job, as outlined in its description and the way you undertake it, towards becoming something that you define.

Some managers will be supportive of skilled staff developing their role by focusing more on tasks that appeal to them and that they enjoy.

For some people, job crafting is also a way to increase the sense of 'purpose' they feel about work. Purpose is a tricky term. You've probably noticed that it is massively overused in corporate puff-pieces and whenever an employer is trying to attract staff. My heart sinks every time I am chairing a panel at a conference and some executive parrots guff about their company's 'purpose-driven work'. It suggests that making money is practically a holy activity.

It isn't, but work, even in money-making enterprises, can and does give a huge amount of pleasure and meaning to our lives. When your ideas and ideals match what your employer is doing (*really* doing, rather than what its mission statements say), that's essentially what a really practical version of purpose looks like.

If you can craft your existing job so it matches the meaning and fulfilment we all seek from work, then you are onto a winner and I'd be very wary of changing things up for the sake of anything except, say, a big pay rise to go to an appealing job elsewhere, or to start up on your own.

One of my favourite organisational psychologists, Tomas Chamorro-Premuzic, wrote about job crafting in the *Harvard Business Review*. Job crafting, he says, is 'the ability to make your job more meaningful by aligning it with your interests and values. This notion is consistent with well-established scientific evidence on the benefits of matching people to a role that is a good fit with their abilities, personalities, and beliefs.'

Let's say you've crafted your job into something that suits you perfectly, and delivers great results for the company. And from your personal career point of view, you have given yourself the 'gift' of creative time because you are so brilliant at the core tasks.

All of this might lead to your next move, after all. Because the right opportunity for you may not come from any of the obvious places. You may even be able to create it yourself.

Yes, intrapreneur is a word

Whenever I talk about intrapreneurs, I get weird looks. Possibly people think it's one of those occasions when apparently smart people just pronounce things completely incorrectly (I do this often).

An intrapreneur is, in fact, someone working within an established organisation to build something new. It's just a fancy term for corporate innovation done by individuals. And it's one example of how you can build your career by creating a new role for yourself, rather than waiting for a promotion. If you have a great idea, or even a refinement of an existing idea, it can be hard to get it past the layers of management and process in a traditional company. Big employers have plenty of resources, but are often not nimble at getting new things off the ground.

If your employer has an 'innovation lab' or hosts regular hackathons, where good ideas get tested out by internal teams with different skills, then you are very lucky and should make the most of it. Big tech companies started the trend of giving staff (or some staff) time built into their work weeks to think about their own projects, new, often off-the-wall, ideas, and problem solving – these are sometimes called 'moonshots'.

The reality, though, for many of us is that we are working beyond our capacity every day, with no space to think, and that makes us unlikely to be very creative.

If you can manage to clear space in your mind and in your calendar to think sideways, ahead, or beyond the present, then that's a realistic start. Have a look at the chapter on productivity (see page 70) to help maximise the efficiency of the work you do without doing any more of it for other people's gain. Keep a part of your week for yourself, your sanity, and potentially, your projects. To be blunt, hybrid work can help with this as at home or in a co-working space you can be free of office distractions.

Creativity, I should note, does not need to be for your employer's benefit. Side hustles start with someone having a good idea, or needing more cash, or finding themselves drawn to a career change without being able to make the leap financially. Whether you are listing on Airtasker or Etsy, your time is worth money, and if you are not committed long term to corporate life, you need time to plan and take your ambition in a far more personal direction.

My favourite intrapreneurs? Spencer Silver and Arthur 'Art' Fry at 3M, who invented the Post-it Note. Spencer (who died in 2021) was a PhD organic chemist in a team working on adhesives, and Art's job was to find new ideas and build them into businesses. When Spencer invented a new sort of adhesive that was sticky but peeled easily, he couldn't immediately find a use for it, but didn't give up. As he told the FT in 2010, 'I felt my adhesive was so obviously unique that I began to give seminars throughout 3M in the hope I would spark an idea among its product developers.'

Some years after seeing one of Spencer's presentations, Art needed to solve a problem. 'I used to sing in a church choir and my bookmark would always fall out, making me lose my place. I needed one that would stick but not so hard that it would damage the book. The next morning, I went to find Spencer and got a sample of his adhesive. I made a bookmark and tried it out at choir practice.'

It took some time, but in 1977 the pair perfected what we now know as the Post-it Note.

The key thing to note here is that Art needed to solve a problem, and Spencer's invention helped to do that. Nearly all good ideas start with a problem that needs fixing, or a gap in the market that you can see but that hasn't been noticed or exploited yet by the wider world (or even your boss).

The second thing to note is that the Post-it Note was a long time coming. But Art remembered Spencer's presentation and acted on it. Even if you don't get results immediately, your ideas, and certainly your enthusiasm, will be remembered by senior leaders.

Need help with the next step? Coaching, and your own personal board of directors

A friend recently got a fantastic new job with a large pay rise. She's very talented, so it wasn't a surprise, but she told me that she had been working with a coach in recent months, and that had helped give her the confidence to clarify what she wanted from her next move, and to go for it.

People often look to coaches for help with a specific professional goal, such as securing a new job or overcoming a block such as public speaking and presentation. Like sports coaches, an executive coach will essentially guide you to deliver your best performance. It's emphatically *not* about telling you what is the best thing to do next. They haven't got a crystal ball. Nor are they therapists, so they can't solve your relationship with your dead mother.

But if you are relatively senior, or have been identified as 'high potential' by your employer (a cringey concept but obviously you should make the most of it), then you may be offered some executive coaching. For more explanation on what this means in practice and how it can help, I turned to an FT colleague, Michael Hepburn, who is also an accredited and practising executive coach. (I have no idea how he finds the energy.)

I asked him what exactly a coach does. In short, they aim to help clients improve performance and reach their full potential. (Who wouldn't want that?) 'Coaching offers a professional and collaborative relationship,' says Michael. 'It is a confidential and non-judgement environment, where clients can talk through the issues and challenges they face as they move into a leadership role. Many executive coaches use a non-directive (questioning, summarising, navigating) approach to the discussion to help the executive build their self-awareness and reflection.'

This can help change mindsets and behaviour, and free you up for fresh ways of thinking. And if you don't think you need fresh thinking, then you definitely do.

Unlike therapy and counselling, coaching is relentlessly focused on how your personal qualities can improve your professional life.

If you have been offered a coach at work, you will probably be allocated to an individual working with a cohort inside the organisation. But for a more general approach (maybe you have managed to get coaching paid for as part of your annual pay and performance review), then the HR department is a good place to start. They usually have a list of approved executive coaches.

If you are paying for this support yourself, then Michael recommends one of the professional bodies. The International Coaching Federation or the European Coaching and Mentoring Council have lists of accredited coaches.

Finding a coach with qualifications is just step one. Michael's tip is to 'ask a prospective coach for a "chemistry session", where you can briefly discuss your objectives and they can talk through their coaching approach so you can decide if you think you are compatible.'

A little beyond coaching lies the concept of the 'personal board of directors'. This would probably be considered 'advanced career-ing' and one for those of you who take a very structured approach to getting ahead in your work. I am . . . less like that but I still really love the concept.

Essentially, the point of having this group of on-call people in your life is to make sure you get really honest advice and feedback.

My former FT colleague Sophia Smith introduced me (and probably most of our *Working It* newsletter readers) to this concept in 2022: 'Many people work with mentors or executive coaches to get support in their professional lives. A personal board takes this a step further; it's a network of people who are there not just to support you, but to offer a critical check on your thinking and provide pushback when needed.

Together, they act as a conduit not only for honest feedback, but they can help you practise self-analysis and healthy communication.'

The beauty of this is that your board members don't actually need to know they are on a board – unless you choose to tell them. If you have a coach, they can certainly be a member of the board but beyond that, Sophia says, 'there are a variety of attributes to consider in compiling your board; you may want to find someone who excels at making connections, someone who keeps you accountable, and even the adversaries or "frenemies" you have at work. You could also include therapists, nutritionists or anyone who helps you achieve your goals.'

If you think that's too much, you could try the following instead. I recently organised a dinner at my house where I invited ten friends round for mediocre food (I am not a cook) and, I think, a really lovely evening. Many of them didn't know each other. There were people there from high school, friends from my days at the primary school gates, and friends I have made at work. If you think your friends might like to meet each other, this is a less formal way to encourage new connections and support – in both personal and professional fields.

And a 'weak connection' – someone who is a friend of a friend or a work contact, not someone in your inner circle – is statistically far more likely to be someone who can help you professionally or give you the 'in' on a job or freelance opportunity.

Future-proof your job

My basic advice to everyone wanting to stay relevant in the workplace is to be curious, alert, and aware that there are many new jobs that didn't exist even a few years ago, as well as some that are yet to be invented.

Some companies now have a Head of Remote Working, a Head of Age and Longevity, or a Director of Wellbeing. These are jobs that didn't exist ten years ago and are focused on the human side of the workplace. But the rapid advance of generative AI into our daily lives and work is going to displace some jobs or tasks (let's hope it's a lot of the boring admin and manual data-extraction work) and create others.

Your next job might not exist yet, or it might be an action point on the end of the agenda in your next meeting. The nature of newness is that it is often unexpected. But by being curious and open-minded you can stay ahead of the curve.

The World Economic Forum, Gensler, Slack, Edelman, and Microsoft are some of the organisations doing big 'future of work' surveys and trend forecasting. Dip into this research, most of which is available free online, and you'll always stay one step ahead – and ready for your next step – whether that's up, sideways, or out.

Takeaways

- We've all spent far too long thinking that careers should be a straight line going upwards. That's an outdated concept. Your career can and should be a messy line, reflecting your life and its fluctuating ambitions and needs – up, down, across, out.

- Status does not equal satisfaction. And your self-worth must not be bound up totally in your professional status – that will lead to disappointment and frustration.

- Learn the difference between management (doing and delivering) and leadership (guiding and inspiring). A great leader doesn't make it all about their own ego; it's actually about having a vision that others buy into.

- If you want leadership, accept that stress and mental health challenges come as part of the job. Are you self-aware about the effect it will have on your life and family commitments?

- Sticking in your current management position might be the right thing to do, right now. It gives you time for yourself and your health, as well as for creativity, ideas, and possibly the space to generate your next job as an 'intrapreneur'.

- Still want to lead? It's a great ambition to have. Find a coach to help you prepare for the transition and overcome any blocks you have. If you don't want to invest in coaching (or your employer won't pay) you can bootstrap your career move with the help of books, LinkedIn learning, and in-depth online resources such as the *Squiggly Careers* podcast.

- You can even get together your own 'board of directors' who are informal advisers (and may not even know it).

Chapter 6: AI and the Never-ending Journey
A snapshot in time, as this hyper-fast reality changes every week

While I have been writing this book, AI has arrived big time. I haven't given it a whole chapter because it would be out of date by the time you read this, and there's nothing future-proof about that.

But here's where we are now, as I finish writing in 2023, with some pointers on how to try to ride the waves of incoming change.

The fast-moving developments in tech were summed up for me when it took four attempts to pull together an episode of the *Working It* podcast about the use of AI in professional workplaces. Every time we thought we'd nailed it, something new happened, and then we had to re-record with the same guests to talk about the new developments.

Part of the issue for us was that AI is an ill-defined term, covering lots of different aspects of technological advance, as well as being confusing and fast-moving. But if you can accept that vagueness, and keep yourself curious and motivated, then that's all you need to move ahead with embracing whatever comes your way at work in future. And if that's all you want to know about AI, then you can stop reading right here. Honestly, much of this stuff is still a totally blank slate.

For those who want more (and why wouldn't you?), I recently attended a dinner with a bunch of people who use AI in their jobs already. Being familiar with this rapidly advancing technology was described by the group as 'a life skill, not a work skill'. That shifted how I thought about it all.

Think how many people have a smart speaker in their kitchens. Somehow, we have disconnected our tacit acceptance of AI at home from its rapid, and sometimes feared, advance in the workplace. Yet those smart speakers are powered by the 'transformer model' technology that came out of Google research in 2017, a development that transformed how computers process language.

Transformers have also made large language models (LLMs) possible. These are the so-called 'generative AI' that mimics the human brain and processes and creates language. The best known of these LLMs is ChatGPT.

The FT's artificial intelligence editor, Madhumita Murgia, succinctly describes generative AI as 'software that can create plausible and sophisticated text, images and computer code at a level that mimics human ability'.

We get worried about the potential for computers to behave like humans. No wonder. People have been thinking about the 'Turing Test' since it was first devised by the computer-science pioneer Alan Turing in 1950. He created a famous benchmark: When a machine can have a text-based conversation with a human without being detected as a machine, the Turing Test has been passed.

Machines have passed the test already, of course, and the most recently hyped advance, ChatGPT-4, is arguably one of them. Its makers, Open AI, claim that it can exhibit 'human level performance' on tests such as the US bar exam. When a business professor at the prestigious Wharton business school in Pennsylvania put the previous version of the software, GPT-3, through the exams on his MBA course module, it performed better than some of the students.

This level of generative artificial intelligence is probably not routinely seen in your workplace – yet. That's going to change very soon.

What is already in use in many companies is a form of AI called machine learning, which essentially helps us to predict, using data, what might happen next (which customers are most likely to cancel, where the biggest demand for your product is going to come from next – that sort of thing). Another term for machine learning is 'predictive analytics'.

Think back to even a couple of years ago. Most of us thought that advances in technology would free us from repetitive and boring tasks. We thought the main beneficiaries of AI (or not) would be those whose jobs relied on trawling through datasets, or inputting data, or any sort of deskless work that relies on (essentially) finding and moving stuff.

Now, a couple of years later, for knowledge workers, the horizon looks very different. Generative AI can already write your emails, summarise papers and meeting notes, and extract the five most important points from a video of a keynote or lecture. It can even attend meetings on your behalf, so you can spend more time on the management that matters.

And when you get a report back from the meeting you didn't attend, you can ask the bot to give you just the action points that relate to your follow-ups. No need to waste time reading through the entire meeting notes. (Although I wonder how 'bot attendance' is going to impact workplace relations. Your team will be furious if you, as their boss, decide not to bother with a meeting – and send a bot instead.)

Other areas where generative AI is really taking off include training and development (now often called upskilling, which I hate) and recruitment and onboarding (formerly known as induction). The terms we use at work are changing almost as quickly as the technology that underpins our work.

There is real progress on AI, with much more to come in the next few years, but it's also important to maintain a sceptical eye on what's known as the 'hype cycle'. We are in the middle of that now. As John Thornhill, the FT's innovation editor, writes, 'Trillion-dollar companies, including Alphabet and Microsoft, declare that AI is the new electricity or fire and are re-engineering their entire businesses around it.'

Think back to November 2021 when Mark Zuckerberg renamed Facebook as Meta and began to plough billions into developing the metaverse? To refresh the minds of those of us who aren't gamers, the metaverse, in the words of the FT's Tim Bradshaw, is 'a three dimensional version of the internet'.

Meta's experiment hasn't gone as expected. We aren't all putting on headsets to take part in meetings as avatars. I did once put on a headset and join a meeting and it was interesting, but clunky. At one point Virtual Me ended up in someone else's lap, which is as much a breach of etiquette in the virtual world as in the real one. I wrote this straight afterwards: 'It's very hard to move about using the controls but it's probably like driving. I am not good at that, either. The main thing was that I wasn't the worst.' Performance anxiety, it turns out, also follows us into virtual worlds.

The hype cycle has turned into befuddlement when it comes to the metaverse, and I mention all of this as a way of cautiously suggesting we don't need to believe everything we read about AI, or are told by our superiors at work. Much tech advance is rooted in experimentation and failure. And that's not a bad thing. The key is to separate 'intelligent failure' – failure we can learn from, and which gives us valuable new knowledge we might not otherwise get – from other types of failure. If you want to dig into this, these ideas are outlined by the Harvard Business School professor Amy Edmondson in her excellent book, *Right Kind of Wrong*, the winner of the FT/Schroders Business Book of the Year prize in 2023.

This is not to say that faith in the metaverse has gone away completely. Augmented, virtual, and mixed reality settings offer huge potential for businesses, especially in areas such as onboarding and training. One VR (virtual reality) expert told me that medical undergraduates are being trained on a 3D human heart in the metaverse, and that his company had arranged metaverse networking for 100 bank interns in different cities, so all of them could meet senior executives.

There's the potential for real parity and fairness here, something that is often missing when people work from home, perhaps in distant cities, and don't get the benefit of face time with bosses in the office. And when I went to the metaverse meeting, I was 'with' people who really were in Europe and North America. It felt exciting and inclusive.

The hardware is currently heavy and clunky, but will become less so. Meta, for example, is developing AR (augmented reality) glasses, which will allow users to interact with holograms of other people. No need for the headset.

If you are a manager now, you can expect more from the metaverse in due course. And the current hype around generative AI brings with it a lot of experimentation, pilot projects, team members' resistance, and, yes, probably some failure.

Layered on top of this are the issues around ethics and privacy. Who controls AI? Will governments step in to regulate it? The technology has the potential to eliminate human biases – when hiring new staff, for example – but in the wrong hands, it can also embed them.

What many experts already working with generative AI are at pains to stress is that its use in everyday work could free us up to be more human. The dream is that we will have more time to cultivate connection with our colleagues, to make teams work well because we can focus on what used to be called 'soft skills', and to do work we like.

Jeff Wong, head of innovation at Ernst & Young, the professional services firm, spoke to me on the podcast about what generative AI experiments are already bringing to his workforce. 'What we see is more productivity – being able to answer more questions for clients and customers. And frankly, what the teams love the most is that they're able to spend their time thinking more using the human part of their brain. For us, it is a booster in every way possible.'

That's the ideal. Unfortunately, nothing about humans' use of tech to date makes me feel upbeat about the potential for AI to generate more free time for thinking, working with clients, or making meaningful connections. Rather, every new development so far has been a chance for us to work even harder. Let's not forget that, in 1930, the economist John Maynard Keynes predicted that his grandchildren would work fifteen hours a week, thanks to advances in technology and productivity. In 2015, an American outlet, NPR, did actually interview some of Keynes's descendants (he didn't have grandchildren) to discover that no, they didn't work fifteen hours a week.

Nearly a century since Keynes's prediction, perhaps things really are about to change. I am an optimist and really hope that AI allows us to embrace more connection with co-workers, and maybe even move more of us towards a more efficient working life – four-day week, anyone?

The future-proofed career is one that fully embraces the coming wave of change, even though nobody fully understands it yet. We are all, in a sense, dancing in the dark. But, by staying curious and informed, you can prepare better for the opportunities, as well as the potential threats – including mass job losses – that AI and tech advances bring to the modern workplace.

Takeaways

- AI is coming for us at work. It may also come for our jobs, but all you can do at this point is to try to stay ahead of the curve by staying curious about it and reading widely around the subject.

- FT writers are good at demystifying AI, especially Madhumita Murgia and John Thornhill. I also seek out commentators on LinkedIn who offer practical context. One good follow is NYU Stern School of Business professor Connor Grenan. If you are in HR, Josh Bersin offers great tech insights. And Steven Bartlett's megahit

Diary of a CEO podcast has a very good – if scary – episode on AI in which entrepreneur and author Mo Gawdat gives the doomier side of the future.

- Experiment with AI as it's rolled out in Microsoft, Google, and other workplace products, and take advantage of any training your employer offers.

- Play around with ChatGPT to see what it can do. You'll be surprised and possibly alarmed. A grounding in what exactly is going on is going to help you in the future. If you have teens, they've probably already been using it.

- We are in what's known as a 'hype cycle' with generative AI. Be mindful that the end results may not be exactly as advertised, and keep in mind the hype around the metaverse a few years ago, which was not justified. A slightly sceptical eye is fine. Generative AI is not perfect and it makes mistakes (and even makes things up!).

- If you are a manager, or someone tasked with bringing AI applications to recruitment, training, or day-to-day workflow, then remember it's okay for things to fail. Admit that you don't know everything. It's definitely better to be upfront about the learning that you and your teams still have to do.

- Start to think about your Plan B in case AI really does come for our office jobs. The jobs that will survive the techpocalypse? Those that deal primarily with people rather than data. These include care work, some kinds of teaching, and healthcare and service jobs.

- The future of work is just that: the future. We don't have a crystal ball, but the smartest thing you can do to prepare for it is to be as fully 'human' as you can be – a good leader, a good listener, and a good colleague and friend. Above all, be someone who embraces change, rather than fighting it.

Acknowledgements

At the end of 2021, I became the host of the FT's new *Working It* podcast. A crack team created a podcast series from scratch in just six weeks, while turning me – a slightly jaded print journalist – into an audio host.

Two years and millions of downloads later, *Working It* is one of the UK's top careers and workplace podcasts, and I also write a fast-growing *Working It* newsletter for FT subscribers. Our aim is to demystify the world of work, management, and leadership, in a jargon-free and easy-to-access way. My approach in this book is, I hope, an extension of that ethos. I'm bringing together everything I've learned over a three-decade career in workplaces.

Many people have helped to make *The Future-Proof Career* into a reality. Lucy Smith at Pavilion books liked the podcast, sent me a DM on Twitter and got this project rolling. Ellen Simmons so ably took over when Lucy went on maternity leave. My agent Anna Pallai has demystified the world of publishing and kept up occasionally flagging spirits. I appreciate everyone's patience, and their trust in this first-time author.

None of this would have happened without the creative team behind *Working It*. I will always be grateful to Renee Kaplan, who had the idea and got it off the ground. A team from Novel podcasts first brought *Working It* to life, led by the gifted Anna Sinfield. Our senior FT workplace and management writers, Pilita Clark, Andrew Hill, and Emma Jacobs, became our regular guests. I am proud to call them friends and have quoted them all in this book. (I learn from the best.)

I am lucky to have a group of go-to external thinkers, whose wise words I've shared in these pages: Jonathan Black, Gabriella Braun, Viv Groskop, Yasmin Jones-Henry, Cydney Roach, Naomi Shragai, and Michael Skapinker.

There's a lot of material in this book from FT podcasts, articles, and newsletters, and I am very grateful for the permission to reproduce it here. My thanks especially to the FT managing editors Tobias Buck and Abbie Scott, and to our lawyer Nigel Hanson, for their help and support.

The Future-Proof Career asks its readers to believe in the potential of corporate work as a force for lasting good in our lives. So here is a dedication to the real people who embody that, former and current colleagues who have become friends and wise guides: Claer Barrett, Esther Bintliff, Camilla Cavendish, Jonathan Derbyshire, Geoff Dyer, Alice Fishburn, Miranda Green, Sophie Hanscombe, Kesewa Hennessy, Siona Jenkins, Brooke Masters, Rebecca Rose, Neil O'Sullivan, Tom O'Sullivan, and Helen Warrell. And the one who got away: Sarah Gordon, who made a stellar career change. (I still miss her.)

The FT's talented *Working It* team – head of audio Cheryl Brumley, and the production team of Manuela Saragosa and Mischa Frankl-Duval – make work a breeze and are full of ideas. Sarah Ebner and Gordon Smith are behind the success of the *Working It* newsletter. These two teams scaffold everything I do, and none of this book would have been possible without their support.

I am, above all, grateful to the FT editor, Roula Khalaf, who has been so supportive of *Working It*, and of this book project.

Obviously I take my best self to work, so that leaves the less appealing parts for the people I love. Michael – who has been on his own, more arduous, journey. And Freya and Gabe, who brought the welcome distraction of tea, talk, and TikToks during the long hours of writing.

Final mentions are for indefatigable friends. The early-morning swimmers who kept me – and this project – afloat: Tabitha Dean, Lisa Hinton, and Katie Roden. Jo Lewis Tabitha Stringer and Sally Whittle, for unrivalled wisdom and compassion. And Helen Wallace, dearest friend and lodestar. Long may we keep talking about work, life, and everything.

London, October 2023

Bibliography

PART I

Chapter 1

Berwick, Isabel, 'Do you see me? Staying visible in a hybrid workplace', *Working It* podcast, May 2023. https://www.ft.com/content/57020d1e-5431-421c-b556 -cac80a9ab019.

Brooks, Arthur C., *From Strength to Strength: Finding Success, Happiness, and Deep Purpose in the Second Half of Life* (Bloomsbury, 2022).

Gannon, Emma, *The Success Myth: Letting Go of Having It All* (Torva, 2023).

Chapter 2

Archie, Ayana, 'Disney employees must return to work in office for at least 4 days a week, CEO says', NPR, January 2023. https://www.npr.org/2023/01/11/1148 334436/bob-iger-disney-return-to-office.

Bartlett, Steven, *The Diary of a CEO* podcast. https://stevenbartlett.com/the -diary-of-a-ceo-podcast.

Berwick, Isabel and Andrew Hill, 'How 1,000 years of work has shaped humanity', *Business Book Club* podcast, March 2018. https://www.ft.com/content /981d9e16-3292-11e8-b5bf-23cb17fd1498.

Berwick, Isabel, 'Are companies walking their diversity talk?' *Working It* podcast, February 2022. https://www.ft.com/content/bf01b9a8-b840-4e1e -845a-1f601b28b986.

Berwick, Isabel, 'Best of: Friendship in the workplace: It's lonely at the top', *Working It* podcast, February 2023. https://www.ft.com/content/6008b34a -e697-4080-bd64-087f7c530940.

Berwick, Isabel, 'The Loneliness of the long Covid employee', *Working It* podcast, November 2022. https://www.ft.com/content/dfb725ec-4c87-4f9d-b3ee-889 186aab5e8.

Berwick, Isabel, 'Trust is hard to come by in the workplace', *Working It* newsletter, October 2022. https://www.ft.com/content/86cd5567-3c05-4848-9c5c-d09b9 5015102.

Cain, Susan, *Bittersweet: How Sorrow and Longing Make us Whole* (Viking, 2022).

Cain, Susan, *Quiet: The Power of Introverts in a World That Can't Stop Talking* (Penguin, 2013).

Edelman, 'Edelman Trust Barometer. Special Report: Trust at Work', Edelman, 2023. https://www.edelman.com/sites/g/files/aatuss191/files/2023-08/Edelman_Trust%20at%20Work%202023_Top10.pdf

Flynn, Maria, 'How AI Can Help Workers At Every Stage Advance', *Forbes*, October 2023. https://www.forbes.com/sites/mariaflynn/2023/10/02/how-ai-can-help-workers-at-every-stage-advance.

Gardner, Heidi K., *Smarter Collaboration: A New Approach to Breaking Down Barriers and Transforming Work* (Harvard Business Review Press, 2022).

Gratton, Lynda, 'Cut the meetings, make more friends', *Financial Times*, July 2022. https://www.ft.com/content/c95da4e0-ecd3-4f4d-9faa-ac2a3dc4fc15.

Gratton, Lynda, *Redesigning Work: How to Transform Your Organisation and Make Hybrid Work for Everyone* (Penguin Business, 2022).

Hatfield, Steve and Lauren Kirby, 'Taking bold actions for equitable outcomes', Deloitte, January 2023. https://www2.deloitte.com/us/en/insights/focus/human-capital-trends/2023/diversity-equity-inclusion-belonging.html.

Hill, Andrew, 'Daniel Pink: Regret can be a rich source of inspiration', *Financial Times*, March 2022, https://www.ft.com/content/df661f84-9c77-4c01-b8fe-1b8508867313.

https://www.tuc.org.uk/news/intrusive-worker-surveillance-tech-risks-spiralling-out-control-without-stronger-regulation.

Komlosy, Andrea, *Work: The Last 1,000 Years* (Verso, 2018).

McGee, Patrick, Hannah Murphy, and Richard Waters, 'Elon Musk demands Tesla employees show up to the office full-time', *Financial Times*, June 2022. https://www.ft.com/content/f8da2592-ed67-4b87-b6d5-a0e1e4ac5a8f.

Megna, Michelle, 'Pet Ownership Statistics 2023', *Forbes*, June 2023. https://www.forbes.com/advisor/pet-insurance/pet-ownership-statistics.

Microsoft, 'Hybrid Work Is Just Work. Are We Doing It Wrong?', Microsoft, September 2022. https://www.microsoft.com/en-us/worklab/work-trend-index/hybrid-work-is-just-work.

Office for National Statistics, 'Characteristics of homeworkers, Great Britain: September 2022 to January 2023', ONS, February 2023. https://www.ons.gov.uk/employmentandlabourmarket/peopleinwork/employmentandemployeetypes/articles/characteristicsofhomeworkersgreatbritain/september2022tojanuary2023.

Office for National Statistics, 'Prevalence of ongoing symptoms following coro—navirus (COVID-19) infection in the UK: 30 March 2023', ONS, March 2023. https://www.ons.gov.uk/peoplepopulationandcommunity/healthandsocial

care/conditionsanddiseases/bulletins/prevalenceofongoingsymptomsfollow
ingcoronaviruscovid19infectionintheuk/30march2023.

Pink, Daniel H., *The Power of Regret: How Looking Backward Moves Us Forward* (Canongate Books, 2022).

Shelton, Ted and Rasmus Wegener, 'Automation's Ultimate Goal: The Augmented Workforce', Bain & Company, March 2023. https://www.bain.com/insights /automations-ultimate-goal-the-augmented-workforce.

Skapinker, Michael, 'From SVB to the BBC: Why did no one see the crisis coming?', *Financial Times*, March 2023. https://www.ft.com/content/4d589d5c-f2cb -4568-93dd-acda6fab931f.

Smart Growth Analytics, 'The Future of Work Report', Summix, November 2022. https://summix.com/the-future-of-work-report.

Thomas, Daniel, 'Finance staff ignoring mandatory office attendance demands, report suggests', *Financial Times*, November 2022. https://www.ft.com/content /5017c0ab-9b95-430f-8fe1-695cf597e5c1.

Trades Union Congress, 'Intrusive worker surveillance tech risks "spiralling out of control" without stronger regulation, TUC warns', TUC, February 2022. https:// www.tuc.org.uk/news/intrusive-worker-surveillance-tech-risks-spiralling -out-control-without-stronger-regulation.

Waters, Tom and Thomas Wernham, 'Long COVID and the labour market', The Institute for Fiscal Studies, July 2022. https://ifs.org.uk/sites/default/files /output_url_files/BN346-Long-COVID-and-the-labour-market.pdf.

Chapter 3

Barrionuevo, Alexei, 'Warning on Enron Recounted', *The New York Times*, March 2006. https://www.nytimes.com/2006/03/16/business/businessspecial3/warning -on-enron-recounted.html.

Berwick, Isabel, 'Are dogs the key to workplace happiness?', *Working It* podcast, March 2022. https://www.ft.com/content/aefbebf8-dfb1-472d-9c5c-da5515 b3da81.

Berwick, Isabel, 'Best of *Working It*: Is it time to be open about pay?', *Working It* podcast, August 2022. https://www.ft.com/content/7052fa12-735c-4257-a487 -335be47018a7.

Berwick, Isabel, 'How to turn around a toxic workplace culture', *Working It* podcast, April 2023. https://www.ft.com/content/b3d1e963-1c11-45e9-a2ba-b68001 dc561e.

Berwick, Isabel, 'Should you know how much your colleagues earn?', *Working It* podcast, February 2023. https://www.ft.com/content/24da96b5-6f91-41f0 -a7fb-45ce40df9556.

Berwick, Isabel, 'Upskilling: Why it makes sense to retrain staff', *Working It* podcast, April 2022. https://www.ft.com/content/eca32716-304e-463f-878d-2db81e89 aec4.

Berwick, Isabel, 'Why fair pay matters more than high pay', *Working It* newsletter, April 2023. https://www.ft.com/content/a9e90987-fb3b-4d57-9f42-de6f9c5a 630c.

Claer, Barrett, *What They Don't Teach You About Money* (Ebury Edge, 2023).

Groysberg, Boris et al., 'The Leader's Guide to Corporate Culture', *Harvard Business Review*, January 2018.

Hill, Andrew, 'Psychological safety: the art of encouraging teams to be open', *Financial Times*, February 2023. https://www.ft.com/content/5d544a25-d7dc -41ad-8b42-fe92406d25d7.

Jacobs, Emma, 'Why modern managers are reviving old-school staff handbooks, *Financial Times*, January 2022. https://www.ft.com/content/b69d4fb7-9b6b -4507-bb0e-ac9a02de37ba.

Neurodiversity in Business. https://neurodiversityinbusiness.org.

Ryan, John and Michael J. Burchell, *Make Work Healthy: Create a Sustainable Organization with High-Performing Employees* (Wiley, 2023).

Stolzoff, Simone, *The Good Enough Job: What We Gain When We Don't Put Work First* (Ebury Edge, 2023).

United Nations, 'Sustainable Development Goal 11: Make cities and human settlements inclusive, safe, resilient and sustainable', United Nations, accessed October 2023. https://sdgs.un.org/goals/goal11.

Chapter 4

Berwick, Isabel, 'Best of: So your boss is a narcissist . . .' *Working It* podcast, April 2023. https://www.ft.com/content/b324efb4-9313-4851-abc0-c3ec0ff0a9f8.

Berwick, Isabel, 'Filthy colleagues are here to stay, even in the best offices', *Financial Times*, November 2019. https://www.ft.com/content/168fa36e-06ba-11ea -a984-fbbacad9e7dd.

Braun, Gabriella, *All That We Are: Uncovering the Hidden Truths Behind Our Behaviour at Work* (Piatkus, 2022).

Brower, Tracy, 'Managers Have Major Impact On Mental Health: How To Lead For Wellbeing', *Forbes*, January 2023. https://www.forbes.com/sites/tracybrower /2023/01/29/managers-have-major-impact-on-mental-health-how-to-lead -for-wellbeing/?sh=14d7df7c2ec1.

Shragai, Naomi, 'How our childhoods help us make sense of work problems', *Financial Times*, August 2021. https://www.ft.com/content/738dc093-759d -4057-8d3c-54fcd7986c48.

Shragai, Naomi, *Work Therapy: Or the Man who Mistook his Job for his Life* (WH Allen, 2023).

Tayan, Brian, 'Are Narcissistic CEOs All That Bad?', Harvard Law School Forum on Corporate Governance, October 2023. https://corpgov.law.harvard.edu/2021 /10/25/are-narcissistic-ceos-all-that-bad.

Chapter 5

Abrahams, Matt, *Talk Fast, Think Smart The Podcast*. https://mattabrahams.com /podcast.

Axios, 'Data: The best time to send an internal communication email', Axios HQ, March 2023. https://www.axioshq.com/insights/data-the-best-time-to-send -an-internal-communication-email.

Berwick, Isabel, 'The non-graduate job market is booming. Why go to uni?', *Working It* newsletter, August 2023. https://www.ft.com/content/4326639a -1d9b-468d-a422-88b91be0adf0.

Berwick, Isabel, 'Why does my boss send such rude emails?' *Working It* podcast', February 2022. https://www.ft.com/content/5943fe5d-739c-49cd-8061-c65a f48eb61f.

Clark, Pilita, 'The awful agony of the misdirected email', *Financial Times*, July 2023. https://www.ft.com/content/06c98b7e-9421-4cc2-b101-e0c0b6487b23.

Clark, Pilita, 'The scourge of work email is far worse than you think', *Financial Times*, February 2021. https://www.ft.com/content/572682e4-d701-4f33-af92 -db597a7d39de.

Dhawan, Erica, *Digital Body Language: How to Build Trust and Connection, No Matter the Distance* (HarperCollins, 2021).

Franklin, Joshua, Ortenca Aliaj, and Stephen Morris, 'Wall Street's $1bn messaging "nightmare"', *Financial Times*, September 2022. https://www.ft.com/content /d766f618-ec3a-449d-8683-84b3f3a73b06.

Groskop, Viv, 'Zoom in on your lockdown meeting techniques', *Financial Times*, April 2020. https://www.ft.com/content/7e0380ee-7044-11ea-89df-41bea05 5720b.

Groskop, Viv, *Happy High Status: How to Be Effortlessly Confident* (Torva, 2023).

Hampson, Laura, 'These emojis make you look 'old' to Gen Z, according to new poll', Yahoo! Life, April 2021. https://www.yahoo.com/entertainment/emojis -make-you-look-old-to-gen-z-125933332.html?guccounter=1.

Hunt, Elle, '"It just doesn't stop!" Do we need a new law to ban out-of-hours emails?', *Guardian*, June 2021. https://www.theguardian.com/money/2021 /jun/29/it-just-doesnt-stop-do-we-need-a-new-law-to-ban-out-of-hours -emails.

Jenkins, Ryan, '50 Percent of Emails and Texts are Misunderstood, But There's An Easy Way to Change That', *Entrepreneur*, February 2020. https://www .entrepreneur.com/growing-a-business/50-percent-of-emails-and-texts-are -misunderstood-but/346802.

Kelly, Jack, 'Netflix Has A "Radical Candor" Culture, But Fires Three Executives For Criticizing Executives On Slack –The Co-CEO Fires Back', *Forbes*, July 2021. https://www.forbes.com/sites/jackkelly/2021/07/19/netflix-has-a-radical -candor-culture-but-fires-three-executives-for-criticizing-executives-on -slack-the-co-ceo-fires-back/?sh=256b7ab919ca.

Newport, Cal, *A World Without Email: Find Focus and Transform the Way You Work Forever* (Portfolio Penguin, 2021).

Perlow, Leslie A., Constance Noonan Hadley, and Eunice Eun, 'Stop the Meeting Madness', *Harvard Business Review*, July 2017. https://hbr.org/2017/07/stop -the-meeting-madness.

Chapter 6

Barbieri, Annalisa, 'My friend is working so hard it's affecting her health and family. How can I help?' *Guardian*, September 2023. https://www.theguardian.com /lifeandstyle/2023/sep/08/my-friend-is-working-so-hard-its-affecting-her -health-and-family-how-can-i-help.

Barbieri, Annalisa, *Conversations* podcast. https://annalisabarbieri.com/2021 /05/14/conversations-with-annalisa-barbieri.

Bell, Amy, 'Productivity hacks to love or loathe', *Financial Times*, February 2020. https://www.ft.com/content/9cf6a48e-395a-11ea-ac3c-f68c10993b04.

Berwick, Isabel, 'Bored at work? How AI could come to the rescue', *Working It* podcast, June 2023. https://www.ft.com/content/d148ba53-e5fd-44bf-bd7a -a39a21d91816.

Berwick, Isabel, 'How to be more productive at work', *Working It* podcast, June 2023. https://www.ft.com/content/29ba2d31-0523-47e2-a030-8b99c626f0ef.

Burkeman, Oliver, *Four Thousand Weeks: Time and How to Use It* (Bodley Head, 2021).

Cameron, Julia, 'Morning Pages: FAQ', The Artist's Way, September 2017. https:// juliacameronlive.com/2017/09/18/morning-pages-faq.

Cameron, Julia, *The Artist's Way: A Course in Discovering and Recovering Your Creative Self* (Pan Books, 1995).

Clear, James, *Atomic Habits* (Random House Business, 2018).

Fishbach, Ayelet, *Get It Done: Surprising Lessons from the Science of Motivation* (Macmillan, 2022).

Jacobs, Emma, 'How the science of motivation helps with New Year's resolutions', *Financial Times*, January 2022. https://www.ft.com/content/66d17f43-6652 -40a5-be47-08ace7f270bb.

Lordan, Grace, 'Starting the day like Jamie Dimon set me up for success', *Financial Times*, August 2023. https://www.ft.com/content/7e47ff11-e533-490f-9286 -54ad628aac08.

Nieva, Richard, 'Google Will Let You Send A Bot To A Meeting On Your Behalf', *Forbes*, August 2023. https://www.forbes.com/sites/richardnieva/2023/08/ 29/google-meet-bot-cloud-next.

Noy, Shakked and Whitney Zhang, 'Experimental evidence on the productivity effects of generative artificial intelligence', *Science*, July 2023. https://www .science.org/doi/10.1126/science.adh2586.

Office for National Statistics, 'Labour productivity', ONS, accessed October 2023. https://www.ons.gov.uk/employmentandlabourmarket/peopleinwork /labourproductivity.

Strauss, Delphine, 'Will anything revive UK productivity?', *Financial Times*, May 2023. https://www.ft.com/content/0bad26d0-92a3-4f70-8ae3-9dff6c77d8f1.

Chapter 7

Ascend, Harvard Business Review. https://www.youtube.com/c/HBRAscend/videos.

Atkins, Ros, *The Art of Explanation: How to Communicate with Clarity and Confidence* (Wildfire, 2023).

Barrett, Claer, 'Money Clinic live: How to get a pay rise', *Money Clinic* podcast, September 2023. https://www.ft.com/content/495e94fa-8e09-4ec0-bb11 -2192dda0da60.

Barrett, Claer, 'Repeat – How to ask for a pay rise – and get one!', *Money Clinic* podcast, January 2022. https://www.ft.com/content/94d310ae-8139-447b -8b7b-3ae0a5b0826c.

BBC, 'BBC's Carrie Gracie 'could not collude' in pay discrimination', BBC News, January 2018. https://www.bbc.co.uk/news/uk-42601477.

Berwick, Isabel, 'Clearer communication is a workplace superpower', *Working It* podcast, September 2023. https://www.ft.com/content/a05d3480-5b10-4c95 -ab6b-5bf569c80d3d.

Berwick, Isabel, 'Why your skills matter more than your degree', *Working It* podcast, May 2023. https://www.ft.com/content/1a04f0ef-c4dd-49fc-ad13 -cbb61106982c.

Black, Jonathan, 'I have been overlooked at work in favour of a less-qualified outsider — how do I address it?', *Financial Times*, June 2023. https://www .ft.com/content/407895da-9b3a-462d-9ee4-1a447b9c0166.

Fawcett Society, 'Equal Pay Advice Service', Fawcett Society, accessed October 2023. https://www.fawcettsociety.org.uk/equal-pay-advice-service.

Fawcett Society, 'Our Equal Pay Bill', Fawcett Society, accessed October 2023. https://www.fawcettsociety.org.uk/right-to-know.

Glassdoor. https://www.glassdoor.co.uk/index.htm.

Gracie, Carrie, *Equal: A Story of Women, Men, and Money* (Virago Press Ltd, 2019).

LinkedIn Learning. https://www.linkedin.com/learning/how-to-use-linkedin -learning/advance-your-skills-with-linkedin-learning.

Lordan, Grace, 'Polish your storytelling skills to win a pay rise', *Financial Times*, January 2022. https://www.ft.com/content/09ce507b-914a-4988-9a56 -cf5181e1678d.

Murgia, Madhumita and Anjli Raval, 'AI in recruitment: the death knell of the CV?', *Financial Times*, June 2023. https://www.ft.com/content/98e5f47a-7d0d-4e63 -9a63-ff36d62782b8.

Tupper, Helen and Sarah Ellis, *Squiggly Careers* podcast. https://www.amazingif .com/listen.

Tupper, Helen and Sarah Ellis, *You Coach You: How To Overcome Challenges and Take Control of Your Career* (Penguin Business, 2022).

Chapter 8

Berwick, Isabel, 'Is maternity leave still a career killer?', *Working It* podcast, January 2023. https://www.ft.com/content/a86c0e7b-4177-4b0c-a3a3-b98d1e0b19bb.

Field, Emily et al., 'Women in the Workplace 2023' McKinsey, October 2023. https://www.mckinsey.com/featured-insights/diversity-and-inclusion /women-in-the-workplace.

Jacobs, Emma, 'Paternity leave in finance: "The more men do it, the less of a big deal it becomes"', *Financial Times*, September 2023. https://www.ft.com /content/1d0357e5-6f44-47de-867a-9e6772a59da8.

Maternity Action, 'Missing: reform of Shared Parental Leave', Maternity Action, August 2022. https://maternityaction.org.uk/wp-content/uploads/Missing -reform-of-SPL-v2-23-08-22.pdf.

Perel, Esther, *The State of Affairs: Rethinking Infidelity* (Harper, 2017).

Petriglieri, Jennifer, 'How Dual-Career Couples Make It Work', *Harvard Business Review*, September 2019. https://hbr.org/2019/09/how-dual-career-couples -make-it-work.

Petriglieri, Jennifer, *Couples That Work: How To Thrive in Love and at Work* (Penguin Life, 2019).

Slack, 'State of Work 2023', Slack, accessed October 2023. https://slack.com/intl /en-gb/resources/why-use-slack/state-of-work.

Topping, Alexandra, '"Measly" paternity rights mean nearly a third of UK fathers take no leave – report', *Guardian*, June 2023. https://www.theguardian.com /money/2023/jun/15/measly-paternity-rights-mean-nearly-third-uk-fathers -take-no-leave-report.

Chapter 9

Berwick, Isabel, 'Menopause in the workplace: breaking taboos', *Working It* podcast, June 2023. https://www.ft.com/content/64d722dc-c25e-4da7-bda4 -250b061209e7.

Brooks, Arthur C., *From Strength to Strength: Finding Success, Happiness, and Deep Purpose in the Second Half of Life* (Bloomsbury, 2022).

Channel 4, 'Menopause Policy', Channel 4, October 2020. https://assets-corporate. channel4.com/_flysystem/s3/2020-10/Channel%204%20Menopause%20 Policy%202020.pdf.

Chartered Management Institute, 'Employers shying away from hiring the over-50s despite labour crunch', CMI, January 2023. https://www.managers.org.uk /about-cmi/media-centre/press-releases/employers-shying-away-from -hiring-the-over-50s-despite-labour-crunch.

Croft, Jane, 'A new generation refuses to keep quiet on age discrimination at work', *Financial Times*, January 2023. https://www.ft.com/content/7dc366e1-3553 -4d86-874f-3ae12ff8effb.

Davina, McCall, *Menopausing* (HQ, 2022).

Frostick, Jonathan, LinkedIn post, 2021, accessed October 2023. https://www .linkedin.com/posts/activity-6787207960864014336-juUs.

Gratton, Lynda and Andrew Scott, *The 100 Year Life: Living and Working in an Age of Longevity* (Bloomsbury Information, 2016).

Haddon, Ed, *The Modern Maverick: Why writing your own rules is better for you, your work and the world* (Bloomsbury Business, 2023).

House of Commons Committee, 'Menopause and the workplace', UK Parliament, July 2022. https://publications.parliament.uk/pa/cm5803/cmselect/cmwomeq /91/report.html.

Stern, Stefan, 'The "third age": how to prepare for life after an intense career', *Financial Times*, July 2021. https://www.ft.com/content/4c412180-bff9-4771 -813f-6dde7abb205b.

Part II
Chapter 1

Au-Yeung, Angel and David Jeans, *Wonder Boy: Tony Hsieh, Zappos and the Myth of Happiness in Silicon Valley* (Transworld Digital, 2023).

Ben-Hur, Shlomo and David Ringood, 'Millennials: Reality vs. Rumor', IMD Business School, 2018. https://imd.widen.net/view/pdf/nivgeubkeb/tc009 -18.pdf.

Berwick, Isabel, 'From Gen X to Gen Z: bridging the workplace generation gap', *Working It* podcast, January 2022. https://www.ft.com/content/3fd34cb7 -13c2-4373-8026-e1a599adfc39.

Berwick, Isabel, 'The truth about "entitled millennials"', *Working It* podcast, January 2023. https://www.ft.com/content/0e63a919-0d8b-4aa4-9ec4-00b8 52e4e043.

Berwick, Isabel, 'Why we love to hate the middle manager', *Working It* podcast, October 2022. https://www.ft.com/content/cd294a10-15b5-45d2-abbc-92 e115104dba.

Berwick, Isabel, Professional failures? Rejections? We've all had a few . . .', *Working It* podcast, January 2023. https://www.ft.com/content/fe2a89a8-2252-4243 -ae62-b2ea2c5b4837.

Black, Jonathan, 'Gen Z: how to recruit and retain them' *Financial Times*, July 2022. https://www.ft.com/content/9eb9e9d2-6340-44e6-9d56-f2a140f7dee9.

Bohnet, Iris, *What Works: Gender Equality by Design* (Harvard University Press, 2016).

Chartered Institute of Personnel and Development (CIPD), Guides. https://www .cipd.org/uk/knowledge/guides.

Chartered Management Institute, 'How Accidental Managers Are Draining Productivity', CMI, September 2017. https://www.managers.org.uk/knowledge -and-insights/article/how-accidental-managers-are-draining-productivity.

Chartered Management Institute, Knowledge and Insights hub. https://www .managers.org.uk/knowledge-and-insights.

Coursera. https://www.coursera.org.

Deloitte Insights, 'New fundamentals for a boundaryless world: 2023 Global Human Capital Trends Report' Deloitte, 2023. https://www2.deloitte.com/content /dam/insights/articles/glob175985_global-human-capital-trends-2023 /GLOB175985_HUMAN-CAPITAL-TRENDS-2023.pdf.

Edelman, 'The Power of Gen Z': Top 10', Edelman, 2021. https://www.edelman .com/sites/g/files/aatuss191/files/2022-04/Gen%20Z%20Top%2010_Apr22 .pdf.

Goodall, Amanda, 'How common are bad bosses?', *Financial Times*, December 2019. https://www.ft.com/content/ca0f3aa0-1522-11ea-b869-0971bffac109.

Goodall, Amanda, *Credible: The Power of Expert Leaders* (Basic Books, 2023).

Granovetter, Mark S, 'The Strength of Weak Ties', *American Journal of Sociology*, vol. 78, no. 6, 1973, pp. 1360–80. http://www.jstor.org/stable/2776392.

Hill, Andrew, 'Having a "threshold" for bullying is out of date', *Financial Times*, April 2023. https://www.ft.com/content/6522f0d4-735e-420f-a19b-25508 d1213bf.

Hill, Andrew, 'Why being a manager matters more than ever', *Financial Times*, April 2022. https://www.ft.com/content/dd340c7b-48e3-459c-84af-bfb704d 37665.

Hill, Andrew, 'Wonder Boy — the rapid rise and tragic fall of Tony Hsieh', *Financial Times*, May 2023. https://www.ft.com/content/9b061f22-5d5b-4e7d-9723 -dc33074f72f0.

Huy, Quy, 'In Praise of Middle Managers', *Harvard Business Review*, September 2001. https://hbr.org/2001/09/in-praise-of-middle-managers.

Jack, Andrew, 'Management research: why are so few of its ideas taken up?', *Financial Times*, February 2023. https://www.ft.com/content/7cf1deb9-f8dd -498e-9cab-e8bf3a615ee9.

Livingston, Robert, *The Conversation: How Talking Honestly About Racism Can Transform Individuals and Organizations* (Penguin Business, 2021).

Lordan, Grace, 'Why ending favouritism is the key to building a diverse workforce', *Financial Times*, July 2022. https://www.ft.com/content/535f7e8c-5ad3-4cf3 -b127-2d5fecdb8004.

Morris, Joanna, 'The majority of Britons have been bullied – and it had a significant impact on most', YouGov, February 2023. https://yougov.co.uk/society /articles/45285-majority-britons-have-been-bullied-and-it-had-sign.

Murphy, Kate, *You're Not Listening: What You are Missing and Why it Matters* (Harvill Secker, 2020).

Newkirk, Pamela, 'Leaders must commit to change if diversity efforts are to work', *Financial Times*, September 2020. https://www.ft.com/content/9ff25da6 -fd55-45b7-96a9-18aee58309c9.

Newkirk, Pamela, *Diversity, Inc.: The Failed Promise of a Billion-Dollar Business* (Bold Type Books, 2019).

Olson, Emily, '"Leave pity city," MillerKnoll CEO tells staff who asked whether they'd lose bonuses', NPR, April 2023. https://www.npr.org/2023/04/19 /1170669245/millerknoll-ceo-andi-owen-video-bonuses.

Storr, Farrah, 'What's your CV hiding?' Substack, September 2022. https://farrah ,substack.com/p/whats-your-cv-hiding.

TEDtalks, 'A blueprint for diversity in the workplace', video playlist, accessed October 2023. https://www.ted.com/playlists/670/a_blueprint_for_diversity _in_the_workplace.

Uviebinene, Elizabeth, 'Make time for the people at the edge of your life', *Financial Times*, July 2021. https://www.ft.com/content/0292a22a-883c-40d3-99ee -5e45af735cab.

Chapter 2

Algoe, Sara, 'Why It's Important to Show Gratitude at Work – and What's the Best Way to Do It', *The Wall Street Journal*, April 2023. https://www.wsj.com /articles/show-gratitude-work-aaf8f20c.

BBC Witness History, 'The "good enough" mother', video, BBC, accessed October 2023. https://www.bbc.co.uk/programmes/w3cszmvv.

Berwick, Isabel, 'Why is sexual harassment and assault still happening at work?', *Working It* podcast, July 2023. https://www.ft.com/content/5d125801-789b-4c13-9ddf-c0e8ce14d1bc.

Berwick, Isabel, 'Why we are all so angry at work', *Working It* newsletter, June 2023. https://www.ft.com/content/41c7717d-8b66-41d8-b33d-231500785dc5.

Bintliff, Esther, 'Positive feedback: the science of criticism that actually works', *FT Magazine*, July 2022. https://www.ft.com/content/a681ac3c-73b8-459b-843c-0d796f15020e.

Cuddy, Amy, 'Calling All Bravehearts! What Is Social Bravery and How Will It Help Us Put An End To Workplace Bullying?', LinkedIn, February 2022. https://www.linkedin.com/pulse/calling-all-bravehearts-what-social-bravery-how-help-us-amy-cuddy.

Davito, Brandon and Alana O'Grady, 'Verkada's 2023 Workplace Safety Survey Reveals Frontline Workers Are in Crisis', Verkada, June 2023. https://www.verkada.com/uk/blog/workplace-safety-survey.

Evans, Rebekah, 'Concert etiquette: why are people behaving badly?', *The Week*, July 2023. https://www.theweek.co.uk/news/media/961530/concert-etiquette-why-are-people-behaving-badly.

FT visual and data journalism team, 'Most of the world's workers are "quiet quitters"', *Financial Times*, June 2023. https://www.ft.com/content/20f50964-9ed6-4c88-87bf-5f1b94574825.

Gallup, 'State of the Global Workplace: 2023 Report', Gallup, accessed October 2023. https://www.gallup.com/workplace/349484/state-of-the-global-workplace.aspx.

Gould, Mark, '8 in 10 teachers say pupils' attention is worse since pandemic', *TES magazine*, June 2023. https://www.tes.com/magazine/news/primary/pupil-behaviour-attention-worse-pandemic.

Marriage, Madison and Sarah O'Connor, 'KPMG partner at centre of bullying claims quits role', *Financial Times*, June 2019. https://www.ft.com/content/8990f14e-86ac-11e9-97ea-05ac2431f453.

Marriage, Madison, Antonia Cundy, and Paul Caruana Galizia, 'How Crispin Odey evaded sexual assault allegations for decades', *FT Magazine*, June 2023. https://www.ft.com/content/e5d14398-e866-44b3-8ecb-4e6371167c6d.

Shragai, Naomi, *Work Therapy: Or the Man who Mistook his Job for his Life* (WH Allen, 2023).

West, Tessa, *Jerks at Work: Toxic Coworkers and What to Do About Them* (Ebury Edge, 2022).

Chapter 3

Bakker, René, 'Businesses must focus on ability, not disability', *Financial Times*, September 2022. https://www.ft.com/content/5f46cb63-087e-46e0-b82f-f5b 22724a8d1.

Berman, Jillian, 'Even Companies That Sell Tampons Are Run By Men', *Huffington Post*, December 2017. https://www.huffingtonpost.co.uk/entry/women -companies_n_5563256.

Berwick, Isabel, 'All hail older workers', *Working It* newsletter, July 2023. https://www.ft.com/content/21d39004-bedf-4aa7-8b7e-db0fb500c53e.

Berwick, Isabel, 'Breaking the silence on disability in the workplace', *Working It* podcast, April 2022. https://www.ft.com/content/1a5a5f37-4036-483d-9985 -15e59daf9f75.

Berwick, Isabel, 'Neurodiversity at work: "I had to kick doors down to be heard"', *Working It* podcast, March 2023. https://www.ft.com/content/de9c5db0 -e673-40e0-975e-489e75ede234.

Berwick, Isabel, 'Politics in the workplace: how to deal with opposing views', *Working It* podcast, November 2022. https://www.ft.com/content/0aa8f2f5 -1b0c-474b-b453-0bbd01aa1fab.

Dixon-Fyle, Sundiatu et al., 'Diversity wins: How inclusion matters', McKinsey, May 2020. https://www.mckinsey.com/featured-insights/diversity-and-inclusion /diversity-wins-how-inclusion-matters.

Future Forum, Slack, accessed October 2023. https://futureforum.com.

Genius Within. https://geniuswithin.myabsorb.eu/#/public-dashboard.

Harris, John, 'The mother of neurodiversity: how Judy Singer changed the world', *Guardian*, July 2023. https://www.theguardian.com/world/2023/jul/05/the -mother-of-neurodiversity-how-judy-singer-changed-the-world.

Jones, Nina, 'Women's health start-ups bloom with no blushes', *Financial Times*, November 2018. https://www.ft.com/content/de0f5b8c-dec0-11e8-b173 -ebef6ab1374a.

Livingston, Robert, *The Conversation: How Talking Honestly About Racism Can Transform Individuals and Organizations* (Penguin Business, 2021).

Lordan, Grace, 'Why ending favouritism is the key to building a diverse workforce', *Financial Times*, July 2022. https://www.ft.com/content/535f7e8c-5ad3-4cf3 -b127-2d5fecdb8004.

Masunaga, Samantha, 'Remote work gave them a reprieve from racism. They don't want to go back', *Los Angeles Times*, August 2023. https://www.latimes.com /business/story/2023-08-08/remote-work-racism-reprieve-return-to-office.

MindGym, 'Respect: Banish bullying and harassment', MindGym, accessed October 2023. https://themindgym.com/solutions/respect.

Peregrine, Michael, 'The Lasting Leadership Lessons From The Challenger Disaster', *Forbes*, January 2021. https://www.forbes.com/sites/michaelperegrine /2021/01/24/the-lasting-leadership-lessons-from-the-challenger-disaster /?sh=11de1cd061c3.

Roland, Denise, 'Employers see the positive side of ADHD and autism', *Financial Times*, May 2023. https://www.ft.com/content/5148bf49-f3eb-4bd4-acb3-7e3 38deed82c.

Sparta Global, 'Equal Tech Report 2023', Sparta Global, February 2023. https:// www.spartaglobal.com/learn-and-media/sparta-global-equal-tech-report -neurodiversity.

Woolley, Anita and Thomas W. Malone, 'Defend Your Research: What Makes a Team Smarter? More Women', *Harvard Business Review*, June 2011. https:// hbr.org/2011/06/defend-your-research-what-makes-a-team-smarter-more -women.

Chapter 4

Abrahams, Matt, *Think Faster, Talk Smarter: How to Speak Successfully When You're Put on the Spot* (Simon Element, 2023).

Berwick, Isabel, 'Do you see me? Staying visible in a hybrid workplace', *Working It* podcast, May 2023. https://www.ft.com/content/57020d1e-5431-421c-b556 -cac80a9ab019.

Berwick, Isabel, 'How to master the art of schmoozing', *Working It* podcast, July 2023. https://www.ft.com/content/5b851166-6825-4a0d-b6eb-f890e43b 9d7c.

Clark, Pilita, 'Top ways to be super schmoozer' *Financial Times*, April 2023. https:// www.ft.com/content/82a79138-ae35-4e50-97f3-4422713a5a64.

Groskop, Viv, *Happy High Status: How to Be Effortlessly Confident* (Torva, 2023).

Licht, Aliza, *On Brand: Shape Your Narrative. Share Your Vision. Shift Their Perception* (Union Square & Co., 2023).

Skapinker, Michael, 'Listen and you might learn something', *Financial Times*, July 2023. https://www.ft.com/content/9d5bfeba-9af9-4fc4-af22-eb7bc262556f.

Chapter 5

Bartlett, Steven, 'Leadership vs Management', *The Diary of a CEO*, video, accessed October 2023. https://youtu.be/ts1pq-egv2o.

Bartlett, Steven, *The Diary of a CEO* podcast. https://stevenbartlett.com/the -diary-of-a-ceo-podcast.

Berg, Justin M. et al., 'Job crafting and meaningful work', *Purpose and meaning in the workplace* (American Psychological Association, 2022).

Berwick, Isabel, 'Boost your career with a personal board of directors', *Working It* newsletter, November 2022. https://www.ft.com/content/1b092713-dede -48bd-b181-2df4953e36aa.

Darke, Tiffanie, 'Do you need the C-suite check-up?', *HTSI*, January 2023. https:// www.ft.com/content/534b130e-4744-4895-a52d-088a40eb1c38.

Fisher, Jen at al., 'As workforce well-being dips, leaders ask: What will it take to move the needle?', Deloitte Insights, June 2023. https://www2.deloitte.com/ uk/en/insights/topics/talent/workplace-well-being-research.html.

Fry, Art and Spencer Silver, 'First person: "We invented the Post-it Note"', *Financial Times*, December 2010. https://www.ft.com/content/f08e8a9a-fcd7-11df -ae2d-00144feab49a.

Kotler, Steven, 'Create a Work Environment that Fosters Flow', *Harvard Business Review*. May 2014. https://hbr.org/2014/05/create-a-work-environment -that-fosters-flow.

Van Vianen, Annalies E. M., 'Person–Environment Fit: A Review of Its Basic Tenets', *Annual Review of Organizational Psychology and Organizational Behavior*, vol. 5, 2018, pp. 75–101, 2018. https://www.annualreviews.org/doi /abs/10.1146/annurev-orgpsych-032117-104702.

Chapter 6

Ahuja, Anjana, 'Should an AI bot making $1mn really be the next Turing test?', *Financial Times*, August 2023. https://www.ft.com/content/4bb0309b-0a68 -4219-ba9d-8b3a188cf502.

Bartlett, Steven, 'EMERGENCY EPISODE: Ex-Google Officer Finally Speaks Out On The Dangers Of AI!', *The Diary of a CEO*, video, accessed October 2023. https://www.youtube.com/watch?feature=shared&v=bk-nQ7HF6k4.

Berwick, Isabel, 'Bored at work? How AI could come to the rescue', *Working It* podcast, June 2023. https://www.ft.com/content/15093108-b6c1-447a-8bec -5ab7ba3ec014.

Berwick, Isabel, 'Meet me in the metaverse?' *Working It* newsletter, May 2023. https://www.ft.com/content/c49344ff-1d74-4523-b73a-bb055c9c 7817.

Edmondson, Amy, *Right Kind of Wrong: Why Learning to Fail Can Teach Us to Thrive* (Cornerstone Press, 2023).

Jack, Andrew, 'AI chatbot's MBA exam pass poses test for business schools', *Financial Times*, January 2023. https://www.ft.com/content/7229ba86-142a -49f6-9821-f55c07536b7c.

Kestenbaum, David, 'Keynes Predicted We Would Be Working 15-Hour Weeks. Why Was He So Wrong?' NPR, August 2015. https://www.npr.org/2015

/08/13/432122637/keynes-predicted-we-would-be-working-15-hour-weeks
-why-was-he-so-wrong.

Murgia, Madhumita et al., 'Generative AI exists because of the transformer', *Financial Times*, September 2013. https://ig.ft.com/generative-ai.

Runciman, David, 'The end of work: which jobs will survive the AI revolution?' *Guardian*, August 2023. https://www.theguardian.com/books/2023/aug/19/the-end-of-work-which-jobs-will-survive-the-ai-revolution.

Thornhill, John, 'The sceptical case on generative AI', *Financial Times*, August 2023. https://www.ft.com/content/ed323f48-fe86-4d22-8151-eed15581c337.